Did Mom Drop Acid?

Michelle Cain

Copyright © 2024 by Michelle Cain and Bird House Publications LLC

All rights reserved.

No portion of this book may be reproduced in any form without written permission from the publisher or author, except as permitted by U.S. copyright law.

Paperback: 9798991646000

Ebook: 9798991646017

Edited by

Cover art by

Bird House Publications LLC

www.birdhousepublications.com

Suit Press

www.suitpress.com

Introduction

Ordinary families have extraordinary stories.

"Life is a lot like my daytime soap opera" Mom once said. When I was younger, I didn't believe her. Older now, I know she was right.

This is not your warm and fuzzy caretaker story. This is a story of a mother and daughter who traverse the delusional world of Lewy body dementia, forcing one of them to unpack decades of dysfunction while staying sober during a global pandemic. I am that daughter, and author, and a reluctant caretaker, who found myself asking the question *"What do I owe you?"*

Lewy body dementia (LBD) may have been the original story in my soap opera, but it was all the things that happened along the way that highlighted my vulnerability as a human being. Family dysfunction, sobriety, mental health, kids, marriage, and a global pandemic are not unique to me, they simply put the extraordinary into everyday ordinary life. My hope is that readers find pieces of themselves as they laugh, cry and gasp at times as they read the short vignettes.

We're all just messy humans!

To Mom, I love you and thank you for a life in technicolor.

Disclaimer: Actual voicemails and text messages are used throughout the book. In addition, I used emails, events on my calendar and conversations with others involved to compile information. I paraphrased conversations from detailed notes I took on my phone after every encounter with Mom. In these notes, I would write down any quotes verbatim I could remember. Unless given specific permission, some of the names of people, details and places were changed to respect privacy. I tell the story from my perspective and respect that others involved had their own experiences and perspectives.

Everyone involved loved Mom and wanted her to live in dignity for as long as possible. Not to mention, Mom had a great sense of humor and loved to laugh!

Chapter 1
Something's Off

Voicemail to Travis, April 20, 2020:

Hi Travis, it's Kay and I'm trying to locate Michelle, I've just got the strangest thing going in my house. I came in last night and people were propped on two of the pillows on my bed, but I don't know who this is, there's no visible person, but you get the feeling that it's Michelle and Danielle. But anyway, it's crazy she has not spoken one word since she's been here over two days. She's not eating anything that I know of. She's just now, just staring at me, the pillow is staring at me. Could you please give me a call before I lose my mind, thank you.

(*Actual voicemails and text messages used throughout book*)

Travis, my husband of twenty-five years, rounded the corner, his expression something I hadn't seen before. His face took on a serious edge with his jaw square and tight, but his eyes, which were focused on me, were confused with his left eyebrow arched like a question mark.

"Michelle, can you listen to this?" he said, jutting his cell phone out in front of him as my mother's voice filled the room on speaker. Her words swirled around in my head like fragments of information that I was unable to piece together. Travis and I stared at each other, our mouths dropped open in utter confusion. An unspoken *What the fuck?* hung in the air. It's hard to get your head around a voicemail where your mom is suddenly talking in a scared, breaking voice about your sister and you staring at her. I live thirty-five minutes away from Mom and my sister, Danielle, lives in California. This voicemail marked the official start of my journey with Lewy body dementia (LBD), or simply Lewy as I've come to refer to her disease.

Travis hit the phone icon next to Mom's

message, dialing her number. I heard ringing then, "Oh good, it's you," Mom said, breathlessly.

Over the next five minutes, he calmly talked her through Danielle being in California and me standing next to him. He left out that I was practically standing on top of him with a horrified expression. Travis didn't carry the familial relationship that only mother daughter baggage can create, therefore he could be a little less emotionally charged. On the other hand, I was playing out a completely different conversation parallel to Travis's in my head that sounded like, *What do you mean the pillow's staring at you? Of course we're not there, I'm on the phone with you, what the hell, are you crazy?* Needless to say, we were all grateful Travis was taking one for the team. My inner dialogue wouldn't have been helpful.

Travis and I did the only thing we could think to do and told Mom we would drive to her house and check in on her. Later in this journey there would be an immeasurable number of these types of voicemails that wouldn't prompt us to stop everything and jump in a car, but when it's the first, it engenders a certain sense of emergency.

Two hours later, Travis and I approached Mom's front door. I noticed my deceased father's tattered, faded, gray baseball cap placed perfectly on a small glass table on the porch. Memories of Dad wearing that old, weathered baseball cap flooded in. I could smell the sweat and see him in matching worn out t-shirts riddled with holes running along the cliffs that overlooked Del Mar beach.

Thump, thump, thump. Travis's knocking jarred me out of the memory. No answer, *thump, thump.* Increasing in intensity, still nothing. Travis grabbed his cell, dialing Mom. We could hear the phone ringing inside. I pressed my nose to the window that offered a clear view of her kitchen island. Flickering bits of light illuminated in unison with the ringing where I saw Mom's cell sitting on a pile of papers stacked on her island. *That's strange, she never leaves her phone behind.* Seriously, Mom was that lady in the grocery store who answered any call with the tenacity of a transplant surgeon waiting on an organ, then carried on a full conversation about what she'd had for lunch while shopping. Not to mention the time she'd broken her pinky toe, hooking it on the leg of a barstool while running for a call rather than letting it go to voicemail. Her separation from her cell phone was a red flag.

Travis tried the door handle; it was unlocked. We slowly proceeded inside, creeping like we might sneak up on someone. I hoped it would be Mom. Everything looked normal, nothing was out of place, and her car was still parked in the garage. It never occurred to me, given our conversation a couple of hours prior, that she might not be there. It was still early in the pandemic. There was quite literally nowhere to go.

"Mom?, Kay?, Mom?" Travis and I called out in tandem while searching the small 1300-square-foot house.

"Is she hiding?" I said, half-joking. We split up, this time looking in closets and under beds. The only thing weirder than my getting down on all fours to peer under beds, would have been to find Mom's steel blue eyes, scared, staring back at me. Minutes later, Travis and I were back in the living room staring at each other.

"Now what?" I said, shrugging my shoulders.

"I guess let's do the loop and see if she's outside, maybe talking to a neighbor?" he said, equally perplexed.

Mom's community consisted of about forty patio homes lining one small road that formed a circle, the layout making it near impossible not to know your neighbors intimately. Travis and I exited the house headed in opposite directions around the circle. After the first two neighbors didn't know where Mom was, my pace accelerated, and I started calling her name. "Mom, Mooooommmm, Mom!" I felt like someone searching for a lost dog, my eyes scanning yards, even looking behind bushes. For the record, I didn't clap my hands or whistle. A full loop completed, Travis and I stood again staring at each other.

"Holy shit am I going to have to put out a Silver Alert" I said, laughing nervously.

In Texas, Silver Alerts are digital billboards alerting people of a missing elderly person along with their home city and, if applicable, make of car, which for the elderly, is a Toyota Camry more times than not. I get it, the Camry is reliable and reasonably priced, two things the elderly love. I knew I was getting up there in years when a Camry pulled up next to me at a light recently and I thought, *The new body style looks pretty sharp.*

Then, out of the corner of my eye, I saw walking casually towards me from a distance, not a care in the world, my Mom. At this point, I was irritated. I could feel the adrenaline coursing through my body, the byproduct of worry. Immediately, I sympathized with Mom for all the times I'd stayed out past curfew as a teenager, causing her to worry. She looked at me now, bewildered by my expression, which displayed a mix of irritation and relief.

"I told you we were coming. We've been looking everywhere for you," I said, out of breath.

"I talked to you before I left. I told you to put on sunscreen and left the hat out for you," she replied, with an "as if" attitude. *That explains Dad's hat on the patio.*

"No, you didn't," I said, confused. "The last time I talked to you was this morning and it wasn't about sunscreen." *It was about pillows that wouldn't eat.*

"You were lying down in the front bedroom, right before I went to Pam's," she said. We both just stood there looking at each other confused.

In some twisted way I could see her reasoning. According to her voicemail, she believed Danielle and I had been at her house. I had no idea then that conversations in which I explained facts, *reality*, and Mom explained hallucinations, *her reality*, would play out again and again over the following years. What I also didn't know was that my conversation with Lewy had just begun.

Our car ride home was filled with stunned silence, Travis and I both staring at the windshield like deer in headlights, leaving me alone with my thoughts. *Something's off.* I couldn't put my finger on it, but something was there, causing an *unsettled, almost queasy feeling* in my stomach. My mind started flipping through other memories where I'd felt that same *unsettled, almost queasy feeling* only to brush it aside, rationalizing it as "typical aging".

One such memory was of sitting in a long booth at Cheesecake Factory, Travis, Mom, and me facing my sons, who sat directly across from us. Mom loved Cheesecake Factory. She had a fondness for all things Southern comfort food, the kind of food where you stop counting calories because the portions are so big or the food is so fried. I stared at her chicken fried steak smothered in thick creamy white gravy and I wondered why she'd tortured my sister and I with "health foods" growing up. In an era before Whole Foods existed, we had unpasteurized milk delivered to our door and choked down carrot juice for breakfast. I was out of elementary school, before I knew Oreos existed; Who does that to a kid!? As I watched her devour this chicken fried steak, which had to have been the entire chicken pounded flat, she made the comment that my sons, Cameron and Connor, were the same age. Cameron and Connor are four years apart. Mom knew this because she had been present at all their birthdays for the past two decades. When Travis mentioned the boys' actual ages, twenty and sixteen, her face looked confused for a second. Then she laughed and said, "Well I am seventy-eight." And there it was that *unsettled, almost queasy feeling*.

At other times on the phone, she would mix up people in a story, which I quickly brushed aside with thoughts like, *Hell, if you catch me on the wrong day, I'll mix up pets with kids*. There were also those phone conversations where she talked about having just seen my sister who lives 1500 miles away at her house, and I chalked it up to her having timing mixed up from prior visits.

Sometime in early 2020, I spent an absurd amount of time with Mom looking for chairs for her outdoor patio table. To this day, I'm not sure exactly what she was envisioning, because we never found it.

Mom had slid out a chair, eyeing it up and down. "These would work," she'd said. "They're the right height for that table."

"Those are barstools, people would be hunched over to eat," I'd said, laughing. Again, that *unsettled, almost queasy feeling,* fleeting but there, then gone. A mind-numbing argument about barstool versus chair heights followed. It's also not uncommon for elderly to have trouble with spatial awareness, so again that feeling was pushed aside.

The sound of our garage door opening snapped me back to the present. "Well, that was interesting," I said, turning to face Travis.

"Uh, that's an understatement," he replied, shaking his head.

"At one point I wondered if she'd dropped acid," I said, laughing, but also still wondering.

Chapter 2
How Much Do You Like Your Family?

One Month Prior, March 2020

Austin issued a stay-at-home order to help stop the spread of COVID-19. All you had to say was 2020 and there was a collective understanding of what that year entailed. Short version, shitty year. Long version, months of quality time with your family, testing just how much you liked your family. Terms like "the new normal" settled in as people started hoarding toilet paper, apparently thinking it would not only clean up their asses, but their problems too. The pandemic was the backdrop for the beginning of my LBD journey which caused confusion when I was trying to decipher real medical symptoms from the effects of pandemic isolation with Mom. Additionally, the added stressors caused by the pandemic affected how I dealt with Mom's LBD.

My older son, Cameron, twenty-one-years-old at the time, had just come home from college for spring break, only to learn he'd be spending months, not a week, with his family. SURPRISE! My younger son, Connor, seventeen-years-old at the time, was a junior in high school and had no idea he wouldn't walk the halls of his school again that year or the following. My husband, Travis, now working remotely, set up his home office in our master bedroom with his desk strategically placed where the entry door to our bedroom was his backdrop on ZOOM. Also in the background, was the dresser filled with my clothes.

"Is your camera off? Are you sure?" I'd say, peering from our master bath, before descending into the bedroom on full display to rummage through drawers for underwear and bras.

There're probably some compromising videos capturing me sneaking into the room that I wouldn't want floating around on the web. Two weeks prior to the stay-at-home order being issued, we'd ripped out part of our master bath to start a remodel, leaving all of us sharing one communal bathroom. As you can imagine, both boys were thrilled to be sharing a bathroom with their parents. Who doesn't want to see their mother's bra on the counter while brushing your teeth in the morning? To round out our quarantine household was one African Grey parrot, named Nigel, who spent his days bossing our two crazy terriers, named Sadie and Finn.

In March, I was working at a drug and alcohol detox facility. These facilities were deemed essential for obvious reasons. If you were trapped in your house, you'd drink too! Also deemed essential were liquor stores, the two producing a steady stream of clients into detox. My exposure at work all but guaranteed I would catch COVID. Our client base turned over approximately every seven days. These clients placed the importance of their immune health, just below wanting to go to detox. Testing for COVID was a joke! If you were lucky enough to obtain a test, you would then have to wait five to seven days to get results. This meant we could tell a client they tested positive, only after they'd infected the entire community and were now leaving the facility. For the record, I'm not being insensitive to people trying to get sober. I'm in recovery; I'm one of those people. I'll touch on this later.

As the stay-at-home order left people isolated, mental health issues became so commonplace, one might say they were as contagious as COVID. The old adage, *People need connection for survival,* is true. Turns out, if we don't talk to others, we'll talk to ourselves, our pets, even the TV. Fortunately, I had a talking pet, therefore my conversations with Nigel were marginally less crazy. Unless I was dressed in a hazmat suit, I limited my exposure to Mom since I was quite literally the riskiest person she would encounter.

Throughout March, Mom would talk about seeing her deceased cream-colored Pomeranian, Porsche, or people in her house. *That's odd,* I'd consider. *Why is she entertaining people during a pandemic?* If Mom talking to her dead dog seems unusual, the way she interacted with Porsche when the dog was alive was stranger. Mom's behavior had been strange, but no stranger than the conversation I'd had at work when a detox client's boyfriend called saying he was going to scale the facility's wall to break out his girlfriend because "they were releasing the prisons."

"There's no walls and she's here voluntarily," I'd replied, envisioning a medieval escalade. Times were strange.

One afternoon, while Mom talked about seeing Porsche, a flood of memories filled my head. Mom had irrational anxiety about Porsche and that anxiety often fixated on Porsche getting enough water. If Mom and Porsche were at my house, she'd place water bowls everywhere, spreading them out like land mines. I never understood her fear of Porsche dehydrating. Travis and I walked through the house constantly kicking over bowls, sending water everywhere. More infuriating, Mom turned our dog's food bowls into additional water bowls. I'd add a handful of dry dog food to a bowl, only to have the pellets float on top of the water. It's a miracle Nigel (parrot) doesn't say "Shhhiiittt" followed by the sound of a sliding ceramic water bowl on the floor. Nigel does say, "You want water?" in my Mom's voice.

Neighborhood Ninjas

May 2, 2020

"I think I need to go to the doctor," Mom blurted out, during a phone conversation.

You never want to go to the doctor, I thought and could hear Mom's typical retort, "I'm fine," to the mere suggestion she see a doctor.

"I'm fine," she'd snapped two years prior, as my family circled her foot to view the deep purplish-blue toe, which resembled late-stage frostbite. "I think it's just a bug bite," she added, wiggling the toe that looked like it was ready to fall off. Seeing everyone's expressions of horror prompted her to slip her foot back into her red leather flat.

"It looks like you could lose the toe," I'd said, as images of brown recluse spiders, scorpions, and centipedes inundated my mind.

Whistle. "Sadie come!" Nigel calling the terriers from the other room, brought me back to the phone conversation.

"Why do you want to go to the doctor?" I said, nervous about her sudden willingness to seek help.

"I keep seeing things," she said casually, as if everyone sees things that aren't there.

"Like what?" The words escaped my lips before I had time to think about whether I wanted the answer.

"Sometimes animals, dogs, um, you know Porsche," she said slowly. "Sometimes people. It's starting to bother me that both of you won't talk or eat and Gene Ann (Mom's sister) just bosses me constantly." Now her voice was irritated. *Both of you, that must be Danielle and I. God you're obsessed with us eating,* I thought. I could hear the April twentieth voicemail playing in my head. *How often do you see things?*

It figured that Mom was worried about pretend

Danielle and me eating. Mom had a long history of trying to control everyone's eating or not eating. I could hear her voice in my head, "That's all you're going to eat?" or "Are you on some kind of diet?" said with the inflection of judgment. Less benign were the comments like "Why don't we start walking in the morning, so you can take off a few pounds?" or "You remember that birthday party when you were a pudge and your pants barely fit?" I could never win! The judgment for being too fat or too skinny was constant, setting off my life-long unhealthy relationship with food and body image.

My whole body felt tense from the memories, as I tried to shake them from my head to refocus on our conversation. "I think you should go to the doctor. I'll make an appointment," I said, knowing if I left it to Mom she'd never call.

As I Googled, *reasons someone might hallucinate*, an image of my ninety-pound, five-foot-nothing Hungarian grandmother, Nana, came to mind. She'd hallucinated with a bladder infection. For those who haven't dealt with the elderly and bladder infections, let me tell you, it's no picnic. In a short period of time, Nana went from mentally sharp, to thinking her upstairs neighbors were entering her home in the middle of the night through the ceiling, apparently dropping down like ninjas. To ward off her upstairs ninjas, Nana started hiding knives in her vertical blinds. The culmination of these events led Mom to call 911. Mental health crisis officers forcibly took Nana from her home while Mom sat on the curb crying, because Nana was screaming, "She's doing this to me! She's trying to kill me!" The thought of replaying the Nana scenario with Mom had me speed dialing Mom's doctor.

Sibling Rivalry

In the days leading up to her doctor's appointment, Mom openly talked about seeing Danielle and me around her house, as well as Gene Ann. Gene Ann sightings were becoming more frequent. Pretend me was slightly offended at being cast aside by pretend Gene Ann. When pretend Gene Ann wasn't taking up residency in the front bedroom, she was in the kitchen bossing Mom and telling her what to do. Annoyed with her sister, Mom started trying to sort out her reality. This resulted in frequent calls to me to verify if the person she was seeing, in this case Gene Ann, was real.

"Mom, Gene Ann is in Bryan. Why don't you call her?" I said, during one of these fact-finding calls. "Then you'll know she's not there, because she'll answer the phone from Bryan."

"Well, she's standing right here telling me what to do, like she always does. She's not in Bryan!" she replied, her tone discernibly angry. She wanted nothing to do with Gene Ann over the phone or in person. I started to worry that Mom's delusions could bleed into reality and possibly cause harm. *Would she think Gene Ann entered through the ceiling like a ninja?*

This delusional world was melding with reality, pulling relationship dynamics into its pretend orbit. Family dynamics are like living organisms, breathing life into our behaviors. Mom and her sister were no exception to this. In this instance, Gene Ann was a hallucination, but the reason Mom was upset with her was based in reality.

Historically, Mom and Gene Ann have been paradoxically both close and distant. Geographically distant, they spent most of their adult lives in different states until Mom moved back to Texas several years after Dad died. Emotionally distant, because Mom seemed jealous of her sister at times. I remembered sitting on Baba's (Mom's mom) sofa as a child listening to Mom wail, "Everything always has to be about her!" from the bathroom she'd locked herself into, after Gene Ann had been given an engagement ring on Christmas Eve. Even as a child, I remembered thinking it was odd for an adult to lock themselves in a bathroom. Here were two grown sisters, staying at their mom's house, playing out childhood patterns. We really are always children around our parents. Unbeknownst to either sister, their lives would come full circle, intersecting back where it started, in Bryan, TX.

Gene Ann called me one afternoon not long after I'd had a conversation with Mom about pretend Gene Ann standing in her kitchen. "I'm thinking of coming in to see my sister," Gene Ann said.

"Okay. She'd like that," I said, trying to figure out how to explain that Mom already hallucinated her being at the house. "You know she hallucinates, right?"

"I know, it won't phase me," she said, quickly.

"She thinks you've been there. I mean you're there now," I stumbled over my words. "And that you're always bossing her. She can get kind of mad, well, and mean."

"Okay. Well, I'm not there...." she said, her words trailing off.

"I don't know the full extent of what she sees or hears," I tried to explain. "But sometimes she's mad at you, or, pretend you."

"Uh. Okay, I'll just deal with it when I'm there I guess," she said, a bit of hesitation in her voice. I made a mental note to check Mom's vertical blinds for knives.

"I'm FINE!"

First Doctor's Appointment, May 4, 2020

I was fixated on the orange-colored damask fabric on the chair Mom was squirming around in trying to evade the doctor's questions. *Why orange fabric?* Before my mind could critique the interior design of the office, I heard Mom say, "I'm seeing things," dismissing the comment with a wave of her hand and a laugh.

If you say, I'm seeing things to a doctor, two questions immediately follow. "Have there been any changes to your medications?" and "Are you taking any drugs that weren't prescribed to you?" *Maybe acid?*

Once it was ruled out that Mom wasn't a drug addict, the doctor asked for a urine sample to test for a bladder infection. Mom and I were convinced it was a bladder infection because of the experience with Nana. Mom excused herself to the bathroom with a little plastic cup, then returned a few minutes later with the same plastic cup wrapped in a neatly folded paper towel.

Five minutes later, the nurse poked her head into the room. "It's all clear," she said, indicating Mom didn't have a bladder infection. *Now what?*

We left with orders for blood work up and an MRI. More questions, no real answers. My hope was that the blood work or MRI would provide answers, a label that would neatly identify Mom's symptoms as *something*. I didn't know what that *something* would be, but I felt a name would give me some sense of control.

Someone Somewhere Is Building an Ark

MRI Appointment, May 12, 2020

The morning of the MRI, rain poured down in sheets, so torrential I joked with my son that someone, somewhere was building an Ark. Rain was no joking matter for Mom. I knew she was sitting in front of her TV watching the weather doppler images on the radar grow with time lapse. The colors starting green, then yellow, then to shades of red centered with pink indicating the heaviest rainfall. She'd be worried, but she'd also be a little excited, because she might have an excuse to get out of doing the MRI.

Mom had an irrational fear of flooding that rooted back to when she and Dad were in grad school living in Pennsylvania. The story, which I've heard almost every time there's rain, is that they lived on the top floor of a three-story apartment building, when a full day of rain turned into flash flooding. The flooding forced the neighbors living on the first floor to flee up to my parent's apartment for safety. Water never entered their apartment, but the experience would leave Mom with a lifelong fear that all rain would ultimately turn into a flash flood. Right on cue, my cell phone rang, *Mom,* scrolled across the caller ID.

"We're fine. I drive in the rain all the time," I said, curtly, as I answered the call. The same conversation about flooding I'd had so many times over the years played out like a script, finally ending with Mom conceding.

Cameron, like everyone during the pandemic, was looking for any opportunity to get out of the house and offered to drive us. The mix of Mom's incessant worry and my son's twenty-one-year-old driving skills produced a car ride worthy of a

Xanax prescription. Mom simultaneously clutched the door for dear life, while giving Cameron painstaking step-by-step driving instructions. Sprinkled in were the, "Be careful!", statements that startled more than helped the driver. When we arrived and learned that only Mom and I could go inside the building due to COVID restrictions, Cameron wasn't upset at all. NOT AT ALL!

We entered the lobby to find social distancing was in full effect. Chairs sat under harsh fluorescent lighting, evenly spaced six feet apart. Medical clinic lobbies are rarely cozy, but the pandemic made them feel uncomfortably organized and impersonal, like an orderly social experiment. If you weren't sitting upright in defined rows, you were standing on circular blue stickers, also spaced six feet apart, forming a line at reception. Introverted, I took a seat, relishing the distance between people. The chance of someone leaning over to start a conversation in the awkward six-foot gap was slim.

Cautiously, keeping space between people, Mom stepped from one blue dot to another, until she received her intake paperwork. As she walked back, I noticed a strange expression on her face. That *unsettled, almost queasy feeling* began to settle in the pit of my stomach. Her face was expressionless, completely flat. The human face always has expression, a tiny crease by the mouth or a microscopic smile. A completely expressionless or flat face makes you take notice. It's a little creepy and it sticks with you, like Samara from *The Ring* movie.

Mom, now sitting in her chair six feet to my right, was staring at her paperwork, but not putting ink to paper.

"Do you want me to fill it out?" I said, my chair teetering on two legs, as I tried to close the six-foot space so she could hear me. She didn't put up a fight, just shoved the stack of papers into my hands. This small interaction would be forever etched in my mind as the beginning of my job as scribe. Mom would never fill out another form.

There's a certain amount of privacy you count on in mother-daughter relationships. That privacy is like a protective coating around a pill. That pill, the embarrassing information about your mom. There was no protective coating when filling out medical paperwork.

Gosh, this is really thorough, I thought, as I continued down the medical history form. I cleared my throat. "Have you ever had a sexually transmitted disease?" I said, as I held my breath in anticipation of the answer.

"No. Well, not that I know of," she replied, laughing.

I'm just going to mark the little box for no and move on. This simple act of filling out medical forms was the beginning of Mom and me reversing roles. My role now, more maternal and her role, more childlike.

"Kay, we're ready for you," a nurse said, smiling, gesturing for us to follow her.

You'll never find an MRI on someone's bucket list. They're loud, the magnetic clanking frays your nerves, and all your phobias about being trapped are brought to the surface. If you're claustrophobic, it's living out your worst nightmare or in therapeutic terms, exposure therapy. That being said, Mom who was riddled with anxiety on a normal day, was pretty unfazed. *She's probably worn out from worrying about flooding,* I thought.

As I sat alone in the private lobby adjacent to the MRI room, I thought about the night I'd sat alone in my living room holding a filled to the brim glass of white wine that I'd sworn I wouldn't have that night. *If you can just get the boys off to college, they won't need you anymore and you can just drink yourself to death,* I'd thought. I'd tried for almost a year to moderate my drinking. First only drinking on weekends, then only on Thursdays, Fridays and Saturdays. When I couldn't miss a night of drinking, I knew I was in trouble. I couldn't imagine my life if I kept drinking, but I also couldn't imagine my life without alcohol.

Now sitting in this lobby six years later, sober, I wondered if I'd be able to get through the pandemic and Mom without relapsing. The pandemic alone was a playbook for relapse. Isolation, no jobs, no accountability, what could go wrong? If you're sober, EVERYTHING!

Let me get this straight, I can isolate without judgment, AA meetings are online, and there's unlimited quality time with my family. Seriously, anyone would understand relapsing, I mean it was just shy of the apocalypse for pete's sake. I'd read a book in early sobriety, where each chapter started with a scenario that the author would justify relapsing. For example, aliens landing on earth or diagnosis of a terminal disease. Just as I was thinking a global pandemic definitely would have been a chapter, I heard Mom's voice.

"Let's go!" she said, grabbing her purse from the seat next to me, throwing it over her shoulder with some urgency.

"You need to change back into your clothes," I

said, looking at her hospital gown now accessorized with her purse. She gave me a half smile and turned back toward the dressing area where her clothes were waiting. I watched her exposed little, veiny legs stroll down the hall, shoeless, with her purse still slung over one shoulder keeping one side of the hospital gown from exposing her naked backside.

Now dressed we headed for the exit, I could hear the rain pummeling the roof. From the lobby I shot Cameron a quick text.

> We're done, can you come grab us out front?

Mom and I stood at the windows that overlooked the parking lot, holding umbrellas, waiting for just the right time to b-line it for the car. Cameron, who had pulled the car into the parking spot directly in front of us, peered through the windshield eyeing us. Rain pelted the ceiling, torrential and loud. I could see Cameron shrug his shoulders, throwing his hands up, the universal "What the fuck" gesture. The minute his hands fell to the side, I heard my phone ring.

"Are you guys going to come out? You're holding umbrellas!" he said, a little bit of sarcasm lacing the word umbrellas.

Our feet sloshed through what was once a parking lot, but now looked more like a lake. I helped Mom get into the car, my umbrella balanced on the roof and door, as I felt water seep into my shoes, pooling, and soaking my socks. I slammed her door shut then waded through puddles, as tiny white caps hit my ankles. Sliding onto the front passenger seat drenched, I heard Mom from the back seat mumbling about flooding under her breath. Cameron rolled his eyes next to me. I glanced at the clock; it was only fucking 10 a.m.

Several days later while I was at work I received a call from the doctor. I quietly stepped out of the common living room at detox where I'd sat down with the clients because like watching a train wreck, I'd been pulled in by an episode of Tiger King. "The MRI was unremarkable," the doctor said.

Unremarkable, what does that mean?

"Okay. I'm not sure what to do with that?" I said, stumped, listening with my free ear to the client's chatter about Joe Exotic in the other room. "What does unremarkable mean?"

"There's atrophy in areas of the brain as people age," the doctor explained. "Your mom's scan is showing typical atrophy for someone her age."

What now? I felt guilty for wishing Mom's brain had atrophied more, thinking that might explain the hallucinations.

"I would recommend seeing a neurologist," the doctor said, filling my awkward silence.

Chapter 3
Clues In the Street View

July 1-21, 2020

The calm of June had lulled my family into a feeling that maybe everything was going to be okay. Cameron decided to move to Miami for his graduate program, sending me into a frenzied search for a sight unseen apartment.

"You see there's no bars on the windows," I said to Cameron, scrolling over an image on Google Street View. "That's a good sign."

Cameron rolled his eyes. "It looks fine to me," he said, giving me that, you're being ridiculous, look.

Undeterred, I continued. "You can tell a lot by what's in these images. Look here's a lady walking alone," I said, pointing to the tiny image. "Women don't walk alone in sketchy neighborhoods."

"You have to stop!" Cameron said, grabbing the computer from me, not wanting to be educated on universal safety indicators.

I hadn't noticed Travis come up behind us to view the listing photos. "Are we living there?" Travis asked, sarcastically. "That's nicer than our house." He wasn't wrong.

I'd inched up the rental budget to ease the anxiety I felt about picking an apartment without knowing the neighborhoods.

The next day at work I hunted down my co-worker who lived in the Miami area before moving to Austin. "Wynwood is cool," my co-worker said, laying back on the small sofa in my office. "The other is kind of ghetto."

And with that it was decided, Wynwood. Prior to his life doing a complete one-eighty in sobriety, my co-worker had spent his time in the Miami area with a heroin addiction. He was a reliable source for "kind of ghetto."

As we inched closer to Cameron leaving for school, I watched Miami Dade County front and center on every news feed as the hot zone of COVID, along with all the southern states lining the gulf from Texas to Florida.

Road Trip Through the Hot Zone

July 29, 2020

Usually, the prospect of twenty hours in a car brought up feelings of dread, but I was excited for the road trip to Miami. My childhood had been spent driving across the country in my family's cream-colored Buick Century, with my sister and me in the back. At times, a strip of masking tape would be installed by Dad, as a divider, separating us so we wouldn't kill each other. I can still hear, "She touched me," echoing through the car followed by Dad's voice, "If I have to pull off the road, you're going to regret it." There was also the time when Dad decided to cook a pot roast using the engine as an oven. He'd stopped at designated points throughout the desert to pop the hood, peel back the tin foil, and check its progress. The engine cooked the pot roast, carrots, and potatoes to perfection, except the whole meal had a smokey exhaust taste.

The morning we were leaving, I went over last-minute details with Connor who would be staying home alone. "All of Nigel's hard-boiled eggs are in the fridge for breakfast. I told Gma (the nickname we called Mom instead of grandmother) you'd pick her up Saturday," I said, and watched Connor roll his eyes. "She knows it's just for the two days before we come back in."

I know what you're thinking, *your parrot eats eggs, isn't that a little cannibalistic?* Eggs are his go to breakfast favorite!

Connor looked annoyed. "I don't really need Gma. I'm fine alone."

I don't think you'll be alone, I thought, as I visualized his girlfriend moving in.

"It'll just make me relax knowing she'll be here to help break up the trip."

The decision to insert Mom into Connor's time alone would later highlight my denial of Mom's condition. I'd frozen in my mind the version of Mom I remembered leaving my kids with for weekend trips. Not the mom who was delusional and hallucinating. My sense of Mom had been skewed by the frayed nerves of taking one kid to an unfamiliar city, while leaving the other kid halfway across the country during a pandemic. Everything would change after this trip. I didn't know it then, but that would be the last time I relied on Mom.

Just after 7 a.m., we hit the road, twenty hours to our final destination. Cameron and I rode in his car while Travis drove our car, playing follow the leader along highway I-10. We'd be running the gauntlet of the COVID hot zone states through Louisiana, Alabama, and Mississippi and then finally into the reddest zone of them all, Florida. Simultaneously, hurricane Isaias with its eighty-seven miles-per-hour winds, was barreling directly at Florida, setting off a cascade of worried text messages and calls from Mom before we even got out of Texas.

Less than an hour into the road trip, I played a message from Mom on speaker, her voice sounded a bit hysterical.

> Do you have water in your car? What about an evacuation plan? Oh, this just makes me really nervous. Give me a call back.

Ding, ding, ding. The sound of constant text messages followed, causing all of us to silence our phones before we hit Louisiana. I saw my phone light up with a text message from Travis.

> Your Mom keeps texting me about the weather.

I sent a text back.

> I KNOW! She called and texted us too.

Highway I-10 was crawling with cars, with traffic bottlenecks at every narrowing of lanes or on-ramp. *When did road trips become so chic?* Cars with so much luggage strapped to their roofs it made the highway look more like the great migration than a vacation. *How long were these people going to be gone for?*

"I guess everyone's tired of being at home," I said to Cameron, eyeing the miles and miles of cars laid out on all sides of us.

Humanity had been limited in where they could go, where they worked, and who they saw for months. Maybe it was the freedom that four wheels rolling along asphalt brought or it was simply somewhere away from the houses they'd been trapped in, but everyone seemed to be on a road trip. I understood, through the window I watched the landscape change from piney woods to coastal marshes feeling my world expand again.

Pit stops were centered around Buc-ee's, a chain of country stores the size of small shopping malls with a baseball capped beaver as a mascot. I was ready for serious road trip food like Buc-ee's bites, chopped beef sandwiches, cookies, and fudge. You can't shame me, it's a road trip, I'll eat Oreos the whole way if I want. Not Cameron; inside the Louisiana Buc-ees, he picked through the salads, scanning their contents like a detective. Gorging on fudge, when Cameron was dipping carrots into hummus, killed my road trip food buzz. Seriously, it's a road trip, why are there carrots in the car?

Buc-ee's acted as a pandemic thermometer. It was a gauge for mask wearing, social distancing, and well, political views, but that's another book. The further east we descended; the less masks were worn. The Alabama Buc-ee's felt like another world, it was crowded with more people than I'd seen in one place in months. The blue social distancing dots laid on the floor, like relics that had been forgotten. People stood on top of each other, maskless, ordering sandwiches. Then there were the bins of condiments, those were a germ picnic. I figured Dr. Anthony Fauci probably had nightmares that looked like this scene. I placed my coffee on the counter, surveying the cartons of milk and creamers placed in a large trough of ice. My hand wavered over the top of the vanilla creamer, before plunging recklessly in for the grab. Before putting the container back into the ice, I fought the urge to wipe it down with a wet wipe.

"If I haven't already had COVID, I just got it," I said to Travis, as we walked back to the car.

Switching into Travis's car, I jumped into the passenger seat to find a giant bag of M&Ms. *Are you kidding me?* "I've been in the accountability car!" I snapped, looking at Travis as he climbed into the driver's seat. "I can't believe you've had M&Ms this whole time."

Just after 8 p.m., exhausted, we caravanned into Gulf Breeze, Florida, a tiny, adorable suburb of Pensacola. Twinkling yellow lights illuminated the long arch of the bridge into Gulf Breeze. The glowing yellow of the lights were mesmerizing against the black of the evening. The vast inky ocean spanned out in every direction with little silvery reflections glittering in the moon's light. If I hadn't been so beat, I'd have gone for a walk to explore, but instead I fell into bed.

The same bridge, now with the sun reflecting off the ocean, started our remaining nine hours into Miami. Our Buc-ee's pit stops transitioned to Florida turnpike service plazas. Just when I thought I couldn't spend another minute in the car, Miami came into view. As we took the exit that would drop us into the heart of the city, I gazed out the window at incredible spray paint art on the sides of buildings. Art deco and modern skyscrapers were scattered throughout this vibrant city and, even during the pandemic, you could feel its energy. The ocean that lined the entire east side of the city looked like a wet aquamarine jewel. Scantily clad people with sun-kissed skin walked with purpose along the streets, most with either a French bulldog or some other kind of small fluffy mix that was perfectly groomed.

As vibrant as Miami felt, the hotels were still gripped by the pandemic. We were greeted by no less than four hotel staff before we made it to the check-in desk. The man behind the check-in counter popped his head up from the computer. "It looks like we were able to upgrade you to one of our luxury suites," he said, smiling.

It's a low bar man, as long as it's not the car, I thought.

As we walked into the suite, I understood why the man had been excited to upgrade us. *Holy shit, I could move in here!* The suite was larger than our first apartment and looked like it fell off the set of Miami Vice. Vibrant red velvet sofas surrounded a mirrored table, with a small glass dining table cast off to the right in front of a wall with some seriously hip geometric wallpaper. The entire back wall of the suite was floor-to-ceiling windows overlooking the water.

We dropped our bags and ordered greasy hamburgers from across the street. Why would we leave this gorgeous suite!

I felt the grease from the hamburger slide down my hand, as I stood gazing out the window watching yachts scurry back into port, with the looming dark sky of Isaias hanging in the distance. Eating hamburgers in this luxury suite felt like wearing Channel to date night at Applebees. Gusting winds whipped up the water forming large white caps along the shoreline that splashed onto the streets in little surges. Gusts of wind and rain began to pelt the window, vibrating my hand resting against the glass.

Although Miami was spared from the wrath of hurricane Isaias, another storm was brewing at home.

Revenge of the Cinnamon Rolls

July 31, 2020

Not even a full twenty-four hours in Miami, Connor called. "She keeps talking about this old man and his grandson standing by dad's desk,"

Connor said, his voice quick and irritated. "She told me she took Nigel over to the neighbors!"

Maybe she did. No, Nigel tolerates her, I considered. Nigel enjoyed Mom's singing, but for the most part Mom treated Nigel like a domesticated dog, and he reminded her with warning bites that he was an undomesticated intelligent bird.

That's a hallucination.

Now exasperated, Connor continued, "Mom! She came out of the room holding her wadded up pants, saying the cinnamon rolls didn't agree with her stomach!"

"Oooookay. Was she doing laundry?" I replied, not quite putting it together.

"She shit her pants!" he said, firmly.

"Oh." I got it.

I glanced over at Travis, who at this point had caught the gist of our conversation. His expression part concern, part trying to hold back a laugh, mouthing, *shit her pants,* to me. I felt horrible, I had unwittingly put Connor in a baby-sitter role. I told Connor to drive Gma home and we would head back tomorrow.

"Let's send him some money so he and Natasha can go out for dinner," Travis suggested. "It's the least we can do."

"What's the appropriate amount of money to

say, *I'm sorry that Gma shit her pants on your watch?*" I said, laughing.

"Uh, priceless?" he said, sounding like the Mastercard commercial.

The Wynwood neighborhood turned out to be a great pick, hip and safe, with tons of walkable restaurants. Cameron's apartment was in a modest pale gray, art deco building with six units. On the same street there were new modern condos intermixed with bungalow-style houses and a large construction project at the end of the street overlooking the water which eventually would be high-end residences. For the record, the other neighborhood, the one my co-worker had referenced as "kind of ghetto" wasn't "kind of ghetto", it was downright sketchy. The ads for the sketchy area had said, *walk to the medical center*. You could walk, but I can't imagine a scenario where someone would actually walk anywhere in that area.

We spent the day buying furniture and setting up Cameron's apartment. That afternoon, I sent pictures of his place to Mom, hoping to distract her. In an earlier conversation, I'd lied about the reason Connor would be taking her home early. There wasn't a good lie for the situation and the truth felt insensitive. *Well Mom, you're seeing things and it's creeping Connor out,* or, *he really doesn't want to hear about you shitting your pants.*

The next morning, the three of us stood on the street in front of Cameron's building to say our goodbyes. Leaving Cameron in Miami felt like the day we left him in the dorms his freshman year of college. We were once again dropping a kid off in an unfamiliar city, all alone, the parting words inadequate for the situation, "Love you, make good choices."

Travis and I now ran the hot zone gauntlet in reverse, Florida, Alabama, Mississippi, Louisiana, and Texas. Hours of shocked chatter about Mom filled the car. Hallucinating wasn't new, but something about Connor's reaction, coupled with the frequency of hallucinations startled me. The backdrop to our twenty-hour car ride back to Austin, was the audio book, *The End of October* by Lawrence Wright, a fabulous book about a global pandemic. Not the best choice, given the current global pandemic. When we weren't scared silent, the occasional "I hope that doesn't happen" or "I had no idea how close we'd come to that," would be uttered after sections of the book that hit a little too close to home. Published in April of 2020, I wondered if the author had somehow foreseen the future.

Chapter 4
The Clock

First Neurologist appointment, August 26, 2020

Humidity hit me like a hot blanket the minute I exited the parking garage. I was so focused on pulling up the confirmation email from the neurologist's office, that I hadn't realized I'd outpaced Mom who was still in the garage. *Am I sprinting?* It didn't feel like it.

"Sorry I was reading an email," I said, lapping back to join her.

"It's these sandals," Mom said, staring down at her feet. "I keep slipping." The sandals, with their beaded crystals running along tiny straps, barely held the foot to the sole. Mom had a pair in every color.

The protective paper on the examination chair crinkled under Mom's fidgeting body, while she stared at the neurologist like she hadn't understood his question. "Are you more easily confused or is it more difficult to multitask?" he repeated the question. I sat to the side of Mom thinking she looked like a small child with her hands tucked under her knees. I found myself also answering his question, *sometimes, I was completely confused by the TV remotes...*, my internal answer was interrupted by Mom's voice

"Sometimes," Mom admitted, then went off on a tangent about her confusing homeowners associations and stacks of bills. "I have all these damn HOAs," she started into a rant. "It's all so crazy and confusing."

I flashed back to an image of Mom's bills spread out over her kitchen island. Some bills were sorted into piles with little yellow handwritten sticky notes stuck on top. Then there were envelopes with checks half filled out, stuffed inside some of the piles. In one pile there was a recipe for a chicken casserole shoved between utility bills. It was chaos. The doctor's voice brought me back to the room.

"Are you having difficulty remembering things?" he asked.

I forgot an appointment the other day. I couldn't remember what I needed at the grocery store. Shit, my memory sucks. Mom's voice snapped my mind out of autopilot.

"I am. It's getting harder, like I just can't find it in my mind," she said, her face now looking stressed. "I feel like I'm going crazy, you know?" The doctor would have made an excellent poker player, save a nod here and there, his face gave nothing away.

Mom was then handed a piece of paper with a few rudimentary pictures that she was asked to identify. She seemed to ace that test.

So did I.

I watched the doctor hand Mom a blank piece of paper. "I'd like you to draw a clock, just like the one on the wall," he gestured up and to his left. "Please include all the numbers."

I didn't know it then, but this simple clock drawing would be something Mom would later reference frequently with utter disdain. I watched judgmentally, as Mom drew a circle about the size of a quarter in the upper left corner of the paper. *Why so small? You'll never get all the numbers into the circle.* She stared at her circle then proceeded to write tiny numbers into it. Quickly running out of room, she then proceeded to crunch the numbers together forcing them to fit. Her clock looked like something out of Alice In Wonderland.

"Urgh, here!" she said, shoving the paper back at the doctor, frustrated.

The doctor glanced at the clock, folded the paper up and put it into his file. "Have you noticed if your walking has slowed down?" he asked.

YES! I thought but didn't say. A flood of memories rushed in. I thought of a time several years prior when Mom and I were visiting Danielle. I hadn't realized how much I'd adjusted my walking pace to fit Moms, until we were in downtown San Rafael, CA. walking with Danielle and Ben who quickly outpaced us. Unaware they had left us in the dust, Danielle and Ben finally looked back. Danielle had given me a confused look and I'd just shrugged my shoulders. Only this morning, I'd had to circle back to Mom in the parking garage.

"No. Not really." Mom said.

I practically fell forward out of my chair. "Yes! Over the last year or so it's slowed." Mom shot me a sideways look. Her look wasn't mad but confused. She genuinely didn't know her pace had slowed.

The doctor acknowledged my answer and turned back to Mom. "I'd like you to just walk down the hall. How you normally do, then come back," he said, helping Mom off the exam table and guiding her towards the doorway.

Mom looked down at her feet. "Okay, but my feet slip in these sandals, so we'll see how it goes," she said, with a little laugh.

He stood at the doorway studying her gait. I stood behind him studying her arms that hung stiffly at her side, lacking that natural swing arms do when we walk.

"I can't diagnose at this point," the doctor said, re-claiming his seat as we took ours. "But, on my short list would be Lewy body dementia. I'd like to have you meet with our neuropsychologist." He also mentioned Mom appeared to display some Parkinsonian traits. *Parkinsonian, you mean Parkinsons?* I felt the *unsettled, not quite queasy feeling* brewing in my stomach. That had never even crossed my mind and it totally threw me for a loop.

The pharmaceutical options for LBD were limited. The doctor explained that most drugs prescribed to help with hallucinations would worsen dementia. I considered, *Would I rather argue about pretend people or repeat myself constantly?* However, he could prescribe a low dose of Quetiapine, brand name Seroquel, which could help with sleep, as well as hallucinations. Seroquel is one of the tiniest pink pills, it's so small you could hold it on the end of your pinky finger and almost miss it. The dose Mom was prescribed required her to split the already tiny pink pill into two. One half so minuscule, it was about the size of a grain of rice. It was ridiculous. In time, this tiny pink pill would become a point of consternation for those of us helping Mom, eventually earning the name, the fucking little pink pill.

Crazy Bird Lady

August 18, 2020

I felt the hot sticky morning air as I balanced my coffee in one hand and used the other to adhere the suction cup on Nigel's window perch onto the outside window. I grabbed Nigel from inside then placed him on the perch like I'd done many times before. He immediately began his preening routine, between fluffing and preening he bobbed up and down on the perch. All of the sudden on a downward bob he spread his wings as I watched his little claws leave the perch. In the blink of an eye he was in flight, flapping his clipped wings down the fairway behind our house.

My husband, who had been working, saw him fly by the master bedroom window. As I stood in disbelief, frozen in place, the patio door flew open, smacking the wall with force. Travis blitzed by me running toward the fairway, then hurdled over the wrought iron fence in one swift motion. I watched Travis's figure get smaller, as he ran after Nigel down the fairway yelling, "NIGEL!". Nigel, at this point looked like a small dot in the distance, headed for a huge oak tree about halfway down the fairway. Just then two birds flew out of the tree and began dive-bombing him in tandem, as if to say, "Not this tree buddy". *OMG those birds are being mean to my feathered baby!* In a matter of minutes, I had gone from pouring my first cup of coffee, to sobbing in my pajamas.

A feeling of loss settled deep in my chest, gripping my heart, and squeezing. Loss was everywhere. I was losing Mom, the world was losing thousands of people a day to COVID, and now my feathered baby was lost.

I'm just ridiculous about this bird! I'm that crazy bird lady, only you won't find me on a park bench, at least not yet. I thought about the odds of getting a parrot back. This wasn't like losing a dog, he could literally be anywhere miles and miles away.

In no time, there wasn't an electric poll or signpost in the neighborhood that wasn't plastered with flyers displaying a picture of Nigel, front and center, staring back at you along with REWARD at the top. In the midst of my heart break, I was witnessing the best of humanity in my neighborhood. It felt like everywhere, people were on the hunt for Nigel.

"Nigel! Nigel! I really want to find that bird! He's so cool," a little boy yelled, hanging off the back of a golf cart that was driving along my back fence. "I wonder if he talks?" An entire family was crammed in the golf cart and calling for Nigel.

I walked up to the wrought iron fence to approach the family. "Thank you for looking for him," I said, tears welling up in my eyes. If the tears hadn't let the family know Nigel was my bird, the two huge speakers on our back patio blasting African Gray sounds would have. Our back yard sounded like the Nature Channel. Also outside was Nigel's large cage, doors wide open, with his favorite foods in a bowl.

"Oh. We're just dying to see him. I'm so sorry," the Mom, holding a little girl in her lap said. "I really hope you get him back."

Me too. I watched them drive off down the fairway, continuing to call "Nigel! Nigel!"

Did Mom Drop Acid?

I consulted a lost parrot website and learned African Grays in the wild congregate with their kind. I hoped the loud speakers would either keep him close or lure him back. We also learned statistics were not in our favor, but if you had a chance, it would be on day three when he would come out of the trees because he'd be hungry and thirsty.

Later that afternoon, two young boys on bikes passed me calling, "Nigel! Nigel!" as they pedaled, racing each other. My neighbors were calling and texting me with Nigel sightings. My neighbor to the left shot me a text the first night.

> My son's neighbor said he saw
> Nigel in a tree two doors down
> from you, the yard with all the bird
> baths!

A silver lining to the pandemic for Nigel was that everyone was home, looking for things to do outside of their houses. A literal army of neighbors were on a mission to find my ten-inch gray and red parrot.

Project "missing parrot" consisted of dawn and dusk searches, key times when birds are most active. Every dusk my family would descend onto the streets and golf course with binoculars. We received a few sideways stares and one or two suspicious comments due to the binoculars. When you don't explain to people that you're looking for a missing bird, you'll have a handful who are convinced you're a peeping Tom.

Connor and Travis stood at the back window the morning after Nigel flew off, watching me put on my make-up, sitting in a lawn chair in the backyard, crying, and calling for Nigel.

"Is Mom going to be okay?" Connor said to his dad.

"Man, I hope so," Travis replied, unsure. If there were a stock image for "crazy bird lady" my morning makeup routine would be it. For the record, it was a lawn chair, not a park bench.

I didn't tell anyone in my extended family Nigel was gone until day two. Saying the words out loud made it true. Driving into work on day two, Mom called. "Hi Babe." she said, and I fell apart.

"Nigel flew off," I said, gasping into between sobs. "He's been gone for two days."

"Oh honey. I'm so sorry. I know how much you love him," she said, sounding like the mom I hadn't heard in months. "Can I help you in any way?"

I was speechless. Not only had Mom acknowledged my feelings, but she'd also engaged in hard emotions. Since Dad died Mom didn't do tough emotions like loss, typically diverting those conversations into something lighter. Her words this morning felt warm and genuine. I wiped tears from my cheek with the back of my hand, thinking about how long it had been since Mom reacted like, well, a mom. As I ended our call, I felt grateful for the glimpse of the mom I knew before Dad died and Lewy took hold.

"Hey"

August 20, 2020

Another dawn putting on makeup outside in the lawn chair crept in. The heat and humidity fogged my hand-held mirror and made it difficult to apply foundation. It was day three and I was emotionally spent, having done more ugly snot crying in the last forty-eight hours than I'd done in decades. To find some kind of peace, I quietly whispered, "Dad, if he's meant to be gone, I'll accept that. But if he's meant to come home, please help him find someone who knows what to do with a parrot. Someone who can help him." With that, I put Nigel in the hands of something greater than myself. I often talk to my deceased father. I also talk to God and I like to think that they talk to each other. Dad would have loved Nigel, he would have called him 'Turkeybird' because Nigel loves a good chicken or turkey leg.

Every co-worker and client at detox knew Nigel was missing. "Any word on the bird?" they'd say, as I walked through the door each day.

"It's day three. That's a good thing. Maybe?" said one well-meaning co-worker, who remembered the third day was a critical marker.

"I know. I'm hoping, but I'm also accepting he may just be gone," I said, choking back tears. I was crying AGAIN. *Good lord you need to get a hold of yourself Michelle.*

A couple hours into work, I heard a d*ing* from my cell phone sitting on my desk. I scurried to grab it thinking it was probably one of the kids. It was a text from Travis.

> Guess who's back?

Three little dots suspended in a gray bubble followed the message. I held my breath waiting. *He better not be fucking with me.*

A small square picture emerged on the screen. I clicked to enlarge the photo, my heart racing. Nigel was home! I immediately called Travis. "How? How did he get home? Did someone find him?" I talked so fast, he cut me off mid-sentence.

"Our neighbor just brought him to the door in a little pet carrier." Travis said, excitedly.

Nigel flew out of an oak tree and walked up to a neighbor who just happened to be on her front patio smoking. Without hesitation she leaned over, held out her finger, and Nigel stepped up. She hadn't seen any of the posters taped up all over the neighborhood but figured there probably wasn't a wild African Gray in the neighborhood. She put Nigel in a pet carrier with a plumb to eat, then walked directly across the street to the nice man that had come out of his house the previous evening to talk to Travis who had been looking for Nigel on the golf course. In that conversation, Travis told him about Nigel and then pointed out our house down the fairway. Pet carrier in hand, she walked directly to our home and rang the doorbell. Connor opened the door to a woman holding a pet carrier. "Animals always find me," she said, jokingly.

You want to know the first thing Nigel said to Connor after being in the wild for three days? He simply said," Hey". He'd also picked up "Cool. Cool" said with all the drawn out slang of a teenager. I wished Nigel had been wearing a tiny

GoPro, just to know what happened during those three days.

Thank you Dad for leading him to this wonderful animal whisperer! Thank you to my neighbor for bringing him home! Thank you to all my neighbors who scoured the neighborhood looking for him. You'll always hold a special place in my heart.

Chapter 5
Speed Dial

September 21, 2020

Ding, ding, ding. I watched my phone light up with incoming text messages. "I'm sorry, let me just make sure this isn't an emergency," I said to the client I was in the middle of a counseling session with. *Where's the fire?* I thought, looking at numerous text messages from Mom, each increasing in intensity, starting at 8:14 a.m.

> Please call me.
>
> I need you to call me!
>
> Call me!

Next came the rapid-fire phone calls back-to-back, that lit up my phone screen like a little strobe light. My client arched a brow watching my phone light up. "That person really wants to get a hold of you," he said, smirking.

"It's my mom," I said, rolling my eyes. "She thinks everything is an emergency."

"I'm up for a cigarette break, if you want to make a quick call," my client said, squirming in anticipation of a nicotine hit. Once outside, I stepped just out of ear shot from my client and phoned Mom.

"I'm at work. Can I call you after I get off?" I said, quickly.

Ignoring me, she replied, "Well, Donald's funeral is Wednesday, but I need to go to my sisters tomorrow."

"Okay. Let me see if I can get someone to cover me tomorrow," I said, a tiny bit annoyed. "You said you didn't want to go, so I didn't take off work." A couple days earlier Mom had been adamant that she wasn't going to attend the funeral, giving me a laundry list of reasons for her decision.

"Everyone's already there," she continued, sounding like a teenager with FOMO. "We can all go to the funeral from Gene Anns'." Mom's brother and sister, along with all the cousins were in Bryan planning to caravan to the funeral.

Watching my client out of the corner of my eye

start to light up a second cigarette, I quickly said, "Call your sister. I'll get someone to cover me at work."

An image of Uncle Donald, Travis and I at an A&M football game came to mind. I remembered being freezing, huddled next to Travis for warmth, thinking, I *don't care who wins, I just want to go home.* My uncle, on the other hand, cared deeply who won. One of the few things I'd known about Donald was that he was one of the biggest Texas A&M Football fans EVER. He also just died from LBD.

Tailgating A Funeral

September 22, 2020

The next morning, after spending the previous afternoon finding coverage at work, my phone started ringing. I glanced over to see, *incoming call, Mom,* scroll across the top of my cell. *It's not even seven. I can't do this before coffee.* I took a deep breath, I knew Mom would be trying to get out of going to Bryan. *Ring, ring. Ugh, she's just going to keep calling.*

"I don't think we should go," Mom said

anxiously, before I could even say hello. "Have you looked at the weather?"

I took a quick glimpse out the window. "It looks like clear skies here."

"Look at the forecast," she said, unwavering. "There's rain coming, and it looks bad."

I pulled up the weather app. on my phone. A small light green area began to form and spread across a portion of Travis County. *You're freaking out about light rain.* I felt irritation turn my checks hot. I completely reworked my schedule at the last minute, today was my birthday, which she hadn't mentioned, and now an hour before I was headed out the door to pick her up, she was wanting to cancel.

"It's your sister's ex-husband and the father of her kid's funeral," I said, angrier than intended. "Your entire family is in town. If you don't want to go, then you can call your sister and explain why." *Deal with your own shit,* I wanted to say, but instead hung up.

I had spent the last decade with Mom playing possum with plans. She'd commit to something, then want to back out at the last minute, tasking me with calling everyone involved to explain her sudden departure. My frustration was the accumulation of years of dealing with Mom ducking hard emotions and conversations after Dad's death. Gene Ann's entire family had flown to San Diego to attend Dad's Celebration of Life and support Mom. I was disappointed Mom couldn't show up in the same way for her sister. *Put on your big girl pants and let's go,* I thought.

Five minutes later Mom was calling again. "Well, I talked with Gene Ann and decided to go," she said.

"I'll pick you up in an hour," I replied, then hung up quickly before she had the chance to reply. I found out later, she never talked to Gene Ann. The idea of calling her sister and having that conversation apparently was enough for her to brave the light rain.

By evening, Mom and I sat in Gene Ann's living room listening to my cousin tell funny stories. Behind his smile was the grief at the loss of his dad. He slipped into his best impersonation of Uncle George (Gene Ann's second husband) pulling a BBQ out in the parking lot of the funeral. "I've got some sausages we could throw on the grill. There's some beer in the cooler," he said, in his best West Texas drawl. "I ran across my friend's, uncle's daughter, and she's going to stop by." We were all rolling with laughter, his humor a welcome distraction to the sadness that hung in the air. George is the, *Not all who wander are lost,* bumper sticker. He'll detour to see attractions, stop at historical markers, find old friends or relatives in just about any town, throw together a chili cook off, and then go fishing. He would definitely tailgate a funeral.

As the night grew late, those not staying at Gene Ann's started to gather their belongings to head to hotels. While we discussed logistics for the caravan the next morning, I realized Mom was standing behind me with her suitcase.

"I thought you wanted to stay with your sister?" I said, confused by the change in plan.

"No," she replied.

Gene Ann came up behind her. "I thought you were staying with me Sister?"

Please say yes. Please say yes. Ignoring us both, she pushed past me outside, headed to my car, then climbed in. I looked at Gene Ann and shrugged my shoulders. *Damn, there goes my evening alone reading tabloid magazines.* Mom was beginning to take up a lot of space in my life.

Me And My Shadow

September 23, 2020

Coffees in hand, Mom and I rejoined the group back at Gene Ann's to start the caravan into Arlington for the funeral. I was the designated driver for all of the Hart siblings, including Mom, Uncle Tommy, and Aunt Gene Ann. We piled inside my Lexus, Tommy sitting shotgun next to me, Mom in the back seat next to her sister.

The first part of the two-hour drive lulled me into a false sense of calm. We drove through small towns with little white chapels. Cows grazed in the pastures enjoying the mild temperatures before the afternoon heat would settle in and send them running for the shade trees.

About an hour into our drive, we hit highway I-35 up through Waco. *Happy feeling gone.* The narrow lanes with large temporary concrete block barriers lining either side, made you feel boxed in. Huge eighteen-wheelers congested the road. Their loud engines and the constant squealing of brakes, frayed my nerves. Between the traffic and the constant comments from my passengers, it was like a double driving endurance test.

"Be careful!" Mom shouted. "Watch out for that truck!"

Gene Ann gripped the door.

"We're really close to those barriers," Mom muttered under her breath.

I was clutching the steering wheel so hard I had to consciously loosen my grip to let the blood flow back through my fingers. By the time we got to Arlington, I imagined myself in the future, a poster child for one of those "We can't protect you from becoming your parents" Progressive Insurance commercials, only with me clenching the door yelling "Be careful" to one of my boys behind the wheel, as Dr. Rick calmly says, "You're not the one driving."

Fortunately, we arrived at the funeral in one piece. I was disappointed not to see George tailgating in the cemetery parking lot. As I parked, I took in the scene, small groups of people stood talking among headstones. In the distance a large canopy covered three rows of chairs. The chairs faced a coffin, and a framed photo of Uncle Donald propped on an easel behind it. Tommy and Gene Ann climbed out of the car and headed down the small, paved street that led to the site. Mom, on the other hand, clung to my side like those koala pencil huggers from the 1980s. As we neared other groups of people, I felt like I was shoving her into conversations the same way I'd done with my kids when they were young. "Look there's Joey, he likes Pokemon too," I'd say, trying to engage the boys with another pre-schooler. Only with Mom, it was, "Hi, I'm Kay's daughter." Then I'd gesture to Mom in hopes she'd interact, but she'd just smile, leaving an awkward silence until the other person introduced themselves.

Everywhere I went, Mom was on my heels less than a foot away. At one point, I went back to the car to grab something and when I turned around, I saw her closing the distance between us. It was hot and she hated to sweat, so this took some effort on her part. I started hearing the song "Me and My Shadow" in my head and felt the *unsettled, almost-queasy feeling* in my stomach. We were surrounded by Mom's entire extended family, relatives I had only heard about growing up, and she wouldn't leave my side.

When Mom did engage in conversation her memories from the distant past were amazingly accurate. I listened as she retold a story from several decades ago, the details were exactly as I'd remembered them. *How can you remember that?* I felt frustrated as I thought about all the times recently, I'd had to tell her something over and over again.

Family members took their place, one-by-one, at the podium in front of the coffin to share memories of Donald. Mom and I stood behind the rows of chairs, grateful the canopy provided some protection from the summer sun. A dreamlike feeling came over me, images of myself standing in front of a podium sharing memories of Mom flashed before me. Cracks started to form in my denial.

After the funeral everyone gathered to exchange stories about Donald over heaping plates of Mexican food. All-the-chicken-fajitas-I-could-eat later, and feeling emotionally drained we piled back into the car to return to Bryan. Again, we dodged eighteen-wheelers through Waco with lane barriers closing in on all sides. There was no worried chatter this time though; just snoring. Mom and Gene Ann were out cold in the back seat, their heads arched back with their mouths open, breathing loudly. Tommy fought the after-lunch nap through Waco then passed out.

Halfway back to Bryan, I concluded I couldn't do another night and wanted to be home. I would have to drive all over Texas to make this happen but damn it I was going to try. The mission to get home would take me from Arlington to Bryan, from Bryan to Lakeway and finally, from Lakeway to Austin—a six-hour drive time if I was lucky.

When I made my plans known, I got a lot of questioning stares. No one could understand why I didn't just stay the night in Bryan and head out in the morning. They weren't wrong, it was crazy. It was also something I felt in my bones. Only later would I realize I was emotionally shutting down. Like my computer when I sent it too many commands, causing it to freeze then power down, I was processing the changes in Mom, along with the looming responsibility those changes posed, and knowledge that whatever happened, it would end in Mom's death. My bones knew I needed to shut down in the comfort of my own home.

As it turned out, the drive back to Austin would be critical for more than one reason. There would be no question at the end of that five-hour drive that Mom's own driving days were over.

After a short pit stop in Bryan to drop off Gene Ann and Tommy, Mom and I pulled out into the evening darkness. Pitch black blanketed the road, so dark without headlights I couldn't have seen my hand in front of my face. Occasionally, my headlights would catch the white paint of the chapels we'd passed earlier, giving me a sense of where I was. Quiet mile after mile clipped past in this manner. I was zoning out on the white paint of the center dividing line when Mom grabbed for the dashboard. "Do you see that truck?" she screeched. "We're going to drive right through it!"

I looked out, alarmed, into vast darkness. "There's nothing in front of us for miles," I said, turning to look at her. An uncomfortable silence fell over us. In the next moment, two things happened. First the voice in my head slowed down, as if to make sure I was really paying attention. *Oh' shit she's hallucinating while I'm driving.* Second, my phone lit up with a text from Travis.

> Hey, why don't you just come here, and I'll take your mom back to Lakeway.

> Okay

I wrote back gratefully.

> I'll be there in about an hour.

I could have cried when I saw my driveway. Travis, who'd heard the garage door opening, emerged like a shadowy figure before it was fully lifted. Leaving the engine running, I jumped out and Travis jumped into the driver's seat. "Be back soon," he said.

Minutes after getting home, I was in pajamas, sprawled out on the sofa and holding a brownie on a little napkin. Some Netflix series played in the background, but I wasn't really watching it, already halfway lapsed into a comatose state. Another text exchange with Travis jolted me back awake.

(Travis)

> Your Mom reeked. Did you not smell her?

(Me)

> A little, I guess.

(Travis)

> I had to roll the windows down. There's no way she had deodorant on. She was totally out of it too! She had no idea where we were, and she was seeing shit.

(Me)

> I know, she thought we were driving through trucks. We're going to have to talk to her about not driving anymore.
> (SCREAMING IN FEAR EMOJI)

Pressing send on the last text, I shoved the last bits of brownie in my mouth and recalled other times I'd wondered recently if Mom had on deodorant. I remembered an article I'd read weeks before about personal hygiene, or the lack thereof, being an early sign of dementia. *I'm probably reading too much into a smelly night.* Maybe she just forgot to put on deodorant. After all, I'd never seen Mom leave the house without her hair brushed, teeth polished, and full makeup applied. *She'd be horrified,* I thought, followed by: *I'd want someone to tell me if I smelled.* I made a mental note to talk with her next time I suspected she hadn't applied deodorant.

Later, I looked at pictures from the funeral and found it hard to miss the Parkinsonian symptoms. In one particular picture, her arms hung like dead weights at her side, palms flat against her pants. The once vibrant full-face smile now looked fake, almost as if someone had startled her in the photo. She reminded me of the nutcracker figurine I'd had on my mantle at Christmas, its wide eyes and painted smile almost garish.

The Ladies at the House

Over the last couple of months, Travis and I were beginning to figure out that we didn't have the whole picture of Mom's condition. Between her thinking I was driving through trucks on the highway and Connor's experience while we were in Miami, I knew I needed a broader picture.

Travis and I pulled up to Mom's for an unannounced visit. *Knock, knock.* "It's me," I yelled through the door. The door slowly pulled open, exposing Mom standing in her blue and white floral pajamas. *It's 2:30 p.m.*, I thought as I surveyed her disheveled hair. She looked like she'd just rolled out of bed. Don't get me wrong, I love a day in pajamas, but her demeanor and face didn't depict someone who was relaxing, binging their favorite TV series. She stood blocking the door, her eyes darted side to side, as if surveying for danger. Nudging our way into the house, Travis said, "How are things going Kay?"

She shifted nervously. "The ladies won't leave! They need to go," she said, annoyed.

I quickly scanned the room for the ladies. "I don't see anyone," I said, still checking the room.

Her shifty eyes focused on her dining room table. "She just sat there and wouldn't move," Mom said, gesturing towards one of the chairs that was pulled out. "I kept asking her to get in the car with the other ladies, but she wouldn't." *Let me get this straight, you're trying to get pretend ladies into your car?*

Apparently, the ladies were unwelcome guests, so much so, that she described trying to take them to the police station at 2 a.m. "The other ladies were in the car, and she just wouldn't get in," she said, her speech quickening. "So, I finally gave up."

Driving pretend people to the police station isn't good. That's a Silver Alert, I thought, my eyes ping ponging around the room nervously.

Travis, noticing the horror in my face, calmly engaged Mom. "Did you drive to the police station this morning?" We both held our breath waiting for the answer.

"No. She wouldn't get in the car," Mom said, glancing back at the chair, annoyed at the lady apparently sitting in it. I was now staring at the chair too, half annoyed that this pretend woman wouldn't get in the car.

At least you were headed to the police station, I

thought, figuring the police would have called me. I couldn't believe that's where my brain was going; That at least she'd have driven the pretend ladies to the police station.

The change in intensity of Mom's voice drew my focus back to the room. "They just stare at me and don't say anything," she said, waving her hand towards the table. "They won't eat, they just stare!" *Good lord, I would want them to leave too. People sitting around staring at you is creepy.* I glanced over at the dining table wondering what the ladies looked like.

"Kay, it concerns me that you were going to leave the house at 2 a.m.," Travis said, in an even tone, as I contemplated calling the police for a mental health check. "I think it's time we start talking about you not driving."

"My neighbors are awful drivers," Mom said, dismissing Travis's comment. "I've been in the car with them, and they've almost killed me."

Pretty sure your neighbors aren't driving around pretend ladies.

Travis looked at me, then back to Mom. "Why don't we just start talking about it?" he said. "Do you remember how scared you were when you thought Michelle was driving through trucks?"

Mom's eyes widened. "That was awful. I thought we were going to die."

"You have your doctor's appointment coming up, why don't we see what the doctor has to say. In the meantime, can we agree that you should limit your driving or ask people to drive you places?"

Mom looked up at Travis with slumped shoulders. "Okay," she said in a whisper. I was mesmerized by her stature, she looked like a little girl in her pajamas looking up at Travis.

I'm so sorry Mom.

As I watched Mom listen to Travis, I flashed back to a memory of a time when Travis and Mom were enmeshed in a power struggle led by Mom. Early in our marriage, Mom would constantly pick fights with Travis for the sole reason of getting me to pick between my new husband and her. I could hear Travis whisper in my ear twenty-one years ago, "I need to get some air or I'm going to kill your Mom," he'd said as he left the hospital, almost missing the birth of Cameron. Mom had been so overbearing that day, my OB-GYN had to ask her to move so she could deliver the baby. "I don't think your daughter is going to want that picture," she'd said, nicely shoving Mom and her camera aside.

The sound of Travis closing the car door startled me. I looked at Mom standing in her doorway and felt nauseated. "What now," I said to Travis, as we pulled out of the driveway.

Travis let out a deep breath. "I'm not sure," he said, staring at the road.

Chapter 6
At What Age Do You Get Through Your Mommy Issues?

Mom and I had a complicated relationship. My new responsibilities with Mom stirred up unresolved issues between us, that up until this point, I'd hoped to never unpack. I had taken the *shove that shit way down,* approach. I write about our relationship issues in the book, not to disparage Mom, but because I know our relationship isn't unique. There're mothers and daughters as I type this page that are on the same path as us. If dysfunction happens on a spectrum, Mom and I would be on the lower end, however it's impact would be felt in every part of my life, from my relationships to my sobriety. Lewy would dismantle and reconstruct my relationship with Mom.

One afternoon, feeling nostalgic, I found

pictures of Mom and Dad's wedding in an old, large memory box that contained everything from my boy's art projects, to Travis's old Star Wars toys. Mom wore a short, stylish, white mini dress with white tights and Dad still had hair. They looked so young, well before kids had aged them. Mostly, they looked like a young couple in love. Another picture portrayed Mom lying on her stomach on a picnic blanket spread across grass. She stared back at the camera with a huge smile on her face, her hand resting gently on the top of my little blonde head. In the picture, Danielle was probably four-years-old, and I was three-years-old. We each laid on either side of Mom, also looking at the camera, smiling from ear-to-ear. It was a snapshot in time, and I could see how much she loved Danielle and I. Tears blurred my vision. The photo captured the idyllic nature of my childhood, but somewhere along the way, my relationship with Mom had changed. A swirl of confusing emotions started to churn in my stomach.

Weeks of complicated, messy, and often contradictory emotions set up residency. My new role as "reluctant caretaker" felt like a game of hot potato, where I'd caught the potato, could feel it burning my hands, but couldn't throw it away.

My childhood was filled with warm memories

of easter egg hunts wearing little frilly dresses or making birthday cakes shaped like ladybugs, where Mom and I placed sliced gum drops for the spots onto the frosted cake. She'd set up little girl tea parties for play dates, that were decorated as if the Queen might stop by. Each memory filled my heart with warmth, then sent me spiraling down a well of resentment. There had been love. Lots of love. I struggled to figure out why I felt so resentful.

In contrast, as I grew into adolescence my memories started to change. These memories were filled with unsteady feelings of walking on eggshells as I tried to placate Mom's ever-changing moods. Mom was a yeller, and her mood could change in an instant. One minute, she seemed content, but in another she could go into a fit of anger. Her words were loud, cutting, and at times hurtful, with vibrations that echoed through my psyche causing me to "hide in plain sight".

Mom also used silence to convey her disapproval of a situation. Her silent treatments would leave the air in the house so tense; I would cave in and apologize even when I didn't know what I was apologizing for. Dad often played peacekeeper, coming to me during stale mates. "Just talk to your mother," he'd plead. I'd be reluctant, because even if I apologized, that didn't guarantee peace. Often it would just turn into another argument.

As I grew into a young adult, the complexity of our relationship grew. At times, I needed her as I traversed life away from home, and in those times, she could be caring and insightful. At other times, when I was forging a new life away from her, she could be controlling and possessive. Her constant expectations, masked as opinions, wore on my identity. Even as an adult, I feared Mom's reactions and disapproval, leading me to constantly bend to her needs to avoid conflict.

Dad's death in 2006 changed our relationship again, this time into something I didn't recognize. His absence highlighted the role he'd played as the glue of our foursome, delicately holding together the women of the family. Both my parents died the morning of November ninth, Dad to cancer and Mom to grief. Mom became emotionally unavailable. Conversations that could have emotionally connected us, she avoided like the plague, diverting the subject as quickly as possible. To compound the issue, when she moved permanently to Texas, she slowly withdrew from friends, was reclusive at times, and looked to me for her social outlet. My sister and I made many attempts to get Mom to talk to a therapist about her grief and depression, each time we were met with defiant resistance.

This isn't to say Mom lacked empathy, she could be quite empathetic. Those moments of empathy felt like when the sun streaked through the clouds, the light warm, brief, and reverent. When that light hit you, it felt incredible. I would spend a lifetime pursuing those moments of light and warmth.

Many nights I sat slouched in a lawn chair on the back porch trying to make sense out of all the conflicting feelings. In the depths of my resentment, there was raw anger at the loss of a mother fifteen years ago when I needed her. "Do you know she never once asked how I was doing when Dad died? Not once!" I ranted to Travis, trying to sort through emotions. "It was as if the only loss had been hers." Then, there was anger at myself that I hadn't found my voice, nor identity, in the shadow of Mom. Now I was losing her again. At what age do we actually get through our mommy issues?

The Letter

October 6, 2020

Danielle and her husband Ben flew into Austin to help with Mom's upcoming neuropsychologist appointment. I caught up with Danielle at her Airbnb in a very hip part of East Austin. Pulling onto her street, I took note of all the eclectic eateries and coffee shops. *I'll definitely need a latte later.* Danielle greeted me at the door, dressed in a Rolling Stones t-shirt, jeans, and platform shoes. Danielle was 5'3" on a good day and lived in shoes that had some kind of heel on them. She was also vibrating in place, her anxious energy swirled all around like a tornado. I walked past her into the living room. "Uh, this is adorable," I said, taking in the 1930's bungalow with an expensive chic Art Deco style. "Good god, those plants are ridiculous. Are they real?" I said, touching a huge palm leaf.

"Right? And, the owner is a guy," Danielle said, flanked by the huge fan leaves of a white bird-of-paradise plant. I thought about Travis taking care of a plant, it would be dead.

Unable to stand in one place for too long, Danielle flitted off to grab something from the bedroom. "I'm kind of nervous," she yelled, from the back room. *I bet you are!* Danielle hadn't seen Mom since the onset of her symptoms, so I knew seeing her would be like walking into a movie halfway through, desperately trying to make sense of the plot. Not to mention, Danielle's relationship with Mom made my relationship with Mom look uncomplicated.

Ben sat on a stylish turquoise sofa looking like a deer in headlights, clearly on his first cup of coffee. I'm sure the drama and anxiety from my sister leading up to this visit, had left him exhausted before they'd even arrived. Confounding the stress, his own father had been air- flighted out of his remote home in Northern California with heart complications the previous evening. When it rains it pours. Danielle came back into the room like a blur, grabbing her purse and heading for the door.

We descended the stairs of the bungalow's mini wrap-around porch. "I wouldn't argue with her about the hallucinations," I said, as we climbed into my car trying to give her a quick playbook on Mom. "She's touchy about her memory, so she'll argue with you about everything." The information just made both of us more anxious.

When Mom opened the door, I knew we were off to a good start. She was dressed, hair brushed, and had an alertness in her eyes. I took a sigh of relief, *it's a good day*. I sat on the couch watching Danielle and Mom interact, just waiting for the other shoe to fall. They hadn't spent more than a couple of days together in the last decade. Their infrequent encounters were a point of contention for Danielle. Their relationship had always been challenging, however, after Dad died, Mom stopped making any effort to see Danielle. Dad's death had made it clear just how much he'd played a role in keeping their relationship afloat.

Hanging in the air, like an unspoken albatross, was, *The Letter*, a piece of paper holding decades of emotions that would never be discussed by the parties involved. Travis and I started calling it *The Letter* because it holds its own space in a room even years later. *The Letter* sums up the decades of baggage their relationship now carries. This background is important to the story because it colors how Danielle approaches Mom's looming mortality.

The Letter was penned after a contentious relationship growing up, but came to a head after Danielle spent years making trips to San Diego, catering to Mom after Dad died, however Mom never reciprocated by going to Danielle's home. After years of trying to get Mom to visit, Danielle put pen to paper, all her grievances, hurts, anger, and sadness inked out to form what would become, *The Letter*.

The Letter was received by Mom, only Danielle wouldn't have known this because Mom never acknowledged receiving it, which did nothing but deepen the hurt. Mom did however discuss *The Letter* with everyone else, just not Danielle.

Although, *The Letter* was between Mom and Danielle, I could relate to the pattern of Mom not accepting her part. When met with someone trying to talk about how she had made them feel, Mom immediately turned the blame on the other person or redirected the conversation back to her own feelings.

The last time Danielle and Mom had been together was when she and I traveled to California for my niece's high school graduation in 2019. In hindsight, Mom was displaying early signs of LBD on that trip. There had been numerous *unsettled, almost queasy feelings,* brushed off as getting older. During that trip I felt more like a parent than a daughter. I flashed back to a memory of us at the airport, my hand placed gently on her back, guiding her through airport check-in and baggage, prompting her when to take out her ID, then following her like a helicopter mom, hovering so close to her at times it felt like if I took my eyes off her, she'd get lost.

The trip was filled with conversations where Mom would inject something out of context, or blurt out a random statement, leaving those involved in the conversation scratching their heads. She also tired easily and would nod off in the middle of the day, sometimes on the couch in a room full of people.

To be fair, that trip was what I refer to as a shit show. The disagreements within Danielle's household made the visit tense, leaving Mom and I uncomfortable. By the time we left for the hotel on the first night we were both drained.

I nervously talked out loud as we drove. "I'm not sure what to do here, it's not good," I said, turning towards Mom for a reaction. "Danielle talked to me, it's not good. Uh. I don't know, maybe they need to spend some time apart till things calm down." Silence filled the car. Deep down I knew Mom would duck the conversation, but I needed my mom. I needed my parent to say, "Here's what we're going to do." Instead, I got...

"He's a good provider. She needs to think about that," Mom said, staring blankly out the window.

I was floored. Did we just drive into the

1950's? What happened to my feminist mom who engrained women's rights into my brain growing up? "That's not helpful" was all I could mutter.

Back at the hotel, Mom fell into bed fully clothed. I sat in the adjoining room wondering if she wanted all the lights on and the television playing some Hallmark movie at a deafening volume. I leaned back onto the sofa, utterly exhausted, but couldn't relax because it felt like Mom's TV was in my room. I peered around her doorway to see what looked like a corpse. Fixating on Mom's ashen face, her eyes were closed, but her mouth gaped open like someone caught in the middle of a scream, I couldn't move. Her arms were laid perfectly at her side with legs stretched straight out in front of her. I felt my stomach tighten. *Is she breathing?* Slowly, I inched close to the bed, my eyes fixed on her white skin. I placed my finger under her nose and held my breath. *Oh' thank God*, I thought, as I felt the slightest bit of air hit my finger. Later, I'd look back on this trip and recognize our parent-child roles had begun to flip.

We're Not at That Point Yet, Are We?

October 7, 2020

After an uneventful first day, I wondered if I was jumping the gun on our morning meeting with Jill, the owner of an in-home care company. Coffees in hand, Danielle and I joined Jill who was already sitting at an outdoor table on the patio of Central Market. Jill had been a referral from my neighbor who was also dealing with her elderly mother. My mind tracked back to the conversation I'd had with my neighbor a month prior. We talked as our four small dogs tangled their leashes around our legs. "It was just getting to be too much," my neighbor had said, recounting starting in-home care for her aging mother. "I still have my kids at home, and it was getting crazy. I had to bring in help." I'd remembered thinking, *That sounds familiar*. My neighbor looked tired. I'd wondered if I looked that tired.

Unwrapping Sadie from the mess of leashes, I'd off-handedly said, "I'm still pretty far off from that, but would you send me who you used just so I have it?"

It felt a bit surreal to be sitting with her referral less than a month later discussing Mom.

"Well, she's also eighty-years-old, so it's hard to

know what's normal," I blurted out in defense of Mom, interrupting Danielle and Jill's discussion of Mom's recent behavior. Danielle shot me a look that said, *seriously?*

I watched Jill's body language straighten before continuing. "Putting care in place before it's needed, will keep you from being in crisis mode," she said, looking directly at me. "There's also a benefit to having a consistent caregiver in place before your mom's needs increase." It was hard to argue with that.

Jill then provided us with the additional referral of a senior care manager. The whole conversation opened my eyes to a whole cottage industry for senior care. Jill pushed a piece of paper full of referrals across the table and I thought, *I guess it's going to take a village to deal with Mom.* We parted ways agreeing to talk to Mom about bringing someone in one day a week.

Danielle and I walked to my car feeling like we'd had a full day, and it wasn't even noon. Danielle placed her latte in the cup holder, then turned towards me, clicking her seat belt into place. "Should we talk to her about it today?"

Do we have to?

I felt the blood drain from my face. "Let's wait and see what the doctor says tomorrow," I said, terrified at the thought of talking to Mom about in-home care. Mom would rather swim with sharks than ask for help, that conversation wasn't going to be fun.

Would Dropping Acid Help Us Relate?

First meeting with Neuropsychologist, October 8, 2020

The morning of the neuropsychologist assessment, nervous energy coursed through my body. By the time I climbed into the car to go pick up Mom, I'd begun to think a neuropsychologist assessment might be in order for me.

Thirty minutes later, I pulled into Mom's driveway hoping she'd be ready to go. It crossed my mind on the drive over that I couldn't actually force Mom to go to the appointment. That thought then led to a succession of other panicked thoughts, *I can't drag her out of the house,* then, *I might be able to pick her up and throw her over my shoulder?* and finally, *No, that would draw the attention of neighbors.*

As I turned the engine off, Mom pulled open the door. *Thank God, she's dressed.* I barely stepped out of the car before I heard, "I don't need to do this," she said, rolling her eyes. "I think you're overreacting."

Here we go. "I think we need to know what we're dealing with," I said, prepared for an argument.

She released a long sigh. "I'll do it for you, but it's ridiculous," she said, as if she was doing me a favor. In one swift movement she pulled her front door shut, situated her huge purse on her shoulder and climbed in my car. *Okay, I guess we're going.*

I turned over the ignition and before I could get too worked up by Mom's attitude, she said, "It's a left up here," gesturing towards the turn I'd made a hundred times to exit her neighborhood.

All of the sudden, she lurched forward and grabbed the dashboard. "Watch out!" she yelped. "Can't you see those orange cones in the road? And you think I shouldn't be driving?"

"There are no orange cones," I said, as I visualized unlocking the door, leaning across her, then pushing the door open to shove her out. Problem solved; you don't have to go to the appointment.

Almost an hour later, we pulled into the parking lot of the medical plaza. Danielle, who'd taken an Uber, waited out front. *Woosh.* The elevator doors opened onto a large lobby area. I glanced around at the other people waiting in the room and was curious what life events had led them to a neuropsychologist. If they were like Mom, this lobby would be crowded with pretend people.

"I'm going to grab the in-take paperwork," I said, plopping Mom down in a chair next to Danielle. The receptionist handed me a thick stack of papers. "I've highlighted the places for signatures," she slowed down her spiel, when she saw my face change. "Oooor, you can sign," she slid me a pen. She'd read my face correctly. Mom hadn't signed a document since our MRI appointment months ago. I barely made it back to Danielle and Mom before I heard behind me, "Kay, we're ready for you."

A smiling brunette probably in her mid-thirties, standing behind a large mahogany desk waved us into the office. Mom smiled and took a seat in the chair directly across from her. Danielle and I sat lined up against the wall adjacent to Mom. Without wasting time, the doctor explained that the first part of the neuropsych assessment would be to gather information from Mom, as well as family.

After a few customary questions, the focus narrowed. "Do you ever act out your dreams?" she asked, looking at Mom.

"No." Mom replied without hesitation.

"Yes, you do!" Danielle and I jumped in at the same time, speaking almost in unison.

Mom had been acting out her dreams for years. "Don't you remember when you and Dad were staying downstairs at my Great Hills house," I said, baffled by her answer. "You were yelling for help. Travis almost came down the stairs half-naked."

"Oh, yeah. Your dad woke me up," she said, laughing at the memory. I couldn't figure out if Mom was purposely being elusive, or if she really didn't remember. To this day I can't sleep in the same room with Mom without ear plugs. Not only does she act out her dreams, but she also has full audible conversations. I would later learn REM sleep disorder is often an early symptom of LBD.

The doctor continued, "Do you hear noises or voices when nobody else is there?"

Mom sat quietly, like she was thinking for a minute before answering. "Not really, they don't talk." This was getting interesting, so I leaned forward.

"Who are they?" the doctor asked.

She's good, I thought, relieved she picked up on Mom's imaginary friends.

"The ladies," Mom said, in a way that made it clear we all should have known she was talking about the ladies. "And, sometimes my sister, which drives me crazy."

Keeping an even tone, the doctor peered up from her papers, "Do you see other things besides people?" *That's a good question*, I thought, then wondered if I really wanted the answer.

"Mostly people. Well, (pause) and dogs," Mom said, shifting in her seat. "But then sometimes I realize what I thought was a dog, was something I just wasn't seeing right. My eyesight isn't great."

Pandora's box was now opened. Mom calmly continued to talk about seeing people, animals, objects, and most recently bugs crawling across her bed sheets. "There were just so many, hundreds of them crawling all over," Mom said, using her hands to act out swatting at the bugs. I felt my whole-body quiver at the thought of hundreds of bugs. *That sounds awful*, I thought, then I was plunged into a dark memory.

Trying to shake off the mix of still drunk from the night before, but also hungover, I'd come out of the master bathroom to catch a glimpse of something, like a shadow, move in the corner. Stopping, I'd turned to inspect the corner and found nothing. *Maybe you are crazy?* I'd thought, then could have sworn I saw a bug on my arm, but then it was gone. Hiding in plain sight had started to unravel. The alcohol I'd used to keep my feelings tucked away was no longer working, wreaking havoc on my sanity. Like a ball of yarn, alcohol pulled at a single thread threatening to unravel my life. I shifted in my seat, the memory left a knot in my stomach.

Mom hadn't started out forthcoming about seeing things, but in the end didn't hold anything back. I understood, the only people who sit around and openly discuss hallucinating are people dropping acid. In that setting, seeing things is not only acceptable but favorable. Mom, on the other hand, was not dropping acid, although if she ever found herself in a group of people who were, she'd feel right at home. I wondered if I dropped acid, would Mom and I be able to relate. We'd both be seeing things, maybe then we could have an actual conversation. Unfortunately, dropping acid is frowned upon in the sober community.

Thinking about dropping acid made me remember the night Travis and I were struggling to relate. At nine months sober I'd laid next to him in bed considering whether our marriage would require us to live in two separate houses to survive. He'd felt the same way. I'd confessed, "I thought about smoking pot, but then realized it would just be another way to avoid feeling. Let's be honest, I'd just end up stoned all the time."

"I wondered if pot was an option for you too," Travis had said, also confessing. "You've been kind of a bitch lately." We'd both laughed.

"You were a teacher..." the doctor continued through lengthy historical questioning, tracking back fifty years to when Mom was a teacher, up to the present day. There were a few things Mom couldn't remember, but it was decades ago. The doctor then explained the next portion of the test would take a couple of hours and that Danielle and I were free to leave and come back. Mom looked relieved at our leaving. Danielle and I spent the next couple of hours drinking coffee in awe of our new reality with Mom.

Two hours later, we gathered Mom from the lobby and made a follow-up appointment for the next week. "I'm exhausted!" Mom said. "I don't know how I did, but it was a lot." I glanced over at Mom in the elevator, she looked like someone had lobotomized her. I tried to remember if I'd ever taken a three-hour test.

Back in the car I could feel tension. My stomach tightened; it reminded me of the tension in the house growing up when Mom was too quiet. "I'm tired of being treated like a child!" Mom snapped, turning towards me, her eyes narrowing. Genuine anger filled her voice as she told Danielle and I in a curt tone, we were the only people who thought she had a problem. Mom could be like Dr. Jekel and Mr. Hyde, compliant and nice to others, then turn on a dime, spewing anger at her daughters.

I shot Danielle a look that conveyed, *This is what I've been dealing with.* "No ones doing this to you," I said, trying to remain calm.

I was grateful Danielle was in town, there was safety in numbers. Once Mom finished explaining that we should just let her live her life and stop trying to control her, she fell into the familiar silent treatment. This time I was grateful for the silence.

As we crested into Lakeway, Mom broke her silence to suggest a place for lunch. We made our way through a dirt parking lot up to what looked like a shabby-chic beach house. Fans swirled overhead as we walked through the main restaurant area to an outside table that overlooked part of Lake Austin. I felt the cool breeze hit my face and thought, *This serene setting is perfect for the fighting that's going to happen.* It didn't take long for Mom's anger to build up steam. We were barely seated before the verbal jabs came in rapid succession, first at Danielle, then at me, then at us. "You two just need to let me live my life," she said, her anger palatable. "You two are always pairing together against me." *There it is,* I thought,"*You two.*"

Those two words, *you two*, triggered an old childhood hurt that brought emotions from decades ago roaring into the present. When I was a child, Mom had constantly thought Danielle and I or *you two* were ganging up on her. Comments like, "It's two against one, how do you think that makes me feel?" or "I know you two are talking behind my back" were intended to be a form of manipulation meant to get us to focus on her, which confused me as a child. My sister and I are eleven months apart; of course, we were close. It felt like picking sides in a game I couldn't win. Later, it would morph into, "You two are conspiring something," contaminated by an undercurrent of distrust that would bleed into everything.

When the server placed my lunch plate down in front of me, I decided one member of the, *you two,* was too tired to fight and too hungry to ignore the cheeseburger in front of me, so I took a bite and changed the subject.

Lewy Joins the Family

Neuropsychologist Follow Up Appointment, October 15, 2020

It felt like Groundhog Day driving to pick up Mom for the follow up Neuropsychologist appointment. Passing familiar landmarks, my mind wandered to possible outcomes from today's visit. I was pretty sure it was Lewy body dementia, but there was the possibility that a different diagnosis could side swipe me. My stomach tightened and swirled as I drove. *I'm nervous. Why am I nervous?* I thought.

When I pulled into the driveway, Mom was standing over her sink at her kitchen window. An image from years ago of Mom standing at her kitchen sink in San Diego, face hardened, scrubbing dishes, hung in my mind like it was yesterday.

"She's really crossed the line Michelle," I could hear Travis's furious voice. "I asked her nicely, and she just wouldn't stop." I could see him, head in hands, sitting next to our screaming toddler who he'd been trying to get to bed as Mom stood over him telling him what he was doing wrong.

I turned off the car engine as I thought, *Why hadn't I told her to back off, instead of trying to placate and break the silent treatment?* I climbed out of the car and gave her a little wave which sent her walking towards the door. "Hi babe," she greeted me smiling. "I just need to find my purse."

She's weirdly calm and in a good mood. I waited for the other shoe to fall. We spent ten minutes locating her huge purse, then piled into the car for the hour-long ride.

Fidgeting with the vents I said, "Are you nervous?" projecting my own feelings across the seat.

"There's nothing I can do about it," she quipped, a little hint of the anger sneaking through.

"Turn left up here." *I know how to get out of your neighborhood.*

An hour later, Mom and I sat across from the doctor, taking the same seats we inhabited just a week prior. I dialed Danielle, placed the phone on speaker, and sat it on the corner of the large mahogany desk.

The doctor shuffled the papers in front of her. "Let's get started," she said, giving Mom a soft smile. "The results take into account your age. Essentially, your results are compared to other people in their eighties."

Mom let out a nervous, abrupt laugh. "That's a relief."

The doctor continued to explain the results in

a systematic fashion, giving us time to process the information. I watched the doctor look up from her papers and make direct eye contact with Mom. *Oh god, here it comes.* "I looked at all the results together to come up with the diagnosis of Lewy body dementia," she said, her eyes warm looking first at Mom, then at me. Mom didn't react.

She continued to impart results until she flipped pages straightening the pile, came to a stop, then looked up from the papers to make eye contact with Mom. "The way you process and react to information is slow," the doctor continued. "For that reason, it affects your ability to react while driving, which could be dangerous." I noted later I'd be able to say, "It's not me taking your car away, it's the doctor."

"I really haven't been driving since that night we came back from Bryan" Mom said, looking at me.

"There're lots of options for transportation now," the doctor said. "I understand it's difficult, but based on these results, if you were in a situation in which you needed to react quickly, it would be dangerous."

"I don't want anything bad to happen," Mom said, cooperatively. I watched Mom and knew the battle line had just been drawn, there was zero chance this conversation was over. My mind went to the dark places of the worst-case scenario. *How do you take someone's car away?* I thought about Mom refusing to hand over her keys. An image of me driving off in her car, with the cops hot on my tail, because she'd reported it stolen, flashed to mind. Before I could run down too much of a rabbit hole, a member of staff cracked the door and poked her head into the room.

"Tammy is going to take you down the hall and get you set up with some referrals," the doctor said to Mom, gesturing towards the door. "Michelle will meet you back in the lobby in about fifteen minutes."

"Bye, Mom," the voice from the desk startled me. I'd forgotten Danielle was on the phone.

The doctor wasted no time once the door closed behind Mom. "I wanted an opportunity to talk with you and your sister alone," she said, her tone warm, but harboring a serious edge. "Your mom really should have someone with her every day at least for a couple of hours. It would be a good time to start looking at assisted living, so you could pull the trigger when that time comes." I felt the room tilt slightly, as my mind went blank. *We're already at that stage?*

I watched the doctor's lips move, but her words

sounded like the teacher in the Charlie Brown cartoon, *wah, wah, who, woh, wah.* The words, *assisted living* and *someone with her*, hung in the air. The same words I'd heard from Jill only a week or so before. I remembered the conversation with my neighbor. *Holy shit, we are at that stage.*

Mom and I drove back to Lakeway in eerie silence. Mom stared out the window, her face looked drawn and pale. I suspected the information was sinking in, zapping any bit of energy left in her body. I too was emotionally drained and thought, *the doctor probably should have told me not to drive.*

Chapter 7
Help Is a Four-Letter Word

First Meeting with Senior Care Manager, October 21, 2020

I was getting good at therapeutic lying, a term I'd first heard from Jill. Essentially, it's a lie told in the best interest of a person with dementia to avoid distress. Makes sense, I wondered if you could apply therapeutic lying to marriages. A lie told in the best interest of a spouse, to avoid the distress of an argument. I knew Mom wouldn't agree to meet with Leslie, she didn't think she needed help. In my therapeutic lie I avoided words like *help*, a four-letter word to Mom, *disease*, and *your diagnosis* since Mom was ignoring her disease. Mom wasn't thrilled the morning of the appointment and I danced around her last-minute questions.

"Why do I have to meet this person? This is completely absurd, I'm fine," she said, adding her favorite, "You're the only one who thinks I'm not okay."

Ding Dong. The sound of the doorbell broke the tension in the room. Eager for a distraction, I sprinted to answer the door. Leslie stood on the porch, clutching a large black binder, wearing a face mask. When she locked eyes with Mom, who had come up behind me, she pulled down her face mask quickly, saying, "I'm going to pull this down so you can see my face." That little gesture was brilliant and immediately disarmed Mom, who also wore a mask, albeit begrudgingly because she thought it made her ears look big.

Leslie, in a pre-game warm up of sorts, asked Mom questions about what she did before having kids and talked about her own mother. Pre-game then bled into discussions about Leslie helping Mom or being her advocate as things progress in the future.

"This is an example," Leslie said, pulling out the black binder. "It organizes all your medical information, contacts, doctors, insurance, basically anything someone would need to help you in an emergency." I glazed over knowing that finding all that information with an uncooperative person would be a test of patience. My body cringed every time Leslie said the word *help*. This little word was like a TKO in a boxing ring, it had me preparing for the fight to come after Leslie's departure.

Mom was like two different people in these situations. With casual acquaintances, she was charming and sweet. She could be witty, dynamic, drawing a person in with undivided attention and excellent conversational skills. This casual acquaintance would often tell me later "Your mom is just so sweet." The minute that acquaintance left, she'd do an about face, giving me an earful. Her tongue sharp and cutting, not sweet.

True to form, Mom walked Leslie to the door thanking her for coming, then I heard the door shut and waited.

"This is ridiculous, I don't need help!" Mom said, pivoting around to face me. *Not sweet!*

"I need the help," I said, defensively. "I have no idea what to do or what's coming." As I said the words, I heard them in my eight-year-old self's voice. As a child I'd felt like a rubber ball anytime I expressed my feelings because Mom took those feelings and bounced them back to how they made her feel, usually triggering anger in the process. I'd stopped expressing my feelings, instead putting on a façade of everything was fine.

Karol K. Truman said, "Feelings buried alive never die." My eight-year-old self had no idea how the façade would crumble in my early forties.

"I don't need you telling me how to live my life," Mom's angry voice pulled me back to the present. "Why don't you just go live your life and let me live mine." *That would be nice.*

I wanted to bolt for the door, run for my car, and go home, but instead I said, "That's not realistic. This isn't easy on either of us, so why don't we call it a day and give each other some time." No response.

When I reached for my keys, I heard, "Everyone is trying to bury me!"

That's dramatic, I took a deep breath. "No one's trying to bury you," I said, unable to hide my annoyance. Now facing me, she eyed me up and down, like someone sizing up an opponent.

"Goodbye!" The word delivered like a command with a hand gesturing toward the door. I left. Battle lines drawn.

The Ladies Play Dress Up

November 9, 2020

Mom was already calling before I'd had a sip of coffee. "Gene Ann keeps siding with them," Mom said, when I picked up.

"Who's Gene Ann siding with?" I said, half awake. "Who's them?"

I could hear Mom audibly sigh. "The ladies!"

"Gene Ann's in Bryan, it's a hallucination," I said. *I haven't had enough caffeine for this.*

"Well, I'm looking at her and she's telling me what to do," Mom said, fed up with pretend Gene Ann. My slow response time allowed Mom to jump back into her rant. "One of them has been wearing my hat."

I thought back to the pillow I'd seen sitting upright in one of Mom's dining room chairs wearing a large-brimmed straw hat. This wasn't the first pillow I'd seen wearing accessories, often the hat was joined with a stylish pair of red sunglasses. I was starting to think the pillow and the ladies were one in the same.

On a recent visit to Mom's, Travis had asked, "Why is there a pillow wearing sunglasses and a hat?" as he came out of the guest room, looking confused.

"It's one of the ladies," I'd replied, like it was common knowledge.

"Ooookaaay" he'd said slowly. His acceptance evidence that our world had digressed to being unconcerned with dressed up pillows.

Mom had also started talking to the pillows, full conversations transpiring in front of Travis and me. On my way to the bathroom one afternoon, I'd witnessed Mom in her guest bedroom facing a pillow that sat in a wicker chair, wearing a navy and white striped pillowcase, straw hat, red sunglasses, and a beaded necklace that looked like it came straight from Mardi Gras. "I told you they were coming," Mom had said, in a quiet voice to the pillow. There was a silent moment, then Mom appeared to answer a question. "I did, this morning, I put it on the bed," she'd said, gesturing towards the bed behind her. I'd wondered if she heard them.

Detouring from the bathroom, I'd popped my head into the room. "Do they talk to you?" I'd asked, curious. My voice startled her, causing her to whip her body around, looking like she got caught with her hand in the cookie jar.

"Sometimes," she'd said, as she pushed past me out of the room towards the kitchen.

I don't know what to say about that.

At times she'd question her reality, asking me, "Do you hear them?"

"No." I'd reply.

She'd stare at me for a minute, then say, "You don't?" genuinely baffled.

"No, they're hallucinations, but I know they seem real to you," I'd say, and then think, *It would be easier if I did hear them.*

Some days she accepted that they were hallucinations, other days she'd become irritated and frustrated, trying desperately to convince me that what she was seeing was real. With the hallucinations becoming more frequent, there'd be days I'd barely make it to my car before tears started streaming down my face. I felt for Mom, when you can't trust your own mind what can you trust? It would be lonely living in a world that only you could see and hear.

Just Get Over the Finish Line Dude

As Mom was contemplating her reality, Connor, a senior at the time, was quietly contemplating how to dig himself out of the abyss of his failing grades. Connor had always been an A, B student, so Travis and I naively didn't think Zoom learning would change that. One afternoon on a whim, I decided to be a responsible parent and check Connor's grades online.

His grades had gone from A's and B's to D's, and one C-. I never thought I'd be so grateful for a C-, that little crescent shaped letter indicated he was at least passing one class. I'd also started receiving the "Your child has missed one or more classes" automated voicemail from the school every couple of days. Schools had been thrust almost overnight into online learning and were still working out the kinks in their attendance process. The pilot attendance system implemented to record online attendance relied on teenagers to record their attendance. These teenagers were as enthusiastic about online classes, as my dogs were when they realized the fun car ride was actually a vet visit.

I wondered if Connor was lying about his attendance, but also questioned if I'd be more upset that he was lying or failing out of school. My distorted thinking spiraled down, descending deeper into an irrational rabbit hole, each thought opening a new door with different endings. *He'd have to take the GED. What kind of jobs would he get with a GED? He wouldn't go to college. He'd be doomed for life without a college degree. Would he live at home forever? Do you want fries with that...?*

I sank into the couch, already in pajamas at 3:30 p.m. *I missed wine.* Those first couple of sips of a chardonnay washing away the day's stress sounded incredible. I didn't have that glass of wine, but what kind of alcoholic would I be if I didn't think about wine. I'll always miss wine. Wine is like a toxic boyfriend you know isn't good for you, but is super-hot and tempting in times of weakness.

Travis came up behind me on the sofa. "I'll talk to him," he said. "I don't think you should."

"What makes you think that?" I replied, giving him a smirk. "Is it the pjs at 3:30?"

He was right, nothing about me screamed this is a mom armed with coping skills. I was so pathetic, Finn, our terrier, had quietly draped his elongated meatloaf shaped body, across my midsection like a faux-fox fur wrap. The combination of pandemic living and dealing with Mom had left me with coping skills of a three-year-old.

I've failed as a mom, I thought. I had been so focused on Mom, I'd forgotten I was a mom. Of course, my teenager was struggling, why would he be unscathed at a time when his whole world had flipped upside down. Grown ass adults were falling apart right and left, embracing the slogan "Don't make me adult today."

I watched Travis walk down the hall toward Connor's room, grateful it wasn't me. Seeing no other option, Connor told his dad he figured he would just take the GED and go to community college. Okay, so it really was a good thing that I didn't talk to him, since the GED had been part of my rabbit hole thinking. Travis did a stellar parent-teenager talk, no one yelled, no one freaked out, and together they came up with a game plan for Connor to talk to his teachers. Turns out teachers knew kids were struggling and wanted them to graduate. I often listened to these teachers trying to engage teenagers in online discussions and would think, they don't get paid enough.

"Just get over the finish line dude" became our mantra for Connor's senior year. Our parenting had morphed into what we coined, pandemic parenting. Once we expected A's and B's, now we expected to just attend a graduation ceremony. How he got to that graduation ceremony was less important.

I Hope I Never Have to Use These

Signing of Legal Documents, November 18, 2020

I could still feel Mom's eyes boring into me as she stood across the kitchen island. "Are you fucking kidding me?" I'd screamed. "You want to put Travis, my marriage, in the middle of our family stuff?" Our argument weeks earlier over the Statutory Power of Attorney document still caused my blood pressure to rise. Even now as I was getting ready to go pick up Mom so she could sign those legal documents, I was having to take deep breaths to calm myself.

"You have absolutely no reason not to trust me!" I'd said, frustrated that she questioned making me POA. "I've never done anything to you but play concierge, drag my family to your house for a million Sunday dinners," I'd had to catch my breath, I'd been so mad. "Right now all I'm trying to do is protect you. It fucking hurts Mom, it just hurts."

As I brushed mascara on my lashes, I thought about her stone-cold face that day. "Fine," she'd finally uttered a word. "Then I'll just make Craig Power of Attorney." I'd known this had been solely to assert control and take another jab at me.

Holding onto the kitchen island I'd felt like a teenager again wanting to hide, but when I'd tried to shove my emotions down, the anger just boiled up.

"Do whatever," I'd said, furious. "Apparently, you have two daughters who have done nothing to you but try to help you, but you can't trust either of us." I'd been so mad, I didn't even remember leaving.

I tried to shake the memory as I grabbed my keys and purse to head out. Nervous, I knew today would be hard, getting Mom to do anything that acknowledged her declining independence was delicate.

When my car rolled to a stop in Mom's driveway, I took a second to steel myself. The front door slowly opened, in the doorway Mom stood completely dressed in her favorite long jean skirt and white ruffled blouse, her ridiculously large purse slung over one shoulder. Mom always had a purse capable of carrying enough snacks, Band-Aids, and other essential items to survive for days. Recently though her large purse sagged in on itself, only holding a wallet and her Seroquel pills, a.k.a fucking little pink pills, both which sat in darkness at the bottom of the huge purse.

As I focused on the sagging purse, I tried to

remember when Mom's compulsive re-organizing of things had started. She'd spend hours shuffling items around in her house, the purse had just become a mobile version of this. An image of Mom's oven came to mind. I couldn't remember when she'd started storing all her bread products in the oven, I just remembered her saying, "It's extra storage, I never use it."

Several weeks ago, Travis had stood, hunched over Mom's open oven peering inside. "This has to be some kind of fire hazard," he'd said, as a box of Triscuits and a loaf of bread fell out onto his shoes.

"I know, just leave it," I'd said, quietly. "I'm not taking that fight on tonight."

Then there was the reorganizing of her daily medications. This alone could have sent me back to drinking. I would find little groups of pills in the tiny soap dish by the kitchen sink or bottles lined up on the counter, some filled with pills, some empty. Occasionally, a solitary pill would inhabit a strange place like the makeup drawer or in a ZipLock bag in the pantry. I'd purchased a plastic daily pill organizer, which quickly became one of Mom's favorite obsessions, because each little daily box sent her into a frenzy of counting and recounting. She'd also move the pills around by color, constantly doubling up medications. Luckily nothing she was taking would kill her in a higher dose.

When she wasn't messing with the pill organizer, she was systematically removing items from her wallet. First it was the credit cards because someone was stealing from her. Then it was the Costco card and eventually her medical ID cards. I learned the hard way her wallet was empty one afternoon standing at the grocery store checkout.

"Why is there nothing in your wallet? Where are all your cards?" I'd said, stumped, staring blankly at the little empty slots.

"I hid them," she'd said matter-of-factly. "You know people are stealing from me." I'd fought the urge to roll my eyes.

Mom threw her huge purse onto the passenger floorboard and we pulled out of the driveway. The passenger seat belt alarm blared as we drove off. "You need to put on your seat belt or that's going to keep screaming at you," I said, wondering how she could ignore the sound.

Mom drew the seatbelt strap across her body. "You're going to make a left up here," she said, at the exit to her neighborhood.

I KNOW! For fucks sake, I KNOW! I knew someday I would look back and appreciate all the time Mom and I had together on these drives, today however, was not that day.

"Watch out for that man!" she blurted out, gripping the passenger door. Frantically looking for the man, it took me a second to realize she was hallucinating.

"There's no man," I said, wondering if I'd ever get used to the pretend obstacles in the road.

"Well, you need to slow down," she replied. I left it alone.

Forty-five minutes later, Mom and I entered a quiet office with no other soul in sight. "It's a little weird being here in person," I said, turning towards Mom as we ventured down a hallway in search of the attorney. At the end of the hall sat the man, who up until this point I'd heard but not seen. Tall, slender, and in his late fifties wearing a mask, the man extended his hand to Mom, a warm, potentially risky, gesture during a pandemic. Mom, also masked, shook his hand, the little creases around her eyes let me know she was smiling.

In the conference room it was hard to miss the thick stack of legal documents that sat looming in the middle of a table with three pens laid out to the side. Mom took a seat at the head of a long oval table, the attorney to her left, and me to her right.

Mom's anxiety was palatable, she tugged at her face mask as if it were actually suffocating her.

"These are the documents," the attorney said, sliding the stack of papers from the middle of the table to in front of him. "I'll explain each one to you before you sign. If you have any questions just stop me. Are you ready?"

"No," Mom blurted out, sounding irritated. "But she says I have to do this."

The attorney laughed thinking she was joking.

I knew she wasn't.

Mom pulled at her mask every couple of minutes, until she finally ripped it from her mouth and tucked it under her chin in one quick movement. "I can't breathe with this on!" she said, inhaling dramatically. Ironically, with the mask tucked under her chin, it pulled on her ears and did make them look big.

I panicked, locking eyes with the attorney waiting for his reaction. He'd have every right to ask her to put her mask back on. My anxiety skyrocketed, I'd had hundreds of mask conversations with Mom, but today I just didn't have the mask fight in me.

Acting as if nothing happened, the attorney continued, "You'll see at the bottom, here, you'll need to sign your name just as it's printed."

I let out the breath I'd been holding behind my mask and caught a glimpse of the clock that hung in the corner of the room. *Twenty minutes! It's only been twenty minutes?* It was going to be a long day.

The attorney went through each document carefully explaining both the legal use and more importantly, the practical use of each document. In essence, situations in which you would use the document. For example, the Medical Power of Attorney, without Statutory Power of Attorney, would grant you the ability to make decisions about care, however you could run into problems without the financial ability to pay for that care.

If these documents were dinosaurs, The Statutory Power of Attorney would be the T-Rex. It states at the top in bold print **THIS IS A VERY POWERFUL DOCUMENT**. That's an understatement, this document could eradicate a person's financial imprint. I thought back to all the Dateline TV episodes I'd watched where someone had finagled power of attorney from an elderly person, only to completely clean them out. Even though Mom was probably convinced I had some ulterior motive, I didn't. I love a good Dateline episode, but I wasn't trying to become the feature of one.

Knowing this document had been the center of

our argument weeks earlier, I held my breath as Mom dangled the pen over the signature line. When she finally put ink to paper, relief washed over my body. In the end, she'd made me POA, but today I wondered if I'd later regret it.

We walked out of the attorney's office stoic and quiet, a folder full of papers under my arm. I glanced over at Mom and thought about the next time I'd be pulling these papers back out. *I'll be using these because I won't recognize you anymore.* I had everything I would need legally; I wished I could say the same for myself emotionally.

Chapter 8
Cry For Help

November 19, 2020

"Mom, I'm at one of those ER clinics, my stomach is so bloated," Cameron's voice frantically came through the phone "Something's wrong."

Cameron's "bloating" wasn't new, Travis and I had begun to suspect anxiety more than actual bloating. He had visited several doctors since transplanting to Miami, causing a little voice somewhere in the back of my mind to question if maybe he wasn't transitioning to Miami smoothly. He'd barely landed in Miami before his graduate program went completely online, taking away the normal social interactions of college that would have helped acclimate him to a new city.

I heard a sigh, then frustrated by my lack of response, he continued, "I feel like the doctor doesn't believe me."

She doesn't, I thought.

I took a deep breath. "Cameron, if you need to go to a specialist, we can do that," I said, calmly. "You'll be home in a week. Is something else going on? I feel like this isn't about your bloating?" What followed broke my heart.

"I just need to come home," he said, his voice soft, almost childlike. In my mind, five-year-old Cameron's quizzical little face stared up at me.

A lump formed in my throat. "Come home. You don't have to wait," I said, quickly, before tears could form. "Dad and I will pay for the ticket. Book it and let us know."

Within the hour, I had a text confirming he'd booked a ticket and would be arriving the following evening. I texted him back.

> Glad you're coming on home,
> Dad and I will pick you up
> Tomorrow. Excited to see you!

An uncomfortable feeling settled into the pit of my stomach, like an alarm waiting to go off. There had been signs that something wasn't quite right. Little things that would send the voice in my head chattering, *Is he ok? Would he tell me?* Countered by, *don't be a helicopter mom*. The voice was soft, so faint, it had been drowned out by the chaos of dealing with Mom.

Cameron had always been an outgoing, social, take-charge child, so I thought it was just the new city, maybe the pressure of grad school, or the pandemic. Boy was I wrong! I should have listened to that little voice, asked more questions, or gone to Miami to lay eyes on him.

Travis and I stood at baggage claim a little after 10 p.m. the following evening, pacing, eyes fixed on the escalator, searching for Cameron. I spotted him and nudged Travis, "He's really thin," I said, under my breath.

"Yeah," was all Travis could get out, but his face conveyed, *he's not okay*.

I quickly forced a smile as Cameron closed the gap between us. The face staring at me was Cameron, but not. His hazel eyes were dull, sunken into the sockets. His normally rosy cheeks were sharp bones jutting out, pressing on his pale skin that had a grayish tone. I wrapped my arms tight around his shrunken body, feeling bones I'd never felt when hugging my son. His pants hung off his waist, their only lifeline a belt cinched to the last hole. *What happened in the months since I dropped you in Miami? How did I not know?* Without speaking, Travis and I exchanged a look that said, *this isn't good,* as we each took a side putting Cameron between us, instinctively surrounding him like animals circle their young in the wild.

We spent the next two months circling Cameron with professionals, forming a village of eating disorder specialists. A psychiatrist, dietician, and treatment center, we threw the kitchen sink at it. Travis and I also made lots of mistakes because we were scared, really scared. Many nights we laid in bed frightened at the dark depression and relentless eating disorder that engulfed our child. We engaged in stupid conversations about calories, conversing with the disease in comments like, "120 calorie tilapia isn't a meal," sounding more like fifth graders fighting, than confident parents. The truth was we felt completely out of control and helpless, grasping at straws.

Depression is sneaky, it comes in like fog, creeping slowly till the cloud snuffs out the light. Then it shrinks your visibility so you can't see a way out. Cameron was knee deep in its murky grasps. That coupled with a brain trying to function on few calories and very little sleep, made him feel hopeless.

One evening, as Travis and Cameron sat out on the back patio, I watched from the living room window, unable to hear words, but keenly aware of body language. That body language conveyed a worried father and defeated son. Both patio chairs faced out overlooking the golf course, Travis's head turned to his left talking to Cameron. His face looked serious, the nuances of fear etched in the lines across his forehead. Cameron sat slouched in the chair, an empty shell of skin stretched over bones, his face tired and defeated, tears forming in his eyes as his dad spoke.

"You can't see it, but I can, trust me," Travis said, recounting their conversation later that evening as we laid in bed. "You will get out of this and be okay. I can see that." This one phrase broke through the fog and had brought the tears I saw through the window into Cameron's eyes. He couldn't see it, but his dad's words opened a crack in his despair. He trusted his dad, so just that his dad could see it, let the tiniest bit of light through that crack. I was so grateful for all the years Travis had spent showing up for his sons, building a well of trust he could pull from in times like this.

"Do you think he heard you?" I said, my voice cracking.

"I hope so," Travis said, the uncertainty in his

voice failed to provide the comfort I was looking for.

I could see Cameron in my mind, two-feet tall standing in front of Shamu, his tiny hand on the shiny black nose of a giant orca at SeaWorld. Behind him a larger version of the same scene displayed on the JumboTron. Travis had taken him to SeaWorld so many times over that summer, studying how the kids were selected to pet Shamu, so he could give Cameron that memory. He couldn't have known it then, but all those moments, even the ones where they fought when Cameron was a teenager, were filling that well of trust drop by drop. Now they both would be peering down into the well, allowing Cameron to lean on his dad's words, holding onto blind faith he would be okay.

Chapter 9
You Need Help

November 20, 2020

For weeks Danielle and I had been busy conspiring, ironically warranting Mom's distrust of "you two." Fully embracing therapeutic lying again, Jill, Danielle and I had been communicating about starting in-home care without telling Mom. The sand in the hourglass now out, I needed to tell Mom in-home care would start next week.

Mom, you need help. I'm worried something will happen, I rehearsed the conversation in my head while driving to Moms. I'd spent my whole life avoiding conflict, especially with Mom, and now Lewy was throwing me into hard conversations and conflict right and left. *Direct is kind,* I told myself, passing Mansfield Dam, a visual marker that always indicated for me I'd entered Lakeway. I thought about all the hard conversations I'd had with my boys over the years, in which I'd reminded myself that I was the parent and not a friend. *I'm the parent. I'm the parent*, I repeated in my head, like a mantra that didn't quite fit.

Mansfield Dam faded in the rearview mirror, as my mind faded into a memory of a time I'd needed help from Mom. After four months of white knuckling sobriety, it had been suggested by Travis that I seek help. The morning that I figured Travis's suggestion might have some merit was when I'd backed into a car leaving yoga—the second car I'd backed into in less than a month. Sobriety had proven to be quite a formidable foe. I can still hear Travis's reaction to the second insurance claim, "Don't you have a backup camera?"

When I'd hung up the phone with the auto insurance rep who'd said, jokingly, "Try not to hit anymore cars this month," I'd reached out to an outpatient substance abuse program.

Mom didn't know I'd quit drinking, nor did she know I was an alcoholic. I'd like to think it was because I hid it so well, but it was more likely that she didn't want to deal with it. The week I was to start treatment, Travis had to go out of town. With no other options left, I'd called Mom for help. "I have outpatient treatment tomorrow night," I'd blurted out, giving no context. "I had to stop drinking. Long story, it was a problem." Silence followed on the other end of the phone. "Can you come stay with the boys while I'm gone at night?"

"Uh," Mom had made her first audible noise, trying to digest what I'd just said. "Of course, yes, do whatever you need to do." To Mom's credit she'd showed up and didn't ask a lot of questions, which I knew had to have been torture for her. Later we would have different struggles with my sobriety, but that week she'd showed up for me and I had been grateful. As I thought about how hard it had been to ask for help, I heard the branch of the huge oak tree in Mom's driveway scraping across the roof of my car.

I approached the door slowly, then knocked. "Come in, it's unlocked," I heard from inside. I entered to find Mom sitting in her white barrel chair watching a Hallmark movie. "Hi Babe. What are you doing here?" she said, taking off her glasses to look at me.

I took a seat on the sofa and wiped my sweaty hands on my pants. "We need to talk about something that's coming up."

"Oh?"

"I've tried to put this off as long as I could," I

said, knowing I'd detoured from my car rehearsal. "Danielle and I scheduled someone to come in once-a-week for just a couple of hours to help you." *Shit.* I'd let the word *help* slip out. Nothing, no response, she just looked at me, her face hardening. *Stay strong.* "I can't be your only driver. This will give you more independence."

"I can just wait till you can take me to the store," she said.

Direct is kind, I reminded myself. "Mom, it's not just about going to the store, the doctor also said I needed to have more people checking in on you." When an uncomfortable silence followed, I continued. "I live thirty minutes away and with the boys and work, well, I also need the help." The word *help* kept slipping out like I had tourettes.

"Do I have a say in this?" she said, irritated. *Not really,* I thought.

"I'm just trying to do what's right here," I said, my eyes starting to fill with tears. "What if something happens? I don't know what to do. I'm just trying to do what the people who know about your disease advise." *Oh god I said it, I said disease.*

She turned to look out the window. "Fine. What am I supposed to do with the person?"

"Go to Target or go to the store," I said. "They

can help you make dinner, whatever you need help with."

She waved her hand dismissively in the air. "Fine, whatever."

I hate this, I thought as I drove home. At this rate, this disease would end with Mom hating me before she died.

No Hard Pants Thanksgiving

November 26, 2020

The scent of roasting turkey, buttery dough, and toasted pecans filled the kitchen. The two terriers camped out under the smell of the turkey, causing a furry barricade to the oven. Christmas is one of my favorite holidays, mostly because the decorations always put me in a festive mood, but Thanksgiving is my favorite meal of the year. To my family's eye rolling, I put up my Christmas tree, adorned in either silver or gold themed decorations the week of Thanksgiving. The combination of cooking for Thanksgiving, with the warm twinkling lights of the tree, is just about as good as it gets. Pandemic Thanksgiving definitely needed twinkly lights, it had been a rough year.

"MOVE!" I said, using my foot to slide the

terriers out from under the oven, so I could baste the turkey. Nigel paced back and forth on his perch making the oven beeping sound and saying, "Chicken, beep, beeeep, you're a good bird."

I grabbed the baster from the drawer, sucked up the juices and told Nigel, "You're a good bird, but you're not getting turkey yet."

The site of the baster brought back childhood memories of Mom standing in pink floral pajamas, rubbing an entire stick of butter onto a raw turkey, then heaving the twenty-pound bird into the oven. I could almost smell the celery and onions sauteing in heaps of butter while she added the little bread cubes for stuffing. She too loved Thanksgiving and butter, lots of butter.

The holidays and dinner parties of my youth were occasions to dig the china out of the hutch and polish the silverware. Mom's tables were gorgeous, each place setting with its own crystal wine glass and goblet for water, fine fabric napkins threaded through gold napkin rings, white table clothes edged in lace, and the warm glow of candles set in the center of a long rectangle antique table. I remember as a young girl lighting those candles, excited to get to strike the match, just as everyone gathered to sit down.

The snap of the oven door closing sent the

terriers running back to take their positions guarding the oven. I leaned against the island. The memories of her cooking got me thinking about recent experiences at Sunday dinners at Mom's. In the months leading up to Thanksgiving, these dinners had become increasingly more challenging for Mom and more adventurous for us. Food seemed to sit longer in her fridge, taking up residency far past the suggested expiration dates.

"Milk doesn't expire," she'd said, one Sunday, watching me study the expiration date on a carton of milk I'd been about to pour into coffee.

"I'm pretty sure it does," I'd replied, then quietly placed the carton back in the fridge.

If she didn't have all the ingredients for a meal, she'd improvise. Think hot dog jambalaya, which, once you got past trying to figure out what the perfectly circular little meat morsels were, was quite tasty. The jambalaya beat the hot dog and cream cheese sandwich I'd seen Mom make, calling the cream cheese mayo. I still get a gag reflex thinking about that one.

Over time, Travis and I adapted by offering to bring dinner to her house. More protection than adapting, if we brought dinner, we knew what we were eating. I would later realize that Lewy had shown up to those Sunday dinners, whispering to deaf ears, "I'm coming."

She'd become increasingly overwhelmed by routine tasks like grocery shopping, constructing a meal, or cleaning out her fridge. Some Sundays, she'd open the door confused, her face wondering why we were standing in her doorway with a bag of food. We'd be equally confused, as we looked at a single glass of wine on the coffee table, a blanket draped across the sofa that looked like it had a person under it minutes before, and a Hallmark movie playing in the background.

"Time must have gotten away from me," she'd say. "I sat down to watch TV and didn't realize what time it was."

Stirring the potatoes that were sloshing boiling water onto the range I thought, *I hope she remembers she's bringing the stuffing*, then I worried about how old the vegetables would be.

I was knee deep in cooking, when I heard Travis and Cameron, who had just come back from picking up Mom, talking as they approached the door. Mom strolled through the door first, making it a foot into the room before coming to a complete stop, blocking the entrance, leaving Travis and Cameron piling up behind her like dominos. The terriers momentarily left their vigil in front of the oven, to jump all over Mom. As she leaned over, the bag she was carrying opened, displaying one bag of stuffing mix, a single stalk of celery, a white onion, and two cans of cranberry sauce. *Crap, I thought you were making stuffing.* My ovens were full and there wasn't a clean pan in sight.

"Excuse me Kay," Travis said, as he edged around her, then shot me a concerned look. Cameron, still behind Mom, also gave me a look that conveyed, *You have no idea what we've been through.*

Travis, who had made his way down the hall to the bathroom, poked his head out the door. "Kay, you said you wanted to use one of our brushes, there's one in here."

"I've been using a toothbrush," Mom said, before turning towards the bathroom.

Cameron whispered to me, "Not on her teeth, on her hair."

She did look a little disheveled, I considered, recalling the image that had just passed me on the way to the bathroom. She was a mess, her hair looked like it had been brushed with a toothbrush. There were sections that appeared brushed, the back of her head looked a bit matted and there were sections that jutted out like antennas. Her black jeans had what looked like smudged dry remnants of food on the thigh. *I hope that was food.*

Travis walked up and took a seat on a barstool. "It's been interesting," he started to say, but was interrupted by Mom yelling from the bathroom. "I can't button these," followed by giggling.

"I'm out," Cameron said, understanding Mom meant her pants.

"I got it," Travis said, as he headed towards the bathroom.

"You're going to have to suck it in Kay," I heard Travis say from down the hall, followed by Mom giggling.

"That's as far as my stomach will suck in," Mom said, sounding like she was holding her breath. *I love that man.*

Emerging from the bathroom with brushed hair, and pants intact, Mom joined me back in the kitchen. I tasked her with chopping the onions and celery. This was an epic failure on my part, not only did I give the lady with dementia, who couldn't button her pants, a sharp knife, she had the attention span of a two-year-old. She'd chop a few pieces, then abandon her station wandering off into the living room.

A half a slice of onion, chopped into little bits and a single stalk of unwashed celery laid on the counter, untouched. "Do you want me to chop this stuff?" I asked, trying to figure out if I should take over her job or if she'd be upset that I was "telling her how to live her life." We ran through this scene two more times, then I just finished the stuffing. I found myself studying her throughout the day. I wondered what she was thinking as she stared out the window or at the wall blankly. Her face looked like her mind had put out a, *back in five minutes,* sign.

I looked around our holiday table at my family with the Christmas tree twinkling in the corner. The meal was familiar, but the family was changing. It was like a scene from Invasion of the Body Snatchers, we looked like the same people, but differences inhabited our bodies. Lewy inhabited Mom, an eating disorder inhabited Cameron, hives from stress inhabited my skin, doubts about pandemic life inhabited Connor, and Travis, the token normal one, was trying to hold it all together. One silver lining to this weird holiday was that most of us wore sweatpants, coined "soft pants" during the pandemic. "Hard pants" were jeans or really anything other than yoga pants. Only Mom wore hard pants, and she couldn't button those, so I figured her future held soft pants.

D-Day

December 2, 2020

The first day a caretaker was to arrive at Mom's, which Danielle and I coined D-day, arrived. I watched the clock all morning anticipating a call from Jill telling me Mom wouldn't let the caretaker or helper, as I called them when not talking to Mom, inside. In my mind, I envisioned the caretaker standing on the front porch knocking, peering through windows, as Mom hid somewhere in the house. I glanced at the oven clock, 2:32 p.m., the helper left at 2 p.m. and I hadn't received angry calls or texts from Mom. When 3 p.m. passed, I called Danielle. "Have you heard anything?" I said.

"Nope, that's good right?" Danielle replied.

"I think so," I said, uncertain. I figured Mom was just planning her revenge.

The calm wouldn't last, in fact the very next morning Mom called. "It's ridiculous! It's weird having someone in my house. It's weird," she spit the words out so fast it was hard to keep up. "She just sat on my couch, and we stared at each other. I don't need this!"

I knew this was coming. "Mom, you agreed to

just try it. Let's at least give it a couple of weeks," I said, defeated from weeks of negotiations.

"Did you find your dogs?" she said, jumping topics.

What?

"Find them? I'm staring at them," I replied, puzzled, looking at terriers who were sitting a foot from me because I was in the vicinity of food.

"They got out yesterday. I was worried."

Did you think you were at my house yesterday or did you think the dogs were at your house? The irony wasn't lost on me that she could tell me she didn't need help in one breath, then in the next talk about hallucinations.

The sound of messages coming through on the app my work used to communicate internally interrupted our call. If the television show *Intervention* had helped me normalize my drinking, my work app helped me normalize the drama with Mom. I hung up and scrolled through messages that depicted the day's happenings. Two clients were caught making out on the side of the building, another client was waiting with his bag for his ride because after two days of detox he could "handle life without heroin" and finally a client I'd counseled two days earlier was making inappropriate comments during group. Mom's drama had nothing on early sobriety.

Little Piles Everywhere

Sunday rolled around, so hamburgers in tow, Travis and I headed up to Mom's for dinner. We'd been unable to convince either of our boys to join us since Sunday dinners with Gma fell somewhere just under doing laundry. Connor had been a hard no since she shit her pants and Cameron, well, he tried to avoid anything that involved food. Hamburgers would have sent him into a calorie counting abyss.

Entering Mom's kitchen, I searched for a place to put down the bag of food I was carrying. On the island, piles of papers scattered the surface like little land mines. The piles were filled with bills, recipes cut out of magazines, blank or half filled out checks and yellow sticky notes stuck everywhere, like binder dividers. This wasn't new, Mom had been organizing her bills into confusing paid, unpaid, important, unimportant piles for months, but there was a new chaos to the piles. I dropped the bag on the counter behind me as Travis trailed in coming to a full stop at the island when he saw the piles.

He plucked one of the yellow sticky notes off a pile to read. "Kay, I think you should let us help you with these," he said, a mix of fear and bewilderment on his face.

Before she could reply, he added, "We'd deal with the HOAs and you wouldn't have all these piles around." Travis has an uncanny ability to be direct, along with highlighting the benefits of the desired outcome he wanted.

"That would be good," Mom said, letting out a sigh. "It's just too much." My mouth fell open waiting for the other shoe to fall, but no argument followed.

This wasn't the first conversation Travis and I had with Mom about taking over her bills. The months leading up to this, Mom's bill paying efforts went from small mistakes to utter mayhem.

"I paid them, but they said I didn't sign my check," Mom had said one afternoon, perplexed by a call from her utility company.

"We could help you put all these on auto pay," I'd said.

"No, I don't want all my personal stuff out there online," she'd said, her tone insinuating I was living dangerously using auto pay.

She'd also started confusing her bank accounts, writing checks off the wrong accounts, or depositing money into the wrong account, then she'd wonder why she had over drafted. There was the occasional double payment made to a vendor, which was the least problematic of the chaos that was ensuing. I'd figured this was how people lost all their money or got taken advantage of by some telemarketer. I remembered having noticed her landline phone in the kitchen for the first time and I'd thought, *I really need to get rid of that. Who even has landlines anymore?* I'd envisioned the landline as a cord linking scammers to Mom.

Travis nudged me. "We need to do this tonight," he whispered. He was right, if we didn't seize the opportunity, she might change her mind tomorrow. One by one, Travis went online obtaining logins to set up auto pay. Paradoxically, we were going through this exercise because of Mom's failing memory, however she also was the person we needed to remember her passwords.

Mom had three homeowner's associations between her properties, two sets of property taxes, medical insurance, and bills. I too started creating little piles everywhere. Not to mention, two of her three HOAs were managed by the same property management company, not on the same property. It was confusing as hell, there would be yellow sticky notes in my future.

I could hear Dad's voice as we set up the different bills on auto pay. "Don't let her piss it away," he'd said, days before dying. His dying proclamation was clear, don't let Mom mess up her finances. Dad's voice triggered another memory of the time I'd spent three days in a car with Mom and Porsche (anxiety ridden Pomeranian), driving from Texas to San Diego. Mom, on a whim, had decided to sell the San Diego condo that was paying her several thousand dollars a month in rental income.

Driving across a stretch of desert somewhere in Arizona, Mom had decided what she'd do with the proceeds of the sale. "I'm going to buy gold bars. Gold has always been a good investment," she'd said, while handing Porche french fries in the back seat. Then I'd heard Dad again. "She'll be set up with the rental income. She won't have to go into the money."

At one point, we'd stopped at what could only be described as a dive motel, only to have Mom bring out a four-pack of tiny wine bottles that could have been placed on the table of my childhood doll house. *Are you kidding me?* I'd thought, *I'm going to slam those in five seconds.* Dad's death had sent my problematic drinking into overdrive. I remembered Mom emerging from the sketchy motel bathroom wearing a towel.

"You already drank yours?" she'd asked, surprised two of the four tiny wine bottles were gone from the cute cardboard carrier.

You think? I almost drank yours too.

Luckily once we were in San Diego, Mom took her neighbors advice, not mine, but her neighbor. "Why would you sell?" the neighbor had said, one evening as we all sat around talking. "You can always sell if you need to but make the rental income until then." I could have kissed the woman, not only for her words of wisdom, but also for having full size bottles of wine.

"Thanks for your help," Travis said, hanging up the phone with the last vendor. I thought about the sense of responsibility I'd felt back then to protect Mom's finances. I felt that same responsibility now, not only to ensure that she would never be destitute, but also to ensure she'd never have to move in with me.

The Art of Regifting

December 25, 2020

A new normal had emerged, I was starting to hate that saying, but that's what it was, a new normal, brought on not only by the pandemic, but also Mom's disease. Mom's hallucinations, delusions, forgetfulness, lots and lots of phone calls, text messages that needed a decoder, were all part of that new normal.

For a month Mom had been talking about Christmas gifts for my boys. She'd drag out random items from around her house to show me, saying, "What do you think about this?" It took me a minute to realize she was shopping for Christmas within her house, as if each room were a different department.

I stared at a blanket from her guest closet that was shoved into my face. "They could always use another blanket," I replied, not knowing how to respond.

I thought back to the time Nana handed Danielle and I sheets of colored dot stickers. "Put these on what you want," she'd said, gesturing around her condo. "It's for after I'm gone."

Nana had a manner of speaking that incorporated abrupt, short sentences, laden with a Hungarian accent that made you stand at attention. Danielle and I looked down and the colorful dots hesitating to lay claim to items. "Why? You seem healthy to me," I'd said, eyeing my ninety-something-year-old grandmother who took an occasional aspirin and walked daily, which unnerved her neighbors because she walked in the middle of the street.

"I could die at any time," she'd said, dismissing my comment with the wave of her hand.

The only thing that defined Nana's interior design was if it looked expensive. After immigrating to the US in her late teens, she'd spent her early years cleaning houses for wealthy New York families. Striving to emulate that wealth, Nana acquired items that she perceived looked expensive. I thought her decor looked gaudy. I remember her judgmental eyes on me as I hesitated to place a colored dot on one of her table lamps that were ornate in an eclectic way.

"That's expensive," she'd said, holding her stare until the little colored dot found its way onto the base of the lamp that made Cesar's Palace look quaint.

Nana lived to ninety-seven-years-old, leaving

Danielle and I to see the colored dots all over our future possessions for years.

My eyes tried to focus on the pink and white plaid blanket Mom held two inches from my face. "What about this one for Connor?" she said, pulling it back and refolding it into a plush square. *Just give the boys colored dot stickers.*

Christmas afternoon, decked out in her favorite Christmas sweater, bedazzled with rhinestones and puffy snowman, Mom opened the door. Her confused expression told me she had no idea why we were standing on her porch. *This would be a good Christmas card*, I thought. Mom in her Christmas sweater, looking at the family in the doorway holding a ham and pie with a blank expression. Spend the Holidays With Those You Love, written underneath the photo in sparkling red ink.

"Merry Christmas Kay," Travis said, interrupting the porch staring contest, as he walked inside.

Mom slid a piece of ham around her plate, quiet, like a stranger had joined us to observe a family dinner. Our attempts to engage her in conversation only led to short, one-or-two-word answers, followed by the *back-in-five* stare.

"Let's do gifts," I suggested, trying to move awkward Christmas along.

Mom was impossible to buy gifts for. I speculated that after a certain age you shift from acquiring shit, to rehoming shit. This year, I'd bought Mom a simple gray sweater, one which I liked, because there was a high probability it would be gifted back to me at a later point. I probably should have just put a colored dot sticker on it, claiming it for later.

"I have some things for y'all," Mom said, as she walked off into the guest bedroom to shop, then re-emerged with two blankets. Everyone stared at the blankets, and I felt like I was in on a secret that no one else knew.

She handed the pink, fuzzy plaid blanket to Connor and the gray fleece blanket to Cameron. Both unwrapped but folded into neat squares. "Uh, thanks grandma," they said, almost in unison, both looking at each other, then at me.

She'd also purchased gift cards for the boys, but then hid them because someone was stealing from her. I figured I'd find them eventually, probably with her pills.

With Mom's bedding hoard folded in our trunk, we headed home, blankets relocated from one closet to another. Awkward Christmas over.

Chapter 10
Scavenger Hunt

Mom tolerated the helpers that came and went every Thursday, but their presence had intensified her hiding behavior. She was obsessed with hiding her pills, particularly the fucking little pink pill. "People are stealing them," Mom said, one afternoon holding the fucking little pink pill container. "It was all over the news." I concluded she'd watched the news coverage of the Oxycontin crisis and somehow substituted her Seroquel for Oxycontin in her rendition of the story. Comparing Seroquel to Oxycontin, was like comparing a light drizzle to a monsoon. One a highly addictive opioid and the other an antipsychotic.

"Mom, no self-respecting drug addict wants a pill that gets rid of hallucinations," I'd tried to reason. "There's literally no secondary market for your pills."

Hints of paranoia began creeping into the hiding behavior, so subtle if you weren't paying attention, you might miss it. Adding to the fun, she moved items she'd hidden like wallet contents, money, insurance cards, jewelry, including fake jewelry, medications, and anything and everything that might have value, from one hiding place to another, several times a day. It was like a one-woman scavenger hunt.

I went to grab toilet paper from under her bathroom sink at one point, only to find a few crystal figurines, a credit card, pills, and a zip lock bag full of jewelry. Holding a little crystal angel in the palm of my hand I'd questioned, *Are you okay to live on your own?*

Just to be clear, the helpers never took anything. Mom would hide something then forget she hid it, thinking someone stole the item, a vicious cycle fueling her paranoia.

Systemically Inflamed Lunatic

January 1-14, 2021

I sat on the sofa, holding my shirt up to expose my stomach. *Did the dogs have fleas?* I thought, as I looked at the tiny raised red bumps that covered the front of my body. It looked as if a hundred bugs bit me in unison. A quick Google search showed horrendous pictures of bug bites, causing me to close the computer screen, ready to Raid my entire house. Bed bugs seemed to fit, with the exception that the tiny red bumps were only on the front side of my body. When I stood in front of the mirror, turning side to side, there was not a single red bump anywhere on the back of my body. It was as if an invisible line had been drawn on my skin, separating the front and back sides of my body in which nothing could cross, not even a bed bug.

I made an appointment with a dermatologist convinced I'd leave with some cream or prescription and the bumps would be history. The morning of the appointment, I sat in a medical gown open exposing the entire front side of my body. As the doctor had me spin around, she said, "That's interesting, there's no bumps on your back." I stayed quiet, feeling uncomfortable in just my underwear standing under unkind fluorescent lighting.

Spinning around, she asked me the same question she'd asked only minutes earlier. "You haven't been in a hot tub?" she said, her tone implying I was either lying, or had forgotten.

"No! I haven't been in a hot tub." *I would remember being in a hot tub.* At my age, you absolutely remember squeezing your body into a swimsuit, especially a winter body, fresh off holiday eating.

A tiny slice was shaved off one of the bumps for a biopsy and I left. No cream, no antibiotics. Two days later I was informed the bumps were harmless, had properties consistent with a bug bite, but that didn't mean it was a bug bite.

At my wits end, I called a pest control specialist, even though I hadn't seen a solitary bug.

Standing in front of the bewildered bug specialist, I pulled up my pants leg to expose the bumps that covered the front side of my shin.

"With that many bites, I'd be seeing bugs or at least signs of them," he said, staring at my shin.

"I feel like I'm going crazy," I replied, sounding crazy. "I haven't seen any bugs."

"There's nothing for me to treat," the man said. "But if you start seeing things just give me a call."

That's funny, I thought, *If I start seeing things, I'll be just like Mom.*

My gut told me the rash had to be something systemic due to its presentation on one half of my body. I started to question whether stress could cause a full body rash.

Around the same time, my estrogen levels spiked, topping out at close to 1000 pg/ml.

"Are you under a lot of stress?" my doctor asked, looking at the blood work up on my hormones.

"Does having a crazy mother qualify?" I joked, then clarified, "She has Lewy body dementia, so she hallucinates and is delusional."

"Oh, I'm sorry to hear that," she said, her initial laugh fading. "Stress does wreak havoc on your hormones."

The memory of another time I'd broken out in a rash rushed into my head. "What are you worried will happen if you stand up for what you need with your Mom?" my therapist had asked six years prior, as I'd watched the red splotches of hives spread on my arms. An awkwardly long silence followed.

"She'll go away," I'd replied, my voice sounding like my eight-year-old self.

"Like she did with your sister," my therapist had gently said. Her words had hit me like someone had thrown cold water on me, shocking and true.

It shouldn't have been a surprise that stress was manifesting externally on my skin and internally hormonally. Essentially, I was a systemically inflamed lunatic. Finding balance in my life sounded like a joke. Mom's disease was progressing at a rate that left me reeling with no time to process one change, before another would hit. Add in eating disorders, Zoom learning and the pandemic and I counted myself lucky it was only a rash.

The evening after my doctor's appointment, I laid in bed staring at the ceiling. "Someone in my family needs to be okay," I said to Travis, defeated. "They can't all be struggling at the same time."

"Life never gives you more than you can handle," he replied, laughing.

"Fuck off," I replied.

Reluctant Uber

The new year brought with it Mom's feeling that something had been taken away from her. To be fair, something had been taken away, her car. Mom had become fixated on places she wanted to go in her car, not driving, but in her car. On the list, Target, lunch, the grocery store, to see friends, trips to Bryan to see her sister, the list was endless. The same lady who a month ago would rarely leave the house, now was a social butterfly, spreading her wings with no car.

I was the reluctant Uber, agreeing to drive Mom places out of guilt, but bitter about driving to Lakeway and back several times a week. At my wits end, I confronted Mom one afternoon about utilizing the helpers. "I can't keep doing this," I said, exhausted. "I've cut back my hours at work, my family needs me, it's just not working. You're going to have to use the caretakers to drive you places."

"You're my daughter," she said, more as a declaration. "Whenever you go grocery shopping, I'll just join you." *If I lived in Lakeway that would be perfect.* Her eyes locked on mine, expressing that a line had been drawn in the sand.

"You're not listening to me," I said, frustrated. "I don't have time to drop everything and take you to the grocery store."

"Whenever you have time," she said, giving me a little smile.

Geesh, you're good at this.

"Why didn't you have the caretaker take you to the grocery store this week?"

"I didn't realize I was out of milk and those cranberry scones I like until after."

Mom was a master manipulator and unwilling to bend our dynamic, even in the light of Lewy. I knew the ball was in my court. *Damn boundaries.* We negotiated a semi-forced routine of Target during the week and dinners on Sundays. I left feeling like I'd been out maneuvered by a woman with dementia.

Mid-way through January, Mom's frustration that she'd never drive again boiled over. I arrived on what I now called, 'Target Tuesday' to find Mom scrubbing a pan like she was angry at the egg remnants stuck in its corners. The minute I entered I could feel the heaviness of anger in the air. My inner child wanted to run and hide. After several attempts at conversation that were met with clip one-word answers and stiff body language, I dove in. "Is something wrong?"

Slamming the pan into the sink, she turned to face me. "I don't appreciate being treated like a child," she said, between gritted teeth. "Who the hell are you to tell me I can't drive and what I can do?"

I'd been waiting for this ever since the day we sat in the neuropsychologist's office. "It's not me, the doctor told you not to drive," I said, throwing the doctor under the bus.

"Target is only two right turns from here," she negotiated, gesturing with her hand like she was giving directions to Target.

"That's not accurate and it doesn't matter how many turns. It's still driving," I snapped.

I could feel the energy in the room shift, anger intensifying and narrowing its aim directly on me. She walked past me, practically bodychecking me, then continued over to the white swivel chair by the window. In dramatic fashion she folded her arms tightly across on her chest, then swiveled to face me. "You're the only one who thinks I have a problem. Just you," she seethed, her eyes now boring into me.

I was mad but couldn't muster the energy to fight. "Do you want to go to Target today?" I said, trying to keep the conversation from turning into a full argument.

"No. I don't!" she said sternly, asserting what probably felt like a little bit of control.

"Fine, I'm going to head out then," I said and pivoted for the door. It wasn't until I was sitting in my car that I realized I had actually left. Our dynamic my whole life had been me placating Mom's feelings, eventually acquiescing, just to break the silent treatment or smooth out the tension. I felt a little liberated, but also angry at my new role and responsibility.

What Do I Owe You?

January 20, 2021

In the days leading up to taking Cameron, who was on the road to recovery, back to his graduate program, Mom and I continued to argue about driving. She'd call multiple times a day, each conversation eventually turning into her snide comments about driving. "Well, if I had my car...", "You're trying to control my life," and "I can't go anywhere."

Halfway into one of these phone conversations, frustrated, I said, "Mom, you've never even asked me how I'm doing with all this. It's hard. My life has been flipped upside down too."

Silence followed, then, "It's happening to me! How do you think that makes me feel?"

I immediately felt like the ghosted child that had stood in front of her Mom as a teenager. "This is me. Why can't you just be okay with that?" I'd said, crying, standing in the board shorts and no makeup that had been met with disapproval. "I can't be the girl that you want me to be. That's not me!" I'd learned many years ago that my feelings didn't count, but today, holding the phone, tears welling up in my eyes, I was hurt by her inability to even acknowledge my feelings before turning it back to herself. *What do I owe you?* I thought. *What's a reasonable sacrifice?* My health, my kids, my marriage, sobriety, or maybe my sanity.

Four days later, I sat in another gorgeous hotel suite in Miami watching the sun fall behind the ocean. It was beautiful, but all I could think about was Cameron slipping back into his eating disorder. I unpackaged the chocolate chip cookies I'd bought at Publix, placing the container in my lap. The image of Cameron looking like a skeleton haunted me while I shoved a chocolate chip cookie into my mouth. As the chocolate melted on my tongue, I thought, *You might not eat, but I'm eating for both of us.*

I knew Mom would get worse and I couldn't imagine what that would look like. I shoved another cookie in my mouth. *She's probably wandering the streets right now.* I looked down at my fingers covered in chocolate and thought, *Both my parents will be dead by the time I turn fifty.* The resentment I had been wearing like armor, shielding me from the sadness of loss, loosened its grip. Now sitting alone in the gorgeous hotel room, I felt my stomach sink, a lump formed in my throat, then tears, lots of tears. Pulling my legs into my chest sent the empty cookie container falling to the floor. Tucked into a little ball, I sobbed.

Chapter 11
Pandemic Wedding

February 5, 2021

The morning of my cousin's wedding, I stood staring at my wardrobe, perplexed by what to wear. It was a rare day that I got out of yoga pants. Adding to the complexity was trying to evaluate what would fit my pandemic body, without having to go through the shame and mental anguish of trying on outfits. Travis on the other hand knew exactly what he wanted to wear, in fact he was downright giddy about it. Before the pandemic he'd bought a navy blue, velvet blazer with matching blue satin lapel that had never seen the light of day. Travis loved this jacket, but I thought it looked like something Hugh Hefner might wear to a disco.

Hugh and I headed out to pick up Mom who would go with us to the wedding then leave with her sister to spend a few days in Bryan. Travis's satin lapel caught the sunlight as we drove, throwing shimmering tiny, blue crystal prisms all over the interior of the car like a disco ball.

We pulled the car to a stop in Mom's driveway. Before I could get out of the car her front door opened and out stepped Mom fully dressed and ready to go, her huge purse hanging off one shoulder.

"I can't believe she's ready," I turned to Travis. "I figured she'd still be in pjs."

"Where are we going?" she said, meeting me at my car door. I felt the hopeful feeling fade.

Gesturing for her to follow, I started for the front door. "Beth's wedding, we're meeting your sister there," I said, my voice trailing off as I rounded the corner to see the dining table filled with a multitude of jackets, an umbrella, a couple of sweaters, several pairs of pants, and an assortment of toiletries.

Coming up behind me I heard Mom say, "Let me grab a jacket, it might be cold."

"What's wrong with one of these," I said, sarcastically, pointing at the pile of jackets on the table. Already in stride to the bedroom, she turned around and looked at the table as if she were seeing it for the first time.

"Is this what you're bringing to Bryan?" I said, waving my hand across the piles on the table. "Do you want to throw this stuff in a suitcase?"

Travis joined us around the piles on the table. "Okay, let's just grab it and go," he said, scooping up the piles. I watched Mom trail behind Travis, as he threw her piles into the back of his car.

Somewhere along highway 290 I caught a glimpse of Mom in the rearview mirror. Sitting turned to her left, she looked to be having a conversation with someone next to her in the back seat.

"Who are you talking to Kay?" Travis asked, turning down the radio. He wasn't trying to call her out on a hallucination, he was trying to figure out if she had said something to him. Abruptly stopping her conversation, she quickly slid into a forward-facing position with her hands clasped between her knees, like a schoolgirl caught passing a note.

"Do you see the little boy here?" she said, in a warm, playful way.

"Just you," Travis said.

"Well, he's really cute," she laughed, then proceeded to describe the little boy. "He just has the cutest brown hair and he's wearing denim shorts with little blue suspenders." He did sound cute and the warmth in Mom's voice told me we were missing out by not being able to see this little boy.

The road changed from asphalt to gravel, as we took the turn for the wedding venue. At the top of a long driveway, sat a modern white farmhouse that looked like it fell off the pages of Southern Living. Hunting for a parking space, we passed the wrap-around porch adorned with gas lanterns that held my Uncle Tom and his wife Susan standing decked out in a tux and sequined gown. The only thing missing were people rocking in chairs with fresh lemonade. Off to one side sat a smaller, equally chic chapel connected by a stone pathway interwoven with flowers.

Travis barely threw the car in park before he popped out and scurried around to help Mom, who was already attempting to exit the car. He rounded the car to find Mom bracing herself on an open door, one foot dangling over the gravel. When her tiny black suede flat hit the ground, the rest of her tried, but it was as if the muscles had lost their memory, coming together discombobulated. Travis lunged forward grabbing her arm, before she completely crumpled to the ground. Unfolding back into an upright position, she brushed herself off. "My leg must have fallen asleep from the long car ride," she said, laughing, but her face was visibly annoyed at the betrayal of her legs.

I haven't seen this many people in one place since the Alabama Buc-ees, I thought as we walked into the venue. Inside, Mom was everywhere I was, the song "Me and my shadow" playing again in my head. If I went to the restroom, so did Mom. It was like having my own personal bathroom attendant. As I moved from group to group, making small talk, so did Mom.

A herd of well-dressed people made their way along the stone path that connected the venue to the chapel. I watched Travis lunge for Mom. "Here let me help you," he said, swooping a hand under her elbow, as she painfully tried to traverse the stone path, losing her balance in the crevasses of the stones. I brought up the rear, watching the bride's ninety-year-old grandfather out pace them.

Seated in beautiful wooden pews, we watched the bride and groom exchange vows in front of a large stained-glass window back lit by the falling sun. After the ceremony, in unison, the herd migrated back to the main hall. Sitting at a table with my aunt, I couldn't help but watch Mom canvas the room, her eyes pausing at times to stare off in a corner. *What are you looking at?* Behind the *back-in-five* stare, lay little hints of paranoia. No one else in the room would have noticed the subtle fearful movements of her eyes, but I saw it, like a weird sixth sense.

Mom and I made our way down the appetizer buffet, returning to the table with food that someone else had cooked, which was exciting during a pandemic. My fork barely planted into a puffed pastry, before Mom stood up and placed her giant purse on her shoulder. The puffed pastry hung on my fork. "Are you going somewhere?" I said, then plunged the pastry into my mouth.

I flashed back to an image of Nana decades before, standing by the front door with her purse. When Nana was ready to leave, she'd just get up, grab her stuff, and head for the door until someone realized she wanted to go home. Apparently at a certain age, all politeness and social etiquette are viewed as needless expenditures of energy. The buttery flavor of the puff pastry brought my attention to the table.

"To the car," she replied, impatiently.

"We haven't had the main course yet," Travis said, hoping to entice her with food. "Why don't you sit down, they'll bring dinner around soon."

Irritated, she dropped down into her seat with her purse still on her shoulder. Throughout the meal, Mom would grab Gene Ann's car key then start walking towards the exit. This would send Travis or me running after her, slowing to a fast walk as we passed guests, before breaking into a sprint to tackle Mom before she reached the door.

"Can you put your car key in your purse," Travis asked Gene Ann after Mom's third attempt for the exit. "Kay keeps taking them and heading for the door. She'll get lost in the parking lot."

I worried tonight would be the night I had to issue a Silver Alert.

Boom, boom, boom, thump, thump. The base vibrated the floor rippling up into my feet. In an instant the quaint southern wedding transformed into a nightclub. Lights dimmed and a colorful spectrum of lasers started striking the walls, dance floor, and ceiling. I thought about all the raves I'd attended in the early nineties and had the urge to throw a beach ball onto the dance floor. It was time for the bride and groom, along with their young bridal party to hit the dance floor as Frank Sinatra faded to Daft Punk.

Dancers in long flowing gowns took to the polished wood dance floor, while the grand nieces, wearing tights, slid to a stop in front of the DJ station, jumping up and down like a tiny person mosh pit.

My eyes came back to our table, landing on

Mom. *Oh God.* Her face looked pale, her eyes bulged and darted around the room like the lasers. The combination of the disco tech, more people than she'd been around in months, and bright colors flickering all over the room, had put her in a catatonic state like a shark flipped on its back. I wondered if hallucinations in laser filled technicolor were beautiful or just scary?

"I think your mom is done," Travis whispered in my ear.

"You think?" I replied, sarcastically.

I mouthed, "It's time" to Gene Ann and tried to nudge Mom who was frozen in the catatonic state toward the exit.

Travis drove us down the long driveway to Gene Ann's car, so we could transition Mom's piles of clothes. When Travis and I hopped out of the car, Mom remained seat belted in place. "Kay, you remember we put all your clothes in the back," Travis said, opening her car door. "You're going with your sister to Bryan."

"I am?" she said, not getting out of the car.

"Come on Sister, let's get your stuff," Gene Ann yelled from her car, which prompted Mom to finally get out of the car. What followed resembled a human conveyor belt of clothes going from one car to another, us putting clothes in Gene Ann's car, then Mom grabbing the clothes out and putting them back into our car. I froze at one point just watching the scene. *They're just walking in circles.*

"Those are yours," Travis said, drawing out the words slowly, placing the sweaters returned to his car in Mom's arms. "They're going with you." The way Travis interacted with Mom reminded me of how we'd talked to our boys as toddlers. Direct, to the point, and just the facts, everything else was confusing filler.

"Come on Sister!" Gene Ann said, climbing into her car, trying to encourage Mom to get in the passenger seat.

Travis guided Mom to the passenger side of her sister's car. "You're going to need to sit down," he said, mimicking taking a seat with his own body, then applied a little pressure to her shoulder. Mom more or less fell into the seat.

"Holy fuck," Travis said, letting out a sigh, as he climbed into our car. "I hope they make it to Bryan." We watched my aunt's Acura drive off into the blackness of the night in the wrong direction.

Halfway back to Austin, we stopped to grab a drink at the roadside convenience store. A young man exiting the convenience store with a bottle of Crown Royal tucked under his arm, held the door open for Travis as he entered. "That's a nice jacket man," I heard the man say as I waited in the car. Travis's head snapped around towards me, an "I told you so" smile beaming across his face.

It's a fly jacket Hugh.

That One

February 11, 2021

A week after the picturesque wedding, I found myself entangled in a familiar circular phone conversation with Mom about in-home care. Trying to stay calm, I said, "I'm not doing this to you. I'm trying to do what's right."

What followed tipped my already waning patience over the edge. "I don't need you meddling in my life," Mom replied, angry. "You aren't responsible for me!"

I wanted to say, "Fine, I'm out, deal with it all on your own," but instead said, "It's not that easy, people call me wondering what's going on with you. They look to me to fix it." The implication from the, "What's with your mom" calls I got regularly was, "Are you handling this?"

"Who?" Mom snapped. "Why are they calling you?" *Shit.* I'd triggered the paranoia.

"Mom, I'm not going into all that with you," I said, deflecting. "I'm tired, I need someone to come in and help once or twice a week. It helps me out."

"I don't need you or anyone else talking about me or telling me what to do," she said, now seething with anger. "Whoever is calling you? I'd like to know who that is."

I felt my blood boil and my ability to be compassionate run out the door. "You know what," I snapped back. "I'm not your only daughter. Call Danielle, you have two daughters." Silence followed. Taking a deep breath, I continued, "I love you, but I need a break for a couple of days. Please just talk to Danielle about this stuff for a bit."

"I don't know how to deal with that one," she replied, in a soft, almost whispered voice. *That one,* the two words suspended in my mind.

"Well, you're going to learn," I said and quickly hung up. *That one. You mean your daughter?* I thought. *That one has a name, it's Danielle.*

A couple of minutes later, I glanced down at my phone and saw the notification, *one missed call, Mom.* I fell back onto the sofa and stared blankly outside at a pint-sized brown bird that landed on a branch. It felt harsh to tell another person you need a break from them, but I didn't know how to deal with *that one, Mom.* My next call was to Danielle, it was only fair to tell, *that one* I had just appointed her as the de facto Mom contact.

My delivery was abrupt. "I just need a break," I said to Danielle, quickly. "I told her she needed to call you for a couple of days. Not me!"

"Okay?" Danielle replied, hesitating some. "Should I call her? Or is there something to do?"

The next day, Danielle called. "She wants me to call her every morning to check in on her," she said.

"You're going to regret that," I said, a little laugh slipping out. "She's been trying to get me to do that for a while and I told her that's not independent living."

This battle between Mom and I had started long before her disease. Mom loved to hang out on the phone, she envisioned us talking multiple times a day. That sounded horrible to me, I hated hanging out on the phone. I didn't even talk to Travis that many times on the phone. Even before her disease, she'd wanted me to call her to check on her every day, saying, "Just a brief check-in first thing. That way if something happened to me, someone would know."

"You live in a neighborhood where everyone knows what's happening with everyone," I'd said.

"Your neighbors are always stopping by, every day in fact."

In recent months she'd tried the same approach to which I'd replied, "Well that's not independent living when I'm having to check on you every day." She quickly dropped it.

Travis often pondered, "What's with your mom and the whole phone thing?"

I heard Danielle nervously laugh. *You should be worried*, I thought. *You just got pulled into one of Mom's games.*

A couple of days later Danielle called again. "I've called Mom a couple of times this morning," she said, more irritated than worried. "She didn't answer and hasn't called me back. Should I be worried?"

"I don't know," I said, suspecting there was no reason to be concerned. "Isn't she the one who wanted you to call every morning?" My voice had an edge to it because it was day three of my break and it felt like Mom was trying to suck me back in by causing worry.

"I'm not going to rush up there," I continued. "If you don't hear from her in a couple of hours let me know."

Danielle called her again later that morning

informing me Mom had been talking with one of her neighbors and missed the call.

The next morning, I hit play on an early morning voicemail as I made coffee. "Michelle! Michelle! I think there's a problem with my credit card and I can't find the number for Wells Fargo," Mom's panicked voice said, then continued "A doctor called, and I don't know if I should call, and I can't find my medical card. I need you to call me!" Break over.

Chapter 12
Sadie Lands in Detox

March 3, 2021

They'll be okay, I thought as I looked at the two terriers sprawled out on the sofa sleeping in the sun. For the first time in almost two years, I was looking at boarding the pets. Mom had always been our pet sitter, but since she was busy with her imaginary pets, that was no longer an option. I reached out to our old pet sitter hoping they were still in business. Travis, Connor, and I were planning a trip to Miami to check in on Cameron.

Thank God, I thought as I confirmed the zoo with the pet sitter. "You guys are going on a little vacation," I said, looking at the terriers who were now sitting attentively under the parrot, who was perched on the ledge of his open cage door, dangling a chicken leg bone over their furry heads. They're the picture of COVID pets, spoiled and rarely alone. *Surely, y'all can survive a couple of days.*

If the forty-five-minute car ride to the pet sitters was any indication of the pet's coping skills, we were fucked. Finn cried an irritating long drawn-out whine, interrupted with smaller yips, that grated on my nerves. Sadie foamed slightly at the mouth, prior to puking up her breakfast all over the back seat. Nigel, contained in his pet carrier, repeated "You're okay" over and over again. *I'm not okay.*

When the wheels of my car hit the gravel of the sitter's driveway, I was ready to throw all of them out of the car. A twinge of worry settled in my stomach, but my real child, not the furry and feathered children, needed his family. I took a breath and handed over the zoo, who were now all completely quiet.

Later that afternoon, I watched the landscape of Austin grow smaller, as our plane slowly merged with the clouds. Dealing with Mom over the last year had been a family affair, the toll of the disease rippled through all our lives. I leaned back in the seat, relaxed, excited to get away and spend time with my family.

Miami's airport was coming back to life. Cinnabon was open again! I made a mental note to grab a gooey bun when we were back at the airport in a few days. The incredible smell of cinnamon, yeast, and warm sugar was interrupted by the, *woosh*, of the sliding doors to the outside opening. Hot air, so humid it felt like a swamp, caused little beads of moisture to form on my skin immediately.

"This makes Austin feel cool," I said, my mind not being able to think of anything except how hot it was.

Miami's sun was intense, penetrating the skin from above and radiating your shins with waves of heat coming off the pavement. I took in the people that bustled around as we waited for our rental car. It was good to see cities coming to life again. I also noticed the people walking around almost naked, I couldn't blame them, I was ready to strip off the clothes that were sticking to my skin like a paper mache project too.

Over lunch I watched Cameron eat most of his lunch. The truth was, I knew exactly how much he ate because I scrutinized each bite with the same attention Mom had scrutinized my high school backpack when she was convinced I was "smoking that marijuana stuff". He was still skinny, but no longer looked like a skeleton and did appear to be eating, or at least in front of us. Because moving in with your adult child is frowned upon, Travis and I had to trust that Cameron was continuing to meet with his therapist and going to his eating disorder groups, so most days we were still holding our breath.

After a full day of playing tourists in South Beach, we settled back into the hotel room. I heard the chime ringtone of my phone, the *unsettled, almost queasy feeling* took hold.

"I'll grab it, it's Sherrie," Travis said, reading the caller ID, his eyes pleading with me not to get worked up. *Why was Sherrie calling?* I looked outside, night had fallen. *She never calls me at night.*

"Where are you," I heard Travis say, after some silence. "Are you at Kay's?"

Brief silence, then Travis said, "Gene Ann isn't there, she's in Bryan."

I was now standing on top of Travis and could hear Sherrie say, "You're sure Gene Ann isn't in town?" Understandably confused, she explained to Travis that Mom had called frantic looking for Gene Ann who needed to go to the hospital. Sherrie and Craig, who lived ten minutes from

Mom, had rushed over to help. The amount of potential Silver Alerts occurring in Mom's orbit was growing.

I sunk into the sofa, wondering if I needed to fly back to Austin. *Bing,* a notification of a voicemail came through my phone.

I have Sadie, she's fine and here with me. Just call when you get this.

What? I didn't recognize the upbeat, friendly, female's voice. I hit the icon to dial the number I didn't recognize back. The same female voice answered.

"You called me about Sadie," I began to say, then the female voice jumped in, "I have her, she's such a little cutie! I work at the detox at the end of the street, and she just showed up here." I could hear a group of people talking in the background.

"She's supposed to be with the pet sitter," I said, still confused.

"I know the place, so I went down the street, but no one answered," she said.

I could hear Sadie barking in the background.

"Do you have a little brown dog too?"

Oh my god, where's Finn?

"I do, Finn, they're there together," I said, panic stricken. "Where is he?"

"He's fine, he's still behind the gate," she said, trying to reassure me. "He's pretty stressed, but fine. I'll keep Sadie here, she's playing with the clients. Just give your pet sitter my number and I'll walk her back down the street."

"Thank you so much, really thank you!" I said, grateful Sadie had landed in detox. Travis and I laughed at the visual of Sadie at detox. "It fits," he said. "She probably needs to be on Xanax." At one point, in fun, we had given our dogs human personas. Finn's persona would be living on a commune making soap and Sadie's persona would be on her third, rich husband and on Xanax, so detox was perfect.

Chapter 13
House Hunting

March 19, 2021

I slowed the car to a park along the street across from Copper Leaf, an assisted living home. It seemed like everyone I encountered lately had asked me if I was prepared for when Mom would need assisted living. *I wouldn't have known this was here,* I thought as I took in the single-story house sitting among other homes in a residential neighborhood.

I thought about one of my last visits with Nana, who at the end of her life, resided in a converted residential home facility like Copper Leaf. During that time, Nana thought people were trying to poison her or communicate through her radio and was so paranoid you questioned your own safety in her presence. I'd remembered thinking, *That's ridiculous, she's only eighty pounds. I can take her.*

I climbed out of the car comparing Mom to Nana. Mom was delusional, but she hadn't reached Nana's paranoia level. I thought of the time I'd brought Nana a bag of mini Reese's peanut butter cups. She'd taken one in her gnarled hand, then slowly held it back out in front of me. "You eat some first," she'd said, skeptically, as if I were her medieval food taster confirming it wasn't poisoned.

I approached the bright-aqua front door the same way I had approached hundreds of doors when I was selling real estate. It felt like house hunting, only missing the excitement that typically accompanies the purchase of a new home, and this buyer, Mom, would definitely be sight unseen. While I listened to the doorbell echo through the house, I quickly strapped on my face mask, fumbling with the rubber band over my ear. The nicely dressed man who opened the door could have doubled as any other homeowner, however his plastic name tag that read Cooper Leaf, Director of Housing reminded me this wasn't just another home.

The house was beautiful with warm modern decor that gave everything an instant serene feeling. Light streamed in through windows lining the back of the home, overlooking a deck and backyard. Outside in a tree, a large squirrel hung upside-down, its little feet holding on for dear life trying to access the bird seed before falling. This could have been any house in an Austin neighborhood, until your eyes landed on its inhabitants.

Around a circular oak breakfast table, a small woman was hunched forward in a wheelchair strapped to an oxygen tank that sat on the floor beside her. Her hand, flecked with large age spots, was wrapped around a fork being used to spear pieces of egg. I watched as she missed the target repeatedly, thinking, *this is why everyone is so thin in these places*. To her left was a woman wearing medical scrubs taking the blood pressure of a man who looked like he had moved from his bed to the breakfast table but hadn't actually woken up.

Caught up in people watching, I suddenly realized the house had unique features that unmasked its real use. There was no carpet anywhere. No area rugs waiting for someone to catch the edge with their walker, not even a welcome mat, just wood and tile. I thought of my own missteps with rugs, truthfully after a certain age rugs are just decorative hip breakers. The walls had strategically placed handrails. Wide gaps made paths between all the furnishings, perfect for wheelchairs. The bathrooms looked more like triage units with stark neutral colored tile everywhere and huge walk-in showers with no doors. Along one wall in the showers hung industrial style facets that could hose down any mess. I thought about Mom's comments to Connor after eating cinnamon rolls and figured the industrial facets and tile were a smart move.

My cheeks hurt from the smile plastered to my face, as the housing director talked about clients needing a lift to get them into the showers. "How big is your mom," he asked. "I ask because it helps me understand if a lift would be needed to assist her."

"Small, she's small," I stuttered.

We turned down a hall, at the end was an open door leading into a bedroom. In the room, a barren mattress lay stripped of all its bedding placed against a wall. There was a reddish-brown stain, about the size of a small pillow in the middle of the mattress. I fixated on the stain. *What caused that?* I heard the voice of the housing director in the background, as I ran through the scenarios in my head that could have caused the stain; diarrhea, blood, bloody diarrhea, or food. I hoped it was food.

"This room just became available," he said. "Joe was here for about a year, but he passed last week." The comment was not said in an unempathetic way, just said by someone who had a familiarity with death.

Back in the living room, we sat in chairs separated by the wheelchair path, as the housing director asked me to tell him about Mom. I recounted all the events that had led me to call for a tour, and conveyed she had a diagnosis of LBD. This would be the first time I realized a LBD diagnosis gave people in the industry pause.

He shifted in his chair, then began talking. "Each case is unique, but we may not be the right facility for your mom," he said, carefully. "There's special training for staff that goes with Lewy body." The words jumped around in my head. Half an hour earlier, I'd stood on the front porch sure Mom would be the highest functioning resident, thinking I'd jumped the gun. Now I was being told they might not accept her. Sensing my shock at the news, he gave an example of a previous client with LBD. "One of our clients, in a delusion, had barricaded himself in a room using the dresser to block the door," he said. "It became a dangerous situation, to himself and others."

I pictured my small mother dragging a dresser in front of her door.

"From what you're telling me about your Mom," he continued, his voice softening. "I could help you find other facilities in town that would be better equipped to provide care for her."

All of the sudden, I felt like a mom sitting across from a school principal who was explaining why my child's behavior required an alternative school.

Later that evening, with a bag of M&Ms on my lap, I said to Travis, "They won't take her."

"What? Why?" he replied, confused.

"Apparently, the delusions can get bad, you know, like paranoid bad," I said, popping a couple of M&Ms in my mouth. "I guess they do things that make it hard on the staff."

"What things?"

"Barricade themselves in a room with dressers blocking the door," I said, shrugging my shoulders.

"Oh shit," he said, as we exchanged a look that conveyed, *I hope that doesn't happen.*

The Goldfish

Second Neurologist Appointment, March 22, 2021

"You won't have to draw a clock," I reassured Mom, when I reminded her of the appointment I'd set with the second neurologist. The first neurologist had fallen onto Mom's bad list due to making her draw a clock and using words like *dementia* and *parkinsonian*. I'd found a female neurologist, hoping the combination of being female and someone different than "that man," as Mom referred to the first neurologist, might make her more amenable to appointments.

A contradiction of sorts, Dr. Stoman was tiny, maybe five-feet tall, wearing cute jeans and a sweater that she probably had to buy in the children's department. However small her stature, she was a spunky, confident woman who held space in a room like someone twice her size. Her direct manner held no punches, but the hit was delivered in a sweet voice disarming any opponent. I immediately liked her, so did Mom.

After asking Mom a series of routine questions she turned to me. "How would you describe your experience with your mom's memory?" she said.

What an interesting question, I thought, a little taken back, because no one had asked me how I experienced Mom's memory loss.

Choosing my words carefully, I looked at Mom who sat next to me, *back-in-five* stare fixed on the picture on the wall. "Sometimes I get frustrated with her," I said, slowly. "Just having to repeat everything, but then I feel bad because it's not her fault."

Without missing a beat, Dr. Stoman lifted her eyes from her notes and looked directly at me. "It's like a goldfish," she said, and I felt my stomach drop. "The short-term memory can't hold things beyond a couple of moments." *Oh my god, did you just compare Mom to a goldfish?* I waited for Mom to get upset, but she didn't react. I struggled not to smile. All I could think about was the orange cartoon-like goldfish with big bubble eyes swimming around in my head.

The doctor's voice interrupted my cartoon fantasy. "I'm going to make a referral for physical therapy. It can help with Parkinson's symptoms," said said, talking directly to Mom now.

Good luck getting her to do that, I thought.

In the elevator on our way to the car, I had a hard time not seeing the orange cartoon goldfish when I looked at Mom. "I think physical therapy is a really good idea," I said to the big bubble eyes.

"I'll think about it," the goldfish replied.

That means no.

Later, I would recount the story to Danielle, who was equally stunned that Mom hadn't reacted. "The goldfish" became a new moniker, never in Mom's presence and only between Danielle and me.

"Were you with the goldfish today?" Danielle would ask.

"The goldfish thinks the ladies are stealing her pills," I'd say and so on.... I had to laugh, or I would literally scream at having to repeat myself all the time. "The goldfish" was like a billboard with a little orange cartoon fish with big bubble eyes staring at me, reminding me to have patience.

We've Been Waiting for A Little Priest

March 23, 2021

It felt like deja-vu as Mom and I pulled into the same stadium parking lot we'd been at a month before when Mom received her first dose of the COVID vaccine. Here for her second dose, we slowly rolled up to our position in line. I rolled down Mom's passenger side window to greet the woman who would inject the shot. "Is this the arm you would like the shot in?" the woman said, prepping the needle.

"Last time they gave it to me in my neck," Mom replied, gesturing dramatically toward her jugular.

The woman looked past Mom, locking worried eyes with me, her expression part quizzical, part horrified.

I shook my head in that way that conveyed, *just ignore that.*

She paused, still trying to process what she'd heard, then proceeded to put the needle in Mom's arm.

Mom and I made small talk as the minutes ticked by in the "adverse reaction" waiting area. A man dressed in a black long-sleeve button up shirt, with a white t-shirt underneath approached the car holding a clipboard.

I rolled Mom's passenger side window down and before the man could utter a word, Mom exclaimed, "Oh good. We've been waiting for a little priest!"

I tried not to laugh at the expression of utter shock on the man's face. Again, I shook my head to indicate, *just ignore that*, then said, "Are we good to go?"

"Yeahhhh," he said, drawing out the word like a question. He ripped off a yellow top copy from the papers on the clipboard then handed it to Mom. In the rearview mirror as we drove off, the little priest stood motionless watching our car.

In less than twenty minutes, Mom had left two workers completely speechless. I wondered if the two, at the end of their workday, would recount stories of the lady who had been given a shot in her jugular and was looking for a little priest.

Chapter 14
The Neighbor's Son

March 24, 2021

Knock, knock.
"It's me," I said, cracking Mom's front door open as I slowly walked inside. Mom sat on the sofa, still in pajamas, looking like she'd been up all night. "We need to get a lawyer!" she exclaimed, before I even reached the living room.

"What? Why do you need a lawyer?" I replied, hesitation in my voice.

She slowly turned towards me, her eyes were serious and almost bulging. "He's trying to take my house!"

"Who's trying to take your house?" I said, realizing I'd unwittingly engaged in a delusion.

She let out a sigh. "My neighbor's son. I saw his truck there, it's always there," she said, talking so fast, she had to pause to catch her breath. "He doesn't live there! Sometimes he just circles the street."

Hello paranoia, I thought, but said, "Your neighbor's son isn't trying to take your house."

"Yes, he is," she replied, like a childish playground retort.

I heard, *not uhhh, I know you are but what am I,* in my mind.

"It's probably the utility truck that has been in the neighborhood doing work." I couldn't tell if she believed me, but she dropped the discussion, at least for a moment. Dropping my purse in the chair, I headed for the kitchen to grab coffee.

"Did you hear I was at the press conference?" she asked, excitement now replacing the paranoia. "I don't know what that man is doing, but I sat next to him and watched him write something down on a little piece of paper."

Don't engage, don't engage, I thought, as I dropped a little sugar in my coffee. "What press conference? Who?" The words slipped out as if on autopilot.

"Governor Newsom, this morning," she said, her tone flippant, like I should have known.

It took me a minute to realize she had watched a press conference on TV that morning with Gov. Newsom and somehow put herself first person into the TV, like an actor in a scene. I had entered the house fifteen minutes ago and was already mentally tired. My brain was like a ping pong ball between delusional paddles.

Trying to move things along, I said, "Why don't you put some clothes on, and we can go to Target?" Her delusions were present outside the house, but it was easier to redirect her when we were out. Target is like Mom's Disneyland and all the merchandise and bright lights made for a wonderland of distraction.

Bits of paranoia flickered throughout the day, emerging as off-handed comments about her neighbor's son or comments such as, "That man keeps looking over here." At times, it had me questioning my own sanity.

When I pulled back into Mom's community, I winced at the sight of the utility truck parked by the mailboxes. I watched Mom purse her lips in a disapproving fashion, as she glared at the utility truck.

Don't ask, don't engage, don't engage, don't engage...

Unwelcome Houseguest

March 25, 2021

The sound of my phone ringing from the bathroom woke me from a sound sleep. Half awake, I grabbed my phone, *Mom, missed call, 5:27 a.m., Mom, missed call, 4:03 a.m.* displayed on the screen. When I began to play her voicemail, her voice sounded scared, which made my whole-body tense.

> He's been here all night. Just sitting in the other room. I just want to get out of here!

I hope she didn't leave, I thought, as I scrambled to call her back.

"Michelle! Michelle! Is that you?" Mom's frantic voice came through the phone.

"Mom, I know it feels real, but your neighbor's son isn't there. It's a hallucination," I said, trying to calm her down. "I'll come up there today and check in on you."

This is how it happens, this is how elderly go missing. I would want to leave my house too if I thought there was a guy just sitting in the other room. Every day Mom inched closer to becoming a Silver Alert.

I called Danielle to update her on the paranoia. She and I briefly entertained the idea of installing a RING camera, then decided with Mom's delusions that would be a bad idea.

"Can you imagine if Mom saw a camera?" I said, laughing. "She'd be even more convinced someone was watching her."

"Yeah, that's true," Danielle replied, also laughing. "She'd totally think the neighbor's son installed the camera."

Before I made it up to Mom's that afternoon I fielded calls from neighbors, Gene Ann, and Sherrie, all concerned with Mom's recent behavior. Her delusions were seeping like water, leaving her house, flowing into the neighborhood. One neighbor informed me that two days prior, Mom had confronted the neighbor to her left about her son trying to take her house. Apparently, Mom had cornered this poor woman in the street, like a scene from West Side Story, which resulted in another neighbor intervening.

I spent the afternoon reassuring Mom I didn't see the neighbor's son in any of the rooms. I did however see a folding table set up in the garage with four chairs set around it and a deck of cards in the middle. "Why is your garage door half open? What's with the table?" I asked.

"Don't be rude Michelle. It's the ladies," she replied, indicating I should have said "hello."

The next day Sherrie called. "Your mom has no idea what's going on," she said, worried and talking fast. "She's talking nonsense. You have to find somewhere for her. I don't think she can live on her own!"

I know. I know! I hung up and frantically started scheduling facility tours.

Cruise Ship on Land

March 26-29, 2021

With the fear of Mom moving into my back bedroom as motivation, I spent the next couple of days touring facilities like there was a fire lit under my ass. When I pulled into the circular drive of the first facility I felt so strung out, I sat in my car for a minute to calm down. Once inside, the community director emerged from one of the offices and gestured for me to join her in the office.

She barely sat down before I started talking. I could hear my own voice, *God I sound crazy*. The words came out fast, manic almost, as I vomited all of Mom's delusional behavior out onto this poor woman, who just smiled and nodded. When there were no more words left, I fell silent. Across the desk the woman's plastered smile told me she was trying to figure out how to respond. There was a lot for this woman to consider, not only had I depicted Mom as paranoid and delusional, but she also probably thought I was too.

She cleared her throat. "I can appreciate the situation you're in with your mom. It sounds like she's unable to be on her own," she paused. "We look at Lewy body on a case-by-case basis, so I'd have to talk with staff about your mom before we could accept her." The words sounded familiar.

It never occurred to me that I would have to paint Mom in a different light in the effort to get her into a facility. When I'd left with more referrals, I again felt like a parent with a problematic child.

Desperate, I phoned Leslie for advice on how to talk about Mom with facilities. Leslie carefully detailed how to navigate the conversation, which sounded a lot like therapeutic lying. She gave an example of another client's father. "She ended up having to medicate her dad with a sedative to get him into a facility," Leslie said.

She's going to be in my back bedroom, I thought. *I'll need a sedative.*

I thought about how I would describe Mom

moving forward, leaving out the paranoia and delusions. I'd say, *She has some anxiety, just normal concerns.* Leaving out, *She thinks the neighbor's son is taking her house.* Adding, *She's pretty mild mannered.* Leaving out, *Unless you try to help her, or tell her what she's seeing isn't real.* Then I'd say, *She's friendly and has always had a lot of friends.* Leaving out, *She isolates except for talking to imaginary people.*

The four facilities I toured shared commonalities. They were all one level, designed to look like a sprawling one-story house from the front, some with small porches or circular drives that arched in front of the entry doors. Access was secured by a blaring alarm triggered anytime the front door was opened, that striked your central nervous system like a bolt. It was unnervingly loud, but I suspected it was needed, given how many residents paced around the door at all times. I wondered if residents ever tried to make a break for it when the door was open. Small business offices typically flanked a common living area, which always had a couple of residents passed out napping on sofas, reminding me of my father after a Thanksgiving meal. Two wings spanned to the right and left of the common living area, each holding a kitchen, dining area, and long hallway filled with residents' rooms. Wreaths, family pictures, bells, and other hanging items adorned the individual doors in an attempt to help residents identify their rooms.

Three levels of house guests resided within the walls of these sprawling one-stories. The first group consisted of residents that at first glance might be staff. They were high functioning, leaving you with the feeling that maybe a family member had jumped the gun on moving them into the facility. The second group consisted of residents that were still fairly mobile, socialized with staff and other residents, but if you paid close attention to those interactions, you'd hear them talking to themselves or repeating themselves over and over again. The third group consisted of residents knocking on an ethereal door, so to speak. Their mobility was limited, often in wheelchairs or in bed completely immobile. Their appearance was pale, almost translucent, with tissue-paper like skin, no body fat, and usually in some state of sleep.

There were activities calendars posted on the walls touting ice cream socials, bingo, movies, and arts/crafts. It reminded me of a cruise ship on land. Community directors eagerly talked about the cognitive benefits of these activities, as I thought about how much Mom hated playing games or engaging in any of the events posted. She might attend an ice cream social for a few minutes, then retreat with the ice cream back to her room.

I could hear Mom's voice say, "You're trying to get rid of me" as I thought about the facilities I'd toured. During this time, Gene Ann expressed wanting to spend time with her sister, asking if I'd considered a facility in Bryan, TX. My initial concern was burdening my aunt with taking care of her sister, but I understood her request, as we both knew deep down that Mom wouldn't see many more years. A sense of urgency would permeate everything until I secured a facility for Mom. I constantly visualized Mom's Silver Alert on a billboard along the highway displaying: SILVER ALERT, Gray 2011 LEXUS RX, TX LIC RX1234.

Two Sisters, Back at The Start

March 27, 2021

I'd roped Travis into touring Victoria Inn, the facility in Bryan. We spent the two-hour drive talking about Mom. Even when she wasn't with us, her energetic imprint rode shotgun. When we pulled into the parking lot for Victoria Inn, I eyed the sprawling white stone one-story. *I remember this place*. Decades prior, I'd pulled up to this same white-stone building to visit Baba. I could see my teenage self-standing next to Baba on her patio, looking out onto the community garden filled with pink and red rose bushes. For the first time in a week my body relaxed.

Becky, the community director, greeted us in the common living area where an old-fashioned popcorn machine spit out fresh popcorn that filled the air with a warm buttery scent. My eyes were immediately drawn to the wall of windows overlooking the community garden, it looked exactly the same as I'd remembered.

"Hello dear," said a female voice, startling me. "Are y'all looking to stay here?" To my side, a woman in her eighties with perfectly coiffed hair stood smiling.

"Yes ma'am, I'm looking for my Mom," I said, my mind neatly organizing this woman into "level one resident". *Women really do outlive men*, I thought, as I realized I hadn't seen a male resident yet.

The facility felt more like an over-sixty community, than an assisted living. Resident units consisted of a living area with a private patio, bedroom with adjoining bath, and small kitchen equipped with a stove, refrigerator, and small breakfast bar, all like small apartments. Travis and I sat across from Becky trying to put language around the confusion we felt with the fluctuating nature of Mom's disease. "On good days, you might not even know anything was wrong," I said, leaving out a description of the bad days.

Becky leaned forward and said, "It sounds like she's in between stages, which is normal. We have lots of people here that are just starting to have issues living alone."

"It's a little more than that," Travis fessed up. "She hallucinates sometimes." *Most of the time,* I thought, but didn't say.

"I understand. We've had others that do also," Becky said, reassuringly. Her reaction was such a stark contrast to the reactions of the facilities I'd spoken with in Austin, that I knew we were benefiting not only from Baba's prior stay, but also that Mom had grown up in this small town. It was as if one of their own was coming home, an unspoken "We'll keep an eye on her" exchanged. We ended our visit discussing deposits for a unit and availability.

Half an hour later we sat in Gene Ann's living room telling tales of Mom. "She confronted her neighbor in the street the other day," I said, trying to make Gene Ann aware of what she would be signing up for. "She thinks you're there all the time, and sometimes isn't happy about it." I hoped she understood Mom could be mean to pretend Gene Ann.

As we drove off, my mind fixated on the full circle life sometimes makes. *Two sisters, back at the start.*

The next day, like a dementia whisper, Leslie coached me through how to tell Mom she was moving. "This is a less is more approach," she said. "Don't overwhelm her with too much information. Keep it positive and talk about all the benefits."

I frantically brainstormed benefits, *All your meals will be made for you* and *Your sister will be right down the street.* It felt like I was trying to psych myself up before a battle.

We Come Bearing Pie

March 29, 2021

As we pulled into Mom's driveway, my eyes fixed on the key lime pie in my lap, Mom's favorite and a peace offering I hoped would sweeten the hard conversation. I lifted my gaze to see Pam and

Karen, Mom's neighbors, coming out the front door, their serious expressions sent my stomach plummeting to the floor.

"That doesn't look friendly," I said, turning to Travis. Mom stood in the doorway watching Pam and Karen leave. The look on her face told me this hadn't been an afternoon wine gathering. The peace offering in my hands might not be enough.

Pam walked up beside me as I got out of the car. "It's been interesting, I'm glad y'all are here," she said, arching an eyebrow. Making sure we were out of Mom's ear shot, she explained that Mom had a fight with someone else in the neighborhood, again about the other neighbor's son trying to take her house.

"That's why we're here," I reassured Pam. "I found an assisted living facility. We're here to tell her she's moving."

"Wish us luck," Travis said, in a friendly but serious tone. *We're going to need it.*

Mom gestured for us to come inside. Travis held up the pie. "We come bearing pie," he said, trying to lighten the mood.

We were barely inside before Mom started in on the neighbor's son. "No one believes me, I know something—"

Travis cut her off mid-sentence. "It's key lime,

I'll cut you a piece," he said, headed for the kitchen.

"What's the occasion?" Mom asked, skeptically.

"No occasion, we just wanted to talk to you about something," Travis said, diving headfirst into dark water.

"Really? What's so important? Did I do something?" she asked, sounding like a child who was in trouble. My heart sank.

Travis gestured toward the outside patio. "Let's get our pie and go sit out on your patio," he said, grabbing two plates with pie. "Danielle wants to be part of the conversation so we're going to get her on FaceTime."

Mom gave him a questioning look. "Now I'm nervous."

"Don't be," Travis said, shoving a plate of key lime pie into her hand. "This is all a good thing." I hovered in the doorway, surveying the environment, waiting for Mom to explode. I was fascinated that Travis's mere presence had kept her from going off on the typical tirade about how I was trying to control her life. Instead, she sat on the outdoor sofa with her shoulders slumped, looking like a child. My heart sank. *It's not your neighbor's son who is taking your house. It's me.*

"Hi, Mom," Danielle said, her face filling the computer screen on the patio table.

Silence followed until Travis broke the ice. "We'd like to talk to you about your living situation," he said, clearing his throat. "Do you remember our conversation this morning when you said you were scared?" It had been another morning full of calls from Mom, starting at 4 a.m.

"No."

"You were scared. You called us at 4 a.m. the last couple mornings and were upset." Travis said, confidently. "Michelle's been looking for a place for you to go. Somewhere you wouldn't have to be scared because there would be people around to help you." I felt the blood drain from my body.

Mom smiled, which took me off guard. "I think that would be good," she said and sounded authentic. "I was just telling my neighbors how all this is just too much," she waved her hands around, gesturing to her house.

Did she just agree? I felt a hesitant relief wash over me.

Danielle, equally surprised, jumped in piggybacking on Travis's comments. "You've talked about being stressed when the TV or remote doesn't work, this way there would be someone to help," she said. The TV remote caused everyone grief; Mom's house was covered in yellow sticky notes with detailed explanations of how to use the remote.

"What did you find for me?" Mom said, looking at me.

Still waiting for her to flip the switch to anger, I felt the words get caught in my throat. "Do you remember where Baba was? Victoria Inn?" I said nervously.

"The place before Crestmoor?" she said. *I can't believe you remember that.*

I grabbed the computer and pulled up images of the Victoria Inn. "Your Baba and I ate here a couple of times," she said, sliding her finger over the image of the main dining room. "Can I go see it?" *Shit, I didn't expect that.* It was a valid request, but not practical, not to mention it would lead to Mom wanting to look at other places, essentially dragging out the process.

"Travis and I did a tour and put a deposit down on a great unit close to the front by the common areas with a little patio," I said, quickly, not answering her question.

Quiet for a minute, it looked like she was trying to access something from the recesses of her mind. "When would I go?"

"In about a week," I said, timidly.

"How would I pack everything by then?" she said, her voice quickening. "I need to see the place so I can figure out what to bring."

Sensing my panic, Travis interjected, "We can take care of all of that," he said, swooping up the pie plates with only crumbs remaining. "Michelle can help you figure out what to bring. We'll get the movers and help you pack."

Travis dropped the plates in the kitchen sink and put the remainder of the pie in the fridge. "Mom, I'm going to take you up to see your sister next week," I said, as we headed for the door. "She can bring you back to Austin next weekend." Therapeutic lying was becoming like second nature. I was actually dropping Mom with her sister to keep her from bogging down the moving process and to keep her safe for the week leading up to the move.

A drought-stained Lake Austin, with its "Sometimes Island" looking like a more permanent land mass, passed by the passenger window while I replayed the day's events. "Well, that went a hundred times better than I expected," I turned to Travis. "Just wait though, when it sinks in, she's going to start blowing up my phone."

The Sleep Over

April 2, 2021

The morning I would take Mom to the babysitter, her sister, started off less than ideal. I had arrived at Mom's to find her purple paisley suitcase cracked open like a clam shell. Folded neatly in the corner were floral pajama bottoms, one pair of underwear, and her sequined parrot t-shirt.

"Is that all you're bringing?" I said, trying to figure out her logic behind the three items. She stood in the office nook that adjoined her bedroom expressionless. "I'm just going to throw a few more things in here for you."

Mom wore a total of two interchangeable outfits. Velour black pants or white denim jeans with a lime green t-shirt bedazzled with tiny beads at the neckline or, a white cotton blouse with a crocheted element on the sleeves. Sometimes she threw in the sequined parrot t-shirt, a shout out to Nigel. I found her two interchangeable outfits, threw them in the suitcase and snapped the clam shell shut.

The drive to Bryan in April was the embodiment of Spring. A mix of wildflowers filled the medians between the highways and scattered all through the green pastures. The coral blooms of Indian Paintbrushes and violet-blue bluebonnets intermixed with the orange and yellow daisy-like blooms of Blanketflowers. It looked like someone drug coral, violet and yellow dipped paint brushes along the highways. Growing up Mom would tell stories of the colorful fields of her youth. "You could see flowers for miles and miles," she'd say, followed by, "You know that's because of Lady Bird's Beautification Campaign?"

Mom reminisced about driving with her family between the small towns that lined Highway 21 during Spring. She pointed out the tiny white chapels that seemed to be in every small town with a population of a couple of hundred people. "There was a time I wanted to take pictures of all these little chapels and make a book of them," she said, looking out the window. *I wish you had.* She would have been a great person to sleuth the stories behind those little chapels and capture their essence on film.

We passed a dilapidated old building that in its prime might have been a diner. Mom gazed out the window at its remaining walls held together by sheer will. "That used to have a little old cafe in it," she said, and I could feel her mind wander back in time. "Out on Sunday drives we'd stop there. It was the only thing between towns, even back then." I felt a little pang of sadness for this building that time had forgotten. As we drove, I wondered what would happen to these stories that felt fragile, like they too would be forgotten.

It was early afternoon when we pulled into Gene Ann's driveway. I stared at the pink-brick house and remembered visiting Baba when she'd lived here, long before Gene Ann moved in to help care for her. I pulled Mom's paisley suitcase from the car and almost threw it on the lawn because it was practically weightless with so few items inside. When I reached the walkway, I turned to say something to Mom and realized she wasn't there. Still seated in the car, her eyes locked on mine through the windshield. *She has no idea where we are.*

"Your sister's inside," I said, opening her car door. I hoped the word *sister* would shake loose some recognition of where we were. She didn't move, so I reached across her body to unlock her seat belt.

"Am I staying here?" she said, still staring at the house.

"Just for a couple of days," I said, helping her get out of the car. As we approached the front door, Mom looked around like she was taking in the front porch for the first time. My concern grew. *I hope she remembers her sister.*

The door creaked open and Gene Ann stood in a fuchsia pink tracksuit. "Hi Sister!" she said, opening the door wider. Gene Ann's voice snapped the confused expression off Mom's face. Two minutes later, Mom and Gene Ann fell into their old routine, each one trying to control the other, leading to bickering. Who would have thought there would be muscle memory to family dynamics?

I placed Mom's suitcase in the guest bedroom and felt like I was dropping a kid off for a sleepover. I did a quick once over of the room assessing it for safety. The window had one simple latch that flipped upward. *She'll figure that out, but the screen will stump her*, I thought. I traced the path from the bedroom to the doors that led outside. Once in the hall, it was a quick left then out the front door or a quick right and out the back door. *That might be a Silver Alert.* The house was filled with dementia traps.

I joined Mom and Gene Ann who sat around the breakfast nook table eating sandwiches. Sometimes it was easy not to see Lewy sitting next to Mom. These little windows of normalcy made me grateful for whatever time I had left with her, but they were also painful, because they illuminated how much had changed.

When I left, Gene Anne followed me to my car where she and I exchanged logistics like undercover operatives, talking in hushed voices, even though Mom was inside. "I'll get the remaining stuff packed up and on the ninth. We'll rent a U-Haul," I whispered. "Her neighbors are having a going away party for her on the eighth."

Like a parent dropping their kid at a sleepover, I relayed important information to Gene Ann. "I wouldn't let her wander alone," I said. "And don't argue about the hallucinations, you'll just be left frustrated. The ladies she talks about at her house aren't real." Gene Ann's eyes widened. "If she doesn't sleep, the next day she'll be confused and it'll be hard on both of you. She goes back and forth between reality and delusions, so you might get a good couple of days, or no good days. It's a crap shoot." I pulled out of the driveway waving goodbye. *Best of luck.*

Alone, with only the sound of the tires rolling along the asphalt, I thought about the events over the last couple of weeks. The commotion of being busy had been like a distracting friend. Finding a place for Mom left no time to think or feel. Now the intrusive thoughts had no corners in my mind to run and hide. It was the beginning of the end and I couldn't ignore it. Mom would never live in her house again. I had spent a lifetime going home to Mom's for visits, dinners, and holidays, but now I questioned what going home would look like. I gazed at my reflection in the rearview mirror, the face staring back at me looked confused, just like Mom's face had hours ago.

Chapter 15
Death at the Party

April 7, 2021

Gene Ann's Texas A&M colored maroon Acura sat in Mom's circular drive. *She's already here? But, she's never early. Hm.* I couldn't recall an occasion when my aunt arrived to anything early. She was always making people wait on her.

"I thought we'd have a little time before they got here," I said to Travis, as we pulled in and parked behind Gene Ann. "Oh well."

"She's probably done with your Mom and her imaginary friends," Travis said, turning off the engine. "I'm sure she's ready to tag you back in after a week with her."

Travis was right. While Gene Ann had supervised her sister, I had spent the last several days boxing up the belongings that would go with Mom to Bryan. Those boxes were now stacked against her living room wall. "Do you think Mom will notice the boxes?" I said to Travis, as we approached the door.

"Do you think she'll remember she's moving?" He laughed.

"That's true." I said, as a nervous high-pitched laugh escaped my lips. "I'll get to tell her all over again about the move. I bet this time it doesn't go well."

We opened the door to find Gene Ann sitting on a bar stool at the island looking tired. Mom was roaming around the kitchen opening drawers like she was looking for something. "How was your drive?" I asked.

"Fine." Mom stopped rummaging through the utensil drawer to look up. "I see the boxes. I want to see what's going with me." *She remembers.*

"Okay. Let's just do dinner tonight, but tomorrow we can dig through stuff," I said, hoping to distract her long enough she'd forget. "Not all your stuff is going to fit in the new place though."

She gave me an inscrutable look.

After dinner I started rinsing dishes in the sink. Everyone else was still at the table when a siren cut through the air. *Nee-naw, Nee-naw.* The loud blaring sound was getting closer. I looked out Mom's kitchen window and saw a streak of red, as a fire engine pulled in and came to an abrupt stop across the street. Immediately behind the fire truck, an ambulance followed hot on its tail. Firefighters jumped out of the truck headed for Mom's neighbor's house. *That's weird, there's no smoke.* Apart from a line of emergency response vehicles, everything looked normal. Then, two people who looked like extras from the movie *Contagion*, dressed in head-to-toe hazmat suits, exited the ambulance, and ran into the house.

The noise had drawn Travis and Gene Ann to the window.

"I wonder what happened?" I mused out loud. I turned around to look at Mom, who was still seated at the dinner table and picking at the ends of her meal.

When she glanced out the window, a Cheshire cat grin spread across her face. A little sparkle twinkled in her eye. "They shouldn't have done this for me," she said, almost giddy.

"What?" I was confused.

"The neighbors. They're throwing me a party," she said. "I hope the fire engine doesn't stay too long. I can't imagine what that'll cost!"

"Mom, that's not what this is," I said. "They're doing a little goodbye party for you tomorrow morning at the pool. This is different. Something's happened." The last time I'd seen a fire engine show up for a party was the last day of elementary school and there definitely hadn't been an ambulance.

Mom, still convinced the emergency response fanfare was for her, got up and headed for the door. A handful of neighbors had started to gather at the edge of Mom's driveway. I watched Mom pause as she opened the door, she eyed the group of neighbors, smiling from ear to ear. *Shit, she thinks the neighbors came for the party.* Mom started down the driveway looking like a debutante walking into a ballroom.

Just as Mom got close to the group, one of the neighbors broke off and headed in the opposite direction. Mom didn't notice. I noticed, because it was the neighbor Mom had aggressively confronted a couple of weeks ago, convinced this woman's son was trying to take her house. *Smart lady*, I thought. The last thing we needed was to add police to the mix.

I watched as Mom began to interact with the group. No one but Mom was smiling. They looked worried.

"Read the room Mom," I said, under my breath heading for the door.

"I'll go out there with her," Travis offered. Stepping back inside, I let him take this one. This episode had shit-show potential written all over it.

Firefighters and EMS personnel walked between the house and their vehicles at a calmer pace now. The flurry of activity minutes ago had given way to routine paperwork. Back at the kitchen window, in the small view between the fire engine and ambulance, I could see a woman walk out of the house. She took a seat on her porch steps, then her head fell into her hands and she began to cry. Her body went limp except for the motion of her shoulders shaking as she sobbed. This was definitely no party! Travis needed to get Mom out of there before she said something insensitive. Another neighbor broke from the group to take a seat next to the crying woman. I watched Travis place his arm around Mom to guide her back towards the house. Respectfully not wanting to gawk, the other neighbors slowly dispersed home.

"I think someone died," Travis whispered in my ear as they came inside.

Oh God, that's awful. That poor woman. I felt like a voyeur, peering through the window. A witness to someone's immense pain. I quietly told

Gene Ann what we suspected. Her eyes bulged as she glanced out the window. Without speaking, the three of us intuitively knew to distract Mom away from the kitchen window. Moments later, two EMS workers carried a stretcher from the house. A white sheet covered what could only be a human body.

It occurred to me that while we'd been eating dinner, another person had lost someone important in her life. All of the sudden, my struggles with Mom paled in comparison. The woman sitting on the steps would be forever changed after tonight. I sat solemn for a bit, feeling a little more empathetic. For the rest of the night, I patiently let Mom sift through a few of her moving boxes knowing one day soon I would be the woman sobbing who had lost someone.

The Power of The Middle Finger

April 8, 2021

The next morning started out like any other morning. Travis on one of many conference calls in our master bedroom, me, trying to get dressed quietly in our master bath. But it wasn't like any other morning, not really. I was more stressed than usual, having spent the last several weeks running all over town looking for a facility for Mom in between making day trips to Bryan and working. Exhausted and fragile, I was a smoldering ember. The slightest provocation would see me ignite.

I'm leaving for Mom's," I said to Travis's back, eyeing the clock. It wasn't even 8:00 a.m. yet, but already I felt hurried and irritable. "I haven't done anything with the pets," I added, before slipping on my shoes.

Travis, who was just then staring at his coworkers in their little ZOOM squares on the computer screen, spun around. "I'm on a call," he hissed, his tone a, *can't-you-see-I'm-busy* indictment.

That's all it took. I exploded. "I'm trying to deal with all my Mom's shit," I yelled. "Can't you help with the pets?"

Travis gaped at me. He tapped the mute button on his cell phone before saying, "What? I've done nothing but help you with your Mom." When I didn't respond, he took his mic off mute to tell the squares on his screen, "I'm sorry, give me just a minute and I'll be back." Then he turned off the camera, swiveled the chair around to face me and let me have it. "Fuck you!" my husband said. "I'm trying to work too and it's not like that just stops because of your mom's stuff."

To be fair, Travis had been incredibly helpful in recent weeks. In addition to working full time, he helped me with Mom, and picked up the slack at home because he knew his wife was teetering on the brink of a meltdown. In that moment, though, I was hurting and couldn't appreciate it. So I picked a fight.

"Fuck you!" I screamed back, throwing him the bird to punctuate my statement. Then, I turned and left, slamming the door on my way out.

I wasn't a block down the road before I felt like an idiot, embarrassed, childish. I hadn't flipped someone off in decades. Why was I now acting like a sixth grader who's just discovered the power of the middle finger? *When I get to Mom's, I'll shoot him a text and apologize,* I thought. Before I arrived at Moms' Travis sent a text.

> I'm sorry for telling you to fuck off. I think we've both been really stressed and it was bound to happen,
>
> love you.

I shot a text back.

I love you, too

I walked the two minutes to the community pool where women were already gathering for the party. Each carried a dish big enough to feed the entire neighborhood. (Southern women knew how to put on a potluck!) Gene Ann was there in an aqua tracksuit, with Foxy Lady, her Pomeranian mix, tucked under one arm. Only Mom, the guest of honor, was missing.

"Where's my mom?" I asked Gene Ann.

"She wasn't ready to come down yet," she said and headed for the food table.

Shit, she's alone with the boxes, I thought. I quickly walked back to gather Mom from her house.

"Your neighbors are already down at the pool," I said, as I entered. "You should head down there." Mom was bent over a box, both arms rummaging through items.

"I think I need to be here, so I know what's going with me," she replied, poking her head up from the box.

"We can do that after your party." I watched her dive back into the box, half her body disappearing. I gently slid the box away causing her to come up for air. "Let's go see your neighbors," I tried again, this time gesturing toward the door. Mom slipped on her impractical, beaded sandals and we headed out.

The three minutes to the pool took ten minutes. Mom was painfully slow and stopped often because she hated to sweat. It was ironic that she'd chosen to come back to Texas, a place so hot and humid, sweating was inescapable. We finally rounded the bend in the road to face the pool verandah, where a table full of food sat under a beautiful stone and wood covered patio placed perfectly in front of a large outdoor fireplace. To the left was a small kidney shaped cocktail pool, its aqua-green water resembled Barton Springs. A slight breeze hit the water sending tiny ripples across the surface that sparkled under the sun. At a time in Mom's life when she had retracted into herself as a widow, this neighborhood's quaint charm and wonderful women had helped pull her from the depths of grief, giving her a footing in life again. Warm tears formed as I thought about how Mom would never live in her adorable patio home with these wonderful women again.

Moving Day

April 9, 2021

The morning sun illuminated my bedroom forcing one sleepy eye to open. When I looked at my phone on the nightstand, I saw no missed calls or texts. Gene Ann had gone back to Bryan after the party leaving Mom for one night by herself before moving day. I'd tried to stay the night or get her to stay with me, but she'd adamantly refused and I'd been unable to muster the energy to fight. Relieved she hadn't exited her home in the middle of the night I made my way to the kitchen to get coffee. Travis, on his second cup of coffee, informed me he hadn't reserved a U-Haul. This caused me to have a minor melt down but lacked my flipping him the bird.

"I don't know where I'm going," Mom said from the doorway, as I got out of my car. I glanced at the suitcase leaning on her leg, it was a crap shoot whether it was actually packed, but at least it meant she knew she was going somewhere.

"We're going to Bryan." I passed her in the doorway headed inside hopefully to find coffee. "Travis and the boys are coming up a little later to get your furniture then they'll meet us at Victoria Inn."

"How will they know what to bring?" She turned and followed me inside.

"You helped me make a list of furniture yesterday," I said, surveying the boxes along the wall for disruption. "Everything else is in the boxes and they'll just grab those."

Not speaking, she walked past me towards the refrigerator, then opened the door, shoving her body inside. I watched her start to sort through lunch meats, milk, old vegetables, and what might have been pimento cheese at one point. "I should bring this. It'll go to waste," she said, placing old lettuce on the island. Dammit, we were about to fall down the rabbit hole of food waste.

Sometime after Mom's seventieth birthday she decided no food could go to waste. Comments like "There're hungry kids in Africa" were replaced with "You can still use that." All food could be salvaged or repurposed into one recipe or another. Leftovers, perishables that were hours from expiring, milk on the brink of curdling, and cheese that had a fuzzy layer that could be "cut off" would never see a trash can. After most Sunday dinners these items were rapped in foil or thrown in

Tupperware then handed to me, where I would take the items and throw them away at my house.

"I'll take all that to my house. The boys are in, they'll eat it," I said, knowing how much she liked to feed the boys.

"Okay." I watched her stop sorting and slowly back up, one hand still holding the refrigerator door. I reached around her and gently pushed the door shut before she could start sorting something else.

~

"There's our newest resident!" Becky approached us as we entered the common living area of Victoria Inn. She introduced Mom to other residents, as we walked through the common areas toward her unit. "Here you are, your new home," Becky said, in a chipper voice. A bright yellow "Welcome Kay" sign hung on the door. Bright yellow ball-like blooms dangled off a plant sitting on the breakfast bar, a single yellow balloon tied to its container.

"That's sweet of ya'll," I said, as Mom passed me on her way to the French doors that lead out onto the small patio.

"I remember this," Mom said, opening the doors. "Your Baba would always leave these open so the little dog, a weiner dog or something like that I think, could come visit."

Bing. I glanced at a text from Travis.

> We're here. I'm going to park the truck out front until someone tells me where to pull it up to get the stuff into her place.

I sent a text back.

> Pull around the left side of the building, You'll see a door propped open that's next to the unit.

If there had been a normal size truck at U-Haul, that wasn't what now rounded the corner casting a shadow along the building. "That's quite a truck," I said, taking in the truck that looked like it was pulling up to move an entire house.

"It was loud as hell the whole two-hour drive," Travis quipped, clearly not in the mood for jokes. He unlatched the lock and slid the back door up to expose Mom's furniture. It looked like someone had taken the furniture out of a doll house and packed it into a huge truck. Gaping amounts of empty space surrounded the furniture and boxes that were secured in the back right corner of the huge compartment.

By the time Gene Ann arrived everything had been emptied from the truck and set up in Mom's unit. Her little apartment looked like a mini version of the house she'd left behind. The entire process of transforming her vacant unit took less than forty-five minutes. Gene Ann took one look at my overdone family laid out on the sofa and said, "Why don't we grab lunch, then y'all can take off?"

Bless her.

After lunch, Gene Ann, Mom and I went back to Victoria Inn to get Mom settled. I watched Mom talk and laugh with her sister on the sofa wondering if she knew she wouldn't be going back with me.

"I'm going to head back," I said after a bit. "I'd like to try and get back in so I have some down time before work tomorrow." I picked up my keys and headed towards the door. I was halfway down the hall before I realized Mom was following me. When I reached the outside, I stopped under the overhang of the entry doors. Mom came up alongside me and stopped too. "I'll be back in a couple of days," I said, leaning in to give her a hug. "We'll get anything you need then. Gene Ann said she'd help you with stuff until then."

As I pulled away, Mom stood there, her face a blank canvas except her eyes which were unsure. "Will we go back to my place then?" she said. I felt like the air had been knocked out of me.

"No. I'm going to come here to see you."

"Where's here? Where are you coming from? Are you about thirty minutes on 620, or I don't know maybe 183?" she said, trying to orient herself with highways.

"You're in Bryan with Gene Ann." I looped my arm into hers to lead her back inside. "At the same place your mom stayed. I'm in Austin, about two hours away." The lady standing behind the visitor's sign-in desk approached, giving me a look that conveyed it was okay to leave. I walked off knowing Mom had no idea where she was, thinking at any minute she'd break into a sprint to catch me.

No One's Home

I rolled into Mom's driveway, easing my foot onto the brake as I surveyed Mom's house. *She's not here.* The sun reflected off the kitchen window, mesmerizing me for a minute. Images of Mom standing at that window over the years washing dishes then heading for the door when she saw me pull in caused my stomach to sink. The breath I hadn't realized I was holding released, as I used the large plastic storage bin in my hands to push the front door open.

Inside it felt surreal, like I should say "hello" and announce myself, but there was no one to alert. The absence of things immediately overtook me. The absence of Mom sitting on the couch in her flowered pink pjs. The absence of the Hallmark channel, playing some Christmas movie I'd seen several times in the background. The absence of items scattered all over the island, sorted into small chaotic piles.

This is weird, I thought and dropped the large plastic storage bin on the island to begin clearing out the kitchen. It didn't take long to realize how woefully unprepared I was. The plastic storage bin would hold half the contents of one cabinet. I started pulling items from the "catch all" drawer that held odds and ins. A white piece of paper folded neatly into so many tiny squares, I wondered if Mom had taken up origami caught my eye. Unfolding the paper puzzle, I found Mom's handwriting staring back at me, its neat flowing cursive letters made rows of names and phone numbers. Michelle's phone was listed at the top.

There had been times I'd wanted my name further down the list. I leaned back against the counter thinking about all the times Mom had called me with what I'd coined the, "you need to" list. "You need to" lists were handed out often and consisted of all the items Mom thought I needed to do. Usually at least one "you need to" would be hurled to keep me from getting too comfortable, just to keep me on my toes. I could hear her voice, "You won't always be pretty, you know. You need to be able to support yourself." She'd then add, "What if Travis has an affair," planting a seed to sprout insecurity. Now as I stared at the piece of paper with my number at the top, I wished she'd call me.

I rummaged through the drawer to find her address book. Images of this address book at every house, in drawers just like this one, conveniently located under the telephone, flipped through my mind like a rolodex. My kids had always looked at Mom's address book like an unearthed artifact.

"What is that?" they'd ask, flipping it in their hands while simultaneously looking at their phones, trying to figure out why anyone would have one.

Before I realized it, everything had been pulled from the drawer and strewn across the counter. It

Did Mom Drop Acid? 239

was a treasure trove of "should I keep this?" items. *This is going to take forever.* I siphoned through dead dogs' collars, keys, and refrigerator magnets. I hadn't factored the trips down memory lane in the clean out process, nor the emotional toll those trips would have on me. Everything inside her house held little bits of Mom, only she wasn't there.

Between day trips to Bryan to visit Mom I gathered moving boxes. On the second trip to Mom's house I found myself again in the kitchen. In addition to hoarding bedding, Mom hoarded kitchen stuff. I'd never seen so many little dishes of all shapes and sizes. Sets of seasonally decorated butter knives took up an entire drawer. Bowls stacked into each other like Russian nesting dolls inhabited one entire cabinet.

I started pawning kitchen stuff on neighbors who stopped by like door prizes. Honing my Home Shopping Network skills, I convinced the neighbors they couldn't live without a mandoline slicer or 4-in-1 chopper. If you stopped by, you didn't leave empty handed.

One night, at a dinner with a family friend I'd yammered on about boxing up Mom's house, when the friend casually said, "Oh God, you know my Mom."

"You're fucked," I replied laughing. Her mom

kept everything from childhood dolls, to moving boxes from two decades ago that would probably disintegrate if you touched one. It made Mom's kitchen look like child's play. I thought about what my boys would say about me and made a mental note to start cleaning out some of the junk I'd kept over the years.

Chapter 16
Adult Tea Party

Mother's Day, May 9, 2021

A memory of Danielle, Mom and me dressed to the nines, sitting at a white-clothed table to enjoy an elaborate Mother's Day buffet hit me as I drove to Bryan. I could hear Dad's voice in my head. "Hey, don't forget to grab a little something for your mom," he'd say, worried I'd forget. You didn't forget Mother's Day, if you did, there would be hell to pay. The sound of a car's muffler passing me on the left brought me back to the present. *Will you even be around next Mother's Day?*

On this day, my Aunt opened the door still wearing pjs. Behind her, my cousin yelled, "You need to get dressed, we're leaving soon." Corralling

Gene Ann onto a schedule was a losing battle. We'd be late. I peered over her shoulder at Mom who sat at the breakfast table with Gene Ann's daughters. I felt a calmness replace the low current of worry that seemed to always be present now.

This is cute, I thought turning into the driveway of a restaurant that looked more like an old country store. A sign with the words "Martha's Bloomers" greeted us at the start of a stone pathway lined with vibrantly colored flowers that led to the door. Inside, I realized it was a country store with everything from specialty spices to books. Connecting the country store to the restaurant was a patio that doubled as a nursery. Plants of all kinds were for sale as we walked along the covered path with wooden rocking chairs where patrons sat waiting on their tables.

The wooden door to the restaurant creaked as I pushed it open and entered a small waiting area that looked like it might have been a covered patio in another life. I flashed back to a childhood memory of one of Mom's tea party's she'd thrown for Danielle and me. A card table covered with a white linen tablecloth held fine china, silverware, and a tiny tea set. Little girls dressed in frilly dresses sat along its edges eating cookies.

The memory left me unsettled. I had never

been a frilly-dress kind of girl, which had left Mom trying to mold me into one. Mom's concern with my outward appearance clashed with my five-minute morning routine growing up. "At least put on some lipstick," Mom would plead with me as I grew up. To this day, if I'm not wearing lipstick, I feel naked, just like one of those dreams where you show up somewhere in public forgetting clothes. At times I'd wished I'd been born male, thinking there would have been fewer comments about my appearance.

Ironically the restaurant looked like an adult tea party. Cobalt blue and buttercream yellow flowered tablecloths adorned the tables that were scattered throughout the dining area. The sound of silverware clanking on fine china filled the room. Wood-planked floors and hanging plants that draped long earthy vines gave the feeling of a cozy patio. *I'm definitely getting the Italian cream cake,* I thought, glancing at a coconut-flaked slice on a dessert platter as we made our way to the table.

I was scooting my chair closer to the table when I heard Mom say, "Someone took him!"

"Who?" Gene Ann said, leaning towards Mom.

"The boy."

The table quieted, everyone glanced at each

other, then to me. I shrugged. A familiar pattern followed; silence while everyone tried to figure out Mom's random comment, then a moment where either someone would ask a clarifying question or just continued on talking as if the comment had never been said. Usually, it was the latter.

Between bites of Italian cream cake, I took in the two generations of women gathered around the table. Flicking a coconut flake from my chin, the understanding that the next time we were together Mom would not be present sank in.

It was late by the time Mom and I pulled into the circular drive at Victoria Inn. When I climbed out of the car I noticed the facility was dark. My nose pressed against the glass door, I could see one faint light in the distance of the common living area.

Where is everyone?

Mom came up beside me and pulled at the entry door's handle. "It's locked," she said.

"Did they give you a key to the outside door?" I said, but was pretty sure they hadn't.

"I don't think so." I could see she was trying to locate the information somewhere in her mind.

I glanced at my phone and saw it was 10:30 p.m. "It's late, they probably lock the doors for safety." I called the phone number listed on the door, while Mom climbed back into the car.

Ring. Ring. I could hear a phone ringing somewhere in the distance. Right as I was about to give up, a man picked up. "Hello," he said, like he was picking up a call at home and I wondered if I'd dialed the wrong number.

"I'm out front with my mom," I said, envisioning Mom back at the hotel with me roaming around the room delusional all night. "We're locked out."

"Let me try to get someone in the nursing care unit to let you in," he said. *Is he offsite? What if he can't get someone in the nursing care unit?* My panicked thoughts were disrupted by a small figure emerging from the darkness of the living area, walking towards the front door. I waved to Mom to get out of the car.

"Hi ladies," the lady with a warm smile opened the door.

"She has her unit key," I said, looking past the woman toward the dark hall that would lead Mom to her unit. "Would you do me a favor? Would you walk her back to her place, it's thirteen?" I pushed Mom forward through the entrance.

"Of course, I'll make sure she gets squared away," the lady said, in a kind tone that made me relax. The doors closed and I watched the two shadowy figures fade into the darkness.

Back in my car, I thought about the time I had been locked out of the dorms in college, probably drunk, forced to wait till another resident, who had remembered their key, wandered home. I laughed at the similarities. Mom and I both had stayed out past the time the doors auto locked, both keyless, and both in an impaired state. My impaired state induced by alcohol; Mom's impaired state induced by Lewy.

The Cable Guy

May 20, 2021

Mom decided she needed internet service. When Mom could find her computer, it was to play solitaire and the thought of her trying to use the remote for streaming services terrified me, but I didn't have the energy to argue, so I set up an installation appointment. Cameron, back from his master's program, who hadn't seen his grandmother since December, agreed to go with me to Bryan for the appointment.

A young bubbly lady stood behind the sign-in desk at Victoria Inn, almost bouncing in place with energy. "Your mom is the sweetest lady," she said, sliding me a pen. "She doesn't socialize much with other residents, but we just love her."

Everyone does. I'd found myself jealous at times of the kindness Mom bestowed on others. *Whatever, she's not barricading herself in the room with a dresser,* I thought, as I shook off the feeling of resentment.

Visits had formed a rhythm, and I was seeing the personality of the facility come to life. Betty, who was always dressed to a tee, with her hair sprayed perfectly into position, sat in one of the chairs that lined the wall of the common living room facing toward the front door, but also offering a line of sight down the halls on either side. It was the perfect position, giving her the best view of all the comings and goings of the facility. I figured Betty had been the lady in her neighborhood who left her front door open, keeping a watchful eye on everything through the screen door. Next to her sat Violet, a petite, equally well-dressed lady with strawberry-blonde hair, cut in a short 1960s doo. The two ladies sat like birds on a perch eyeing everything.

"She's down there," Betty said, gesturing down the hall as Cameron and I approached.

"Thanks Betty. I like the sparkle on your nails."

A genuine smile spread across her face as she looked down at her bright pink nails, the light reflecting the fuchsia glitter in the polish. *I should just buy a bedazzling kit now*, I considered. From the looks of the clothes, pillows, and accessories of the women here, it seemed to be in my future.

Knock, knock. I lightly rapped on Mom's door while I fished the key from my purse. "Mom," I called out, poking my head into the room slowly. Mom sat on the sofa, TV remote in her hand, pointed at the TV that displayed "No signal" in the bottom left corner. Her fingers pressed buttons wildly, barely realizing we'd entered the room.

I sighed, grabbing the remote. "Mom, if you just use the up and down channel button this won't happen," I said, switching the input back to Cable. The TV remote had become my arch nemesis. I couldn't get Mom to leave it alone, she was like a moth to light. I started to grab one of the notes taped all over her place, each with step-by-step instructions for the remote, along with hand drawn pictures on how to get back to the cable input, but then decided it was a waste of time. Adding the streaming services was going to be an abyss of confusion.

As I placed the TV remote in the furthest corner of the room, I noticed Mom's black and white ceramic Shih Tzu dog placed by the open patio door, looking like a statue replica of our family dog Chelsea from several decades ago.

"She likes to go outside," Mom said, noticing me eyeing the dog.

"Ooooh," I said, as I realized she had also placed a small water dish next to the dog's paw. *Here we go with the water bowls.* Cameron and I exchanged a, *Yep she thinks the dog is real,* look.

Still eyeing the water dish, I replied, "She probably likes that."

A few minutes later, Cameron, who now regretted his decision to come, went on a BBQ run while Mom and I waited for the internet guy. I snacked on Flamin' Hot Doritos and Oreos to kill time and figured my stomach would pay for the combination later.

Knock. Knock. I opened the door to see a man who looked like he fell off the cover of Outdoor Life. I gestured for the good-looking man wearing dungarees with brown-leather boots to come inside. "Help yourself if you're hungry," I said, pointing at the counter of BBQ ribs, turkey, and brisket Cameron had brought back. Next to the BBQ was a half-eaten tray of Oreos and a bag of Flamin' Hot Doritos that looked like an ape had torn into it.

"Thanks," he said, eyeing our poor lifestyle choices. "It looks good, but I just ate."

Twenty minutes later, Dave stood in front of the TV holding the remote, as Mom marveled at how easy he made it look. I watched him step backward.

"Be careful she's right behind your foot," Mom blurted out. Dave had unknowingly backed his boot-clad foot up inches away from the ceramic dog. Dave surveyed the ground with a perplexed look. Cameron smirked at me from the corner.

Dave grabbed a piece of paper with instructions from his bag and handed it to Mom. "That should do it," he said. "Let me run you through how to use this."

Good luck with that. He must have noticed the little paper notes with hand-drawn pictures of the remote taped to the coffee table and console.

Mom barely glanced at the paper, laying it down in front of her. "Isn't she cute when she smiles," she said, gazing up at Dave. "I think she likes you."

Dave's eyes darted around the room.

She added, "Her little tail is wagging."

I watched Dave look down and could see the puzzle pieces click together in his mind as he looked at the ceramic dog.

"She's cute," Dave said, smiling at Mom. "What's her name?" Dave was also cute, quick on his feet, and good with old people. I immediately ran through the women I knew that I could set him up with in my head. Damn it, they were all married or lesbians.

Chapter 17
A Guy in the Hall

June 18, 2021

Buzz, buzz, buzz. I could feel my phone vibrate in the back pocket of my biking jersey. I was in the middle of pedaling up a steep hill, answering the phone was not an option. Whoever it was could wait till I found my way to the top and caught my breath. *Bing,* the chime of a text message came through my ear buds. *Someone's persistent.* I picked up my pace, which was a chore since June's summer heat and humidity was kicking my ass. Finally at the top of the hill, I perched under the shade of a tree, one foot on the sidewalk and the other still clipped into the bike pedal. A bead of sweat dropped onto my screen and saw I had missed several calls from Victoria

Inn. *That's not good*, I thought, as I read the first text from Becky.

> Give me a call please.

My sweaty finger hit the call icon above Becky's name. "Your Mom's okay, Gene Ann fell," she said, immediately as the line connected. "She may have broken something. Your Mom's with her in the ambulance. They just pulled out about five minutes ago."

Oh god, she's in the ambulance. An image of the ambulance with its lights flashing and sirens blaring, while Mom rode shotgun hallucinating plastered itself in my mind.

"I'll give her a call," I said, still processing what I'd heard. "Thanks for getting in touch with me. Has anyone called Gene Ann's daughter?"

"No, we don't have her information in our files," she replied. I thanked her again and said I would call Gene Ann's daughter.

"We have a little problem," Mom answered my call before the first ring finished. I could hear my aunt talking in the background to one of the EMTs.

"I'm out riding, I'm heading back now," I said, pausing to catch my breath. "I've got to shower, but then I'll get on the road to Bryan."

"I think that would be good," she replied.

I dialed my cousin's number, then carefully as to not incite panic, left her a message. "Your Mom is okay" I said, then continued to explain what I knew, which wasn't much. I ended the message letting her know I would be headed to Bryan shortly and would update her once I had more information. I slid the phone back into my sweaty jersey, hopped on the bike, and peddled faster than I had in years for home. By noon Mom and her sister were at the hospital and their two daughters were trying to get on the road to join them.

Mom's a horrible chaperon. The chaperon needs a chaperon, I thought, as I sped to Bryan. Images of Mom roaming the hospital, lost, filled my mind as I pressed the gas pedal down. "Shit," I said out loud, looking at the odometer reading ninety-five miles per hour. I slowly released pressure from the pedal watching the odometer decrease to seventy miles per hour.

Just under two hours later I pulled into the hospital parking lot. Finding the section of the hospital Mom described felt like being in a mirrored fun house at a fair. One person would direct me down a hall to another person, who would direct me to another hall, ending in another lobby, until I almost made a full loop. When I'd finally found the right lobby, the receptionist, who appeared worn out, gave me the formal pandemic visitor rules, reciting them in a robotic tone. "One person is allowed back with the patient," she said, staring past me." That visitor is allowed to come to the lobby to update you." Seemed reasonable, however, the visitor was Mom and she'd never be able to find her way to the lobby.

"My mom has Lewy body dementia, she hallucinates, gets super confused," my voice sounding high-pitched and tinny, like a teenage boy in puberty. "I'm worried about her trying to go back and forth between my aunt and the lobby." I sounded a little panicked.

She slowly eyed me up and down, probably trying to assess if she needed to call the psych ward. "Let me go ask the nurse in the back to grab your mom and bring her out here," she said. "Then you can go back."

"Thank you, I really appreciate that," I said, trying to calm my voice.

"You still can't go back together," she reiterated, unsure if I would bolt for the doors behind her. "But you can switch spots and she can just sit here in the lobby."

Swoosh, swoosh. I turned to take a seat in the lobby when I heard the large automatic sliding entry doors open and close. *Would she bolt out the doors?* Before I could play out that catastrophizing thought, I heard Mom's voice. "It took you long enough," she said, then smiled and thanked the nurse for escorting her to the lobby.

"I was on my bike, then had to drive two hours," I said, feeling defensive. "I had to hunt down the right area of the hospital. I think I did pretty good."

She stared at me blankly. "Where were you that you had to drive two hours?" she asked.

I dropped it, it was clear she had no idea I'd been in Austin.

I led her to a chair tucked in the back corner of the lobby, furthest from the sliding doors, but in clear view of reception. "Only one of us can go back," I said, plunking her down in the chair. "I'm going to check on Gene Ann, then I'll come back out." I watched her eyes dart around the room and grow larger.

"You don't need to do anything but sit right here," I said, trying to disguise my worry. "The nice lady right there knows where I'll be and can come get me if you need something," I said, gesturing to the receptionist.

The receptionist punched the code in for the doors and I heard a *click*, as the lock released. I quickly turned to look at Mom one last time. She was still sitting in the chair, staring at the plant that sat in the opposite corner, studying the large palm leaves like it was the first plant she'd ever seen. It felt like I was abandoning a child in the lobby.

A hand landed softly on my forearm. "I'll keep an eye on her," the receptionist said, picking up on my concern.

"Thank you so much," I said, then walked into the busy Emergency Room.

The chaos of the lobby was nothing compared to the ER. The nurses station sat in the center of the room, the sound of phones ringing and the clacking of fingers on keyboards echoed through the room. Balancing the phone receiver between her shoulder and ear, one of the nurses behind the counter said, "What can I do for you hon?"

"I'm looking for my aunt, Gene Ann. She just came in a few hours ago," I said, impressed as I watched her juggle the call she was on while pulling my aunt's chart with only a first name.

"She's right over there in 109," she said, pointing directly behind me. "I think transport just came to grab her and take her over to the main hospital. They're working on getting her approved to go to the rehab facility."

I rounded the corner into my aunt's room to

find three EMS workers trying to transfer her from the bed to a gurney. Gene Ann was sprawled on a navy-blue sheet, with three men pulling the sheet tautly, lifting her off the bed onto the gurney. I watched Gene Ann's face contort as she let out little grunts in pain. I moved to the side, my back pressing into the door jamb as the gurney was pushed through.

"I'll meet you over at the rehab," I said, as she passed. "Your daughter's on her way." I thought of all the things my aunt had been through in life, she was tough, but her face told me she was in a lot of pain.

Beep, beep, beep. The nurse entered the code for the door leading back into the lobby. When the doors opened, I quickly located Mom, still in her seat and still staring at the plant.

"They're transferring her to the rehab facility," I said to Mom. "She broke her pelvis."

Mom climbed out of the chair. "What do you think happened to the guy laying in the hall?"

"What guy?" I said, confused.

"At my place, I looked down the hall and he was just lying there," she said, concern in her voice.

"Your sister?" I said. "Your sister fell in the hall this morning."

"Oh."

I could see the wheels spinning in her brain. *Your sister is going to be pissed you thought she was a guy.*

If the Blinds Could Talk?

Thank goodness the rehab facility was easy to find. It was past 7 p.m. and I was tired, so I knew Mom had to be exhausted. We were also entering sundowners hour, which was a little like Cinderella kicking off the slipper. We were on the clock, each minute that ticked by took Mom's cognitive functioning with it.

The sun was starting to go down by the time we met up with Gene Ann in her room. Mom and I took seats next to her bed as I fished a power bar out of my purse, broke it in half, and gave one half to Mom. Then I sent my cousin an update text.

A woman wearing rose pink scrubs came into the room. "Hi Mrs. Robbins," she said, flipping through papers on a clipboard. "I just need to get a little information from you."

Gene Ann looked up at the woman with stoned, dilated eyes that looked like glass marbles. I figured she was flying high on morphine. I heard Mom next to me mumble something. I turned to look at her and saw she was turned completely sideways staring at the vertical window blinds. *Who are you talking to?*

My aunt laughed, causing me to turn to see what was so funny. The lady in scrubs turned to me, looking confused by the laugh.

She has to know she's high, I thought.

Trying to regain ground, the lady in scrubs looked at Mom and said, "Are you two related?"

Mom snapped her head forward, as if she'd been caught doing something she shouldn't. "She's my mom," she said.

I felt for this poor lady. "They're sisters," I said, jumping in.

Mom turned back to the vertical blinds. "I don't think they know you're here," she said to the blinds, as she motioned with her hand like one does when speaking casually, laughed, then continued. "I know. I was telling them the same thing."

The lady in scrubs remained silent, unsure, her eyes moving between Gene Ann who was now petting her blanket, fixated on its softness and Mom, who was talking to the vertical blinds. *I'm your best bet lady.*

As if she could hear my internal thoughts, she said, "Do you know your aunt's medical history?"

"I know some of it. I'll do my best," I replied, as

I listened to Mom talk to the blinds with my left ear. "Her daughter will be in town in a few hours."

I spent the next fifteen minutes piecing together what I knew of Gene Ann's medical history, then quietly exited with Mom while Gene Ann slept. I dropped Mom back at Victoria Inn, dumping her with the night desk person who was just about to lock the front doors.

Back at the hotel, I laid fully clothed in bed and called Travis. "How'd it go?" he said.

"My aunt's high on morphine and Mom talked to the vertical blinds all night," I said, staring at the ceiling.

"Sooooo, good," he said, laughing.

Please Clean Up After Your Pet

June 19, 2021

The next morning, I made my way past Betty, who was already in full makeup perched in her chair. *You're up and at 'em early this morning,* I thought.

I rounded the corner and noticed Mom's door was open at the end of the hall. When I walked inside, I saw Mom, wearing the outfit I'd dropped her off in the night before, sitting on the sofa. Her pale, expressionless face stared at a blank TV screen with "No signal" displayed in the bottom of the screen.

"Everything okay?" I said, knowing the events of the prior day had left her out-of-sorts.

Her head slowly swiveled toward me. "You're here?" she said, noticing me for the first time. Her face looked drawn and tired, with skin so thin it accentuated the bone structure.

"Let's go check in on your sister," I said, gesturing for her to get up off the sofa. "We can go to lunch after." Signs of life hit her eyes when she heard lunch.

I could hear my cousin's voice before we rounded the corner into Gene Ann's room. My cousin, who had driven all day yesterday, stood at the foot of her mom's bed. Every family has a person that is the glue. The glue that puts the pieces of its members back together, seals the edges, and provides the adhesive that keeps everyone intact. My cousin is the glue of her family.

"Your dog is having a hard time with you not being there," my cousin said to her mom. "She's leaving little presents everywhere." I stayed back, observing the interaction between mother and daughter.

My aunt speared a piece of cantaloupe on the

plate in front of her. "If you just let them dry, it's easier to pick up," she said, like the information was common knowledge.

"Yeah, I'm not going to do that," my cousin replied.

I started to laugh, then thought back to all the times Mom had picked up Porsche's turds only to put them in my kitchen trash where an aroma of shit would loft through the air all day.

"How are you doing this morning Sister?" Gene Ann asked, noticing Mom and I had entered the room. Mom, who had been motionless next to me, came to life at the sound of her sister's voice.

"Better than you," she answered, laughing.

When Mom and I returned from lunch, my cousin generously offered to take Mom back when she headed out.

Does she know what she's signing up for? I contemplated.

"Thanks, that would be great," I said, and headed out.

Back at home, exhausted and laying on the sofa, a text came in from my cousin.

> Honey Kay (Everyone from Texas who knew Mom called her Honey Kay.) wants to come with me tomorrow and sleep over here. I just wanted to make sure that is ok with you?

That's brave, I thought, then shot a text back.

> That's fine, thanks for asking.

Four days later I received a call from my cousin that Mom was still with her and she needed my help to get Mom to return to Victoria Inn. My first attempt to call Mom led to her voicemail. *She's ignoring my call.* Second attempt, *ring, ring, ring.* "Can I call you back?" Mom said, quickly. I knew her finger was hovering over the end call button, so I quickly said, "Hey, give me a second."

"What?" she said, impatiently.

"You need to go back to Victoria Inn. All your stuff is there, and you need to take your pills," I said.

I could hear her let out a harumph. "I have my pills. I need to help out with Foxy."

"Look, your sister and her daughter are trying to deal with the rehab stuff, plus they need time to themselves."

"Fine! Fine!" she said, sounding like a toddler throwing a fit. "You're always telling me what to do!" *Click*, and the call was gone. I laughed out loud, normally this would have pissed me off, but I couldn't take her seriously when she sounded like a toddler. Bless my cousin, I can't believe she made it four days with Mom.

You Should Really Talk to Someone

The heaviness of a "funk" settled in on my lethargic body as I lay in bed contemplating the energy expenditure it would take to move to the couch. *Too much,* I thought. As far back as I could remember, I've had periods of time I'd coined, funks. Cycling every few months and lasting about a week, the funks would paint my world gray, confiscate all my motivation, isolate me from friends, and leave me alone with my thoughts. As I lay in bed, feeling the heaviness of my body press into the mattress, I knew the funk was turning to darkness.

Funks at times had turned dark, really dark. An image of myself the year after I'd graduated from college flashed to mind. I could see my twenty-three-year-old body curled up in the fetal position lying in the bed of our guest bedroom. The room was dark, all the blinds drawn, except for little slivers of daylight peeking through the slits of the vertical blinds. I'd called in sick to work, not being able to muster the energy for anything but to move from my bedroom to the guest bedroom. In my mind I could see my face, with a blanket pulled up under my neck, exposing tear-stained cheeks. I remembered feeling numb. Thoughts of not wanting to go on plagued my mind, but fortunately I'd lacked the energy to act on those thoughts.

The next image was of me standing alone on the back patio of our townhouse in Hayward California, hours after Travis had retired to bed, a cigarette in one hand and a beer in the other. I remembered the buzz that had given way to full body anesthesia on those nights. It would take me years to realize I'd used alcohol to manage my anxiety and depression. At the time, I'd relished the quietness of the night, where I could be alone and feel nothing.

Over the years, I've managed the ups and downs of my mental state with an arsenal of mindfulness, gratitude, exercise, and meditation. When Mom's condition worsened, it seemed as if the effectiveness of my meditation or wellness practices decreased. For weeks Travis had been making comments about my ever-changing moods. "Maybe meditation isn't enough right now?" he'd say. A crying outburst with me reciting everything I was doing to manage my moods between sobs, would follow. In addition to the crying outbursts, irritation lurked at every turn, and depression came and went like the wind. Dealing with Mom had left me wondering how I'd keep the darkness at bay.

One morning, a couple of days after returning from Bryan, I threw two pieces of toast into the toaster oven, slamming the door shut.

"Wooooooo," Nigel said, followed by a drawn-out *Whistle*, then, "You're okay."

"Am I?" I looked over at Nigel who was now back to shredding his toy. I felt tears stream down my face and before I knew it, I was standing in front of the toaster sobbing. I felt Travis come up behind me.

"You should talk to someone," he said, his eyes filled with warmth and concern. *I know*. Defeated, waving the white flag, I set up an appointment with a psychiatrist.

∼

Be honest, don't hide, I told myself over and over again in my head, as I sat across from the psychiatrist. My hand rested on my knee in an effort to stop the nervous bouncing of my leg. I looked up, locking eyes with a petite doctor who even wearing a face mask, managed to come off warm and personable. "Sorry," I cleared my throat. "My husband encouraged me to," I said, in response to her question inquiring why I had decided to make an appointment. I watched her type something quickly into the computer. She continued to ask questions and before I realized it, she had skillfully lured me into a conversation about my funks.

"Do you ever wish you just wouldn't wake up?"

I heard her words, but they sounded faded and far away. "Sometimes," I said slowly, then paused. "Well, not so much now, but yeah in the past I have."

"Tell me about those times," she said. I could hear my own voice saying the same words to my clients. I discussed my early twenties, then found myself talking about the nights I'd stayed up late, alone, drinking wine in my thirties and forties. "I got sober six years ago," I said, the words feeling like I'd dropped a bomb into her notes, as I watched her fingers fly across the keyboard. "At the end, um, I mean the end of my drinking, I didn't really care if I lived." I heard the words fall from my mouth, but it felt like someone else was saying them.

An image of my hand holding a glass of white wine six years ago, poured from the second bottle of the evening, came to mind. I could see the moisture forming on the outside of the wine glass, then a single droplet falling onto my hand. Drunk again, after I'd promised myself I'd only have two glasses. I'd come to the realization that evening that I'd eventually die from alcoholism. I could still feel how that realization hadn't scared me, in fact there had been a certain comfort in it.

The memory planted an uneasy feeling in the pit of my stomach.

"Do you have times where you feel like you have an abundance of energy?" she asked, and I knew where she was going with the question.

"I don't get manic," I blurted out.

"Are there times when you have high levels of energy behind ideas, maybe feel creative?" she asked.

I heard the words trail off, as my mind wandered to another time. I thought back to the many ideas I'd had for companies over the years. I'd feel flushed with energy and ideas, often paying hundreds to thousands of dollars to create different aspects of the company, only to lose interest as the energy faded. *I'm not manic*, I thought, as I recalled the clients I'd counseled who had described their manic episodes. I never became delusional, grandiose or stayed up for days riding a manic wave.

I heard the keyboard clicking as the psychiatrist typed more notes. Seconds later she looked up from the screen, slid her chair away from the computer and looked directly at me. "You fit the criteria for Bipolar II." she said, explaining I don't have manic episodes, but hypomanic episodes with depression. *Hypomanic*, the word flipped around in my mind. Her explanation of hypomania fit my experience. I would have days of increased energy, excitement, feeling like I could take on anything, that would typically lead me to start new projects.

I worked to process what I was hearing, letting my leg shake and vibrate up and down without trying to stop it. I remembered the time I'd sat in a circle of chairs at the outpatient substance use treatment, staring at a white board with different psychiatric disorders detailed out in rows. I'd fixated on the row under Bipolar II, thinking, *that sounds like me*, then dismissing it as related to my abuse of alcohol. Many of the criteria for psych disorders, like erratic moods, emotional instability, and personal relationship impacts also sounded like early sobriety. Everyone's unstable and erratic in early sobriety. It's a shit show.

"I'd like to prescribe you Lamictal," she said, then discussed side effects. I heard bits and pieces of the next statement. "Extremely rare" and "a red or a purplish color rash that forms blisters" her voice sounded far away. I looked down at my torso remembering the strange rash that had inhabited one side of my body only six months before. *Extremely rare, unless you're me.*

I pulled the car door shut, then sat stunned, staring out the windshield analyzing everything I'd experienced in life through my new Bipolar II glasses. There was some relief in having a diagnosis that put language around my experiences, but I also felt the shame of the stigma that followed most psychiatric disorders. My thoughts raced from, *I am crazy? Could I have saved myself from years of alcoholism if I'd just been diagnosed earlier?* Then, *Do I tell my kids?* And *Is it hereditary?*

Chapter 18
The Family in the Attic

July 21, 2021

"My $250 is gone!" Mom said, frantically through the phone. "They left the hot water on in the bathroom and water went everywhere."

"What? Why would they leave the faucets on?" I asked, then realized I had played right into her hallucination. "I'll see you in a couple of hours. Sherrie's coming with me today to visit." I hung up quickly, figuring she'd be onto the next hallucination by the time I saw her.

I glanced over at Sherrie, sitting in the passenger seat, watching her leg vibrate with anxious energy. She hadn't seen Mom since she moved to Bryan. Feeling the need to prepare her, I spent our two-hour drive trying to disseminate just enough information on Mom's decline that it wouldn't cause her more distress.

"Honestly, it's hard to predict," I said. "If we get her on a good day, she'll be pretty easy. A bad day, well, then it's really just unpredictable, anything could happen." I watched Sherrie's mouth drop open. "Unpredictability makes life interesting." I tried to ease her concern, but a nervous laugh slipped out.

"Okay. Poor Kay, I just feel so bad this is happening to her," she said, both legs vibrating now.

Once at Victoria Inn, I introduced Sherrie to Betty and Violet who sat perched in their chairs surveying the common area, then we hung a left down Mom's hall. Halfway down the hall I could see the back of a woman talking to the maintenance man. As we got closer, I caught just a few words, "In my attic...you need to check...."

The maintenance man's face looked puzzled.

"Hi Mom," I said, realizing the woman causing the confusion was Mom.

She slowly turned around and eyed me up and down, irritated I had interrupted her conversation. *I know those eyes. Hello paranoia.*

"Kay, it's been a few months," Sherrie interjected, leaning in to hug her friend. A smile formed across Mom's face, softening her irritation with me.

Mom pivoted away from the maintenance man and led us into her unit. "Isn't she cute," Mom said, pointing to her ceramic dog, which was now laying in the kitchen. "She wags her tail and moves her head when she's excited." I glanced down and saw two bowls, one with dog food and the other with water. *Where did she get dog food?* When I looked back up, Mom was standing by the breakfast bar with her head thrown back looking up at the ceiling. "They're driving me crazy," she said to Sherrie, gesturing towards the ceiling with a hand. "There's a family in my attic." For a second I thought the ladies had moved into the attic, but since she'd referred to them as a family, I figured this was a new set of imaginary people.

"Well, they're probably hot," Sherrie replied and I almost laughed.

I appreciated Sherrie pointing out the obvious. It was summer in Texas, the attic family would die living in the attic. In fact, Mom should start putting water bowls out for the attic family. Sherrie and I exchanged a look that conveyed, it's a bad day. *Buckle up, it just got started,* I thought.

We made our way back down the hall discussing options for lunch, although I knew Mom would pick Cracker Barrel. Out of the corner of my eye I saw Mom cross one leg in front of the other and start to fall. I lunged for her arm, catching her just before she crumpled to the ground.

"Why did you push me?" she asked, looking at me like I'd just shoved her for no reason.

"I didn't. You were falling," I said, defensively, yet a part of me now wanted to push her. Travis had nicknamed Mom "creeper" because her gait had recently changed from long strides to the kind of tiny steps someone would take if they were sneaking up on you.

For the town's population, there was a disproportionate number of places that served biscuits and chicken fried steak in Bryan. Again, I found myself sitting across from Mom watching her devour an entire plate of chicken fried steak smothered in gravy, while Sherrie and I tried to engage her in conversation to no avail. When Mom did engage, it was random comments about hallucinations, making the interaction exhausting for all parties. On our way to the car after lunch, I elbowed Sherrie and whispered, "I usually leave before 3 p.m. because she starts to fade." I wanted to say, "If you think the first couple of hours were exciting, wait till sundowners' hits; it'll be a damn festival."

We barely got into Mom's unit before she started talking about her "night pill" a.k.a the fucking little pink pill.

"On TV this morning they were talking about that little pill I take at night," she said. "It's killing people. They use it as an herbicide, and it causes Parkinsons."

"I haven't heard anything about that." *Don't engage. Don't engage.*

"They're getting addicted to it," she continued. "It's really a bad thing."

"Addicted to the herbicide? I asked, then realized she'd probably seen something on TV about opioids. "Why don't you talk to your doctor about it next time you have an appointment?" I suggested, trying to end the conversation. The thought of the doctor's face as Mom explained the addictive qualities of herbicides made me laugh.

"Is that a typical day with her?" Sherrie asked as we climbed in my car to head back to Austin.

"Yeah. Some days she's a little better and some days she's worse," I replied, nonchalantly.

"I can't imagine worse," she said, shaking her head in disbelief.

Have Attic Family, Will Travel

August 1, 2021

Incoming call, Mom, scrolled across my caller ID. Before I could utter a word, the shrill of her voice came over the line.

"Gene Ann was here last night, but now I can't find her," she said. "The bed isn't messed up, so I don't know. She was playing cards with the family in the attic last night. Maybe she left with them this morning?" *Damn it, the attic people are still there.* It figured that Gene Ann was playing cards with the attic family, in real life, she played cards with a group of women every week.

"How did Gene Ann get to your place?" I asked, thinking Gene Ann was still recovering from a broken pelvis.

"She doesn't really know the family in the attic," she said, ignoring my question. "They were vacuuming this morning."

"Who? The attic people?" I asked, thinking, *Well, at least they're clean.*

"Also, there's a huge snake that's been wrapped around my air conditioning unit for days," she continued. "I think it eats and gets bigger, then shrinks back down, hiding."

Hmm. I wasn't going to ask about the attic people again, but I was tempted to ask about the snake. Snakes aren't uncommon in Texas, maybe there really was a snake wrapped around her air conditioning unit. Which would be scarier: a giant snake, or learning that the snake, too, was in her head?

The next morning, I heard a text come in from Gene Ann.

> Good morning. Honey Kay has spent the weekend here with me and I will take her back today. Her pill is still a major problem! She never has them with her when she is here. I need a supply and someone needs to be giving them to her daily at her home.
>
> She swears she is nearly out of pills and that you are picking them up to bring this week. I know the prescription is filled and in her apartment, but I can't make it down the hall walking yet and she refuses to open that side door for me to enter.

> I drove to pick her up since they don't have motor service available on the weekend. Another issue: She says her eyes are a problem and a result of her syndrome and that she will eventually go blind. Is that correct? She cannot see well at all. What is the deal with that?

Huh. Apparently, yesterday's call had been made from Gene Ann's house. *Great, the attic family is now traveling.* I made a mental note to look for a snake on Gene Ann's air conditioning unit, then shot her back a text.

> She's not going blind. That isn't a symptom of her disease. Good luck getting her to an optometrist, I've tried many times. I'll be in Bryan tomorrow. Is there a snake on your air conditioning unit?

> No, why?

Gene Ann replied.

> Nevermind.

I'd explored medication management in April, opting not to set it up due to the constant push back from Mom. At times, I just got tired of arguing with her. I didn't know how much time she had left and didn't want my memories to be of us constantly arguing. Also, the fucking little pink pill wasn't critical. It did help her sleep, however it helped minimally, if at all, with hallucinations. Now, I knew I was on borrowed time and would need to set up medication management.

BBQ Roadkill

August 3, 2021

I entered Mom's apartment to find a spread of Texas BBQ laid out on the counter, including a tiny piece of brisket placed on a paper towel. Mom was staring at the ground telling an invisible dog (probably inspired by the ceramic dog she thought was real), that she had saved a piece of brisket for her. *What kind of dog is it?* I wondered. *How does she know it's female? Does it have a name?* Questions tumbled through my mind until the sight of Mom's outfit snapped me back to the present. Dressed in a thick winter sweater, a bright floral long skirt, and a pair of black sweatpants under the skirt, she was a busy canvas to take in. *Is she cold? Maybe she threw the skirt on over the pants and then forgot to take them off?*

I was still taking in the pants when Mom began to tell the saga of the barbecue. "We picked it up from JJ's BBQ, you know, we got to talking and laughing, and well, we just didn't notice the back hatch hadn't latched. So off we went, spilling smoked brisket and sausage all over the road, wondering why everyone was honking at us."

The mental image made me laugh. Texans take their barbecue seriously. BBQ roadkill was downright criminal!

"Wait, please tell me you didn't pick this barbecue up off the road," I said, staring at the brisket.

She giggled. "Oh, no! This was a replacement order."

There wasn't much left, and it looked good. I wondered if Mom would notice my eating the pretend dog's brisket.

Little Pills Everywhere

A week later, I entered Mom's kitchen to find her pill organizer laying on the breakfast bar, some of the day's lids popped open and little piles of pills strewn all over the counter. I couldn't sort the pills back into the appropriate daily trays many more times without completely losing my mind. I'd become a proficient pill counter, my ability to put small objects into slightly larger boxes labeled with the days of the week was pretty impressive. Mom's latest anxiety loop of reorganizing her pills over and over again had honed my skills. The term *reorganize* is used loosely, as a nicer way of saying, she liked to go back through her weekly pill box and mess up everything I or her sister had just done.

"We need to bring in someone to help with the pills," I said, letting out a frustrated breath. "We could start with someone coming in just for an hour or so, a couple of times a week." I waited for the inevitable argument.

"I don't need help," she replied, staring at me as if my suggestion was completely absurd. "I take the pills every night."

"Let's see, shall we?" I counted the remaining pills and explained how, by Thursday, she should only have had six pills left for the week. More worrisome was the fact that two daily trays had double blood pressure pills and no cholesterol pills and only one tray had a Prevagen capsule (meant to boost Mom's memory). Although, I was pretty sure the ship had sailed on the memory boosting benefits of Prevagen. It was chaos!

"It's not my fault," she blurted out defensively. "The guy in the attic comes down and messes with my pills. I've been taking them every night!"

The attic guy sounds like kind of a bastard, I thought, but didn't say.

On my way home, I filled Danielle in on the family in the attic and the pill chaos. I asked her to help set up three-days-a-week medication management. As we both had PTSD from the in-home care experience in Lakeway, we talked through our boundaries.

"We can't get into constant arguments with her about it," I said, putting on a strong facade. "Yes," Danielle agreed. "We'll need to ignore her calls on the days the helpers come in." One upside to Mom remembering very little was that you could ignore phone calls and she wouldn't remember it. For the record, that's not mean, it's just survival.

Attic People; Free to a Good Home

August 15, 2021

Sitting in a car, waiting for Travis to come out of the Denton Buc-ees, I received a text from Gene Ann.

> I picked her up yesterday afternoon and she ran errands with me, CVS and Walmart. She was doing good, enjoyed having her along. I totally forgot about the person coming to be sure she takes that little pill. She gets so defensive about all that.
>
> I finally heard enough yesterday and told her I was sick of hearing about the taking of that damn little pill, that I was on seven prescriptions a day and had five different women coming in each week. At least one a day telling me what I needed to do and watching me do it before they would leave! She shut up. She went to lunch today with her friend Ellen. When we got back to Victoria Inn yesterday, she tried to get the kids that live upstairs in the attic to help her unload my trunk.

When Travis climbed back into the car I asked, "Do you think I should remind Mom I'm coming tomorrow for her doctor's appointment?"

"Only if you want her dressed when you get there," he said, smiling.

The reminder voicemail was a mistake. Later that evening, exhausted from dropping Connor off for his freshman year in the dorms, I listened to a voicemail from Mom.

> Well, I'm wondering how close you are to home. I don't even know if it's close. I'm completely dressed, I don't have any idea if I'm supposed to be going somewhere or doing something. So, if you could just give me a call back and let me know about the doctor's appointment. I'm just trying not to waste time getting dressed or dressing again and again and again. Talk to me. Talk to you later.

Travis's comment, "Only if you want her dressed..." played in my head. *Well at least she'd be dressed.*

A Stranger Among Us

August 16, 2021

The next morning, barely back from Denton, I climbed back into the car to drive to Bryan for Mom's doctor's appointment and wondered if I should just start sleeping in my car. Two hours later, I approached the same energetic, bubbly woman behind the sign-in desk. "I haven't seen her yet this morning," she said, pushing a pen towards me on the counter. "Maybe she spent the night at her sister's house?"

"I'll go see," I said, a little worried. When I opened Mom's door, I was overtaken by the feeling you get when something isn't quite right, where everything looks the same, but the energy in the room feels different. Mom sat on the sofa, her eyes fixated on the TV. When she finally turned towards me, she looked confused and didn't acknowledge my presence. *Weird*, I thought and began to rummage through the kitchen.

"Mom you're almost out of coffee," I said, turning back to look at her, as a jolt of panic ran through me at the thought of no caffeine. Just like that, I felt the energy in the room change, like a light switch had been thrown.

"Oh. Hi. It's you," Mom said, a warm smile spreading across her face.

Oh my god she didn't know who I was. I didn't know how to feel. My mother of forty-nine years thought I was a total stranger. If I hadn't said *Mom*, essentially handing her the book, *Who Am I For Dummies*, we'd still be staring at each other in confusion. I heard my phone ring in my purse, I grabbed it to see, *Incoming call, Gene Ann,* scrolling across the caller ID.

"Is my sister there?" Gene Ann said, almost whispering. "Can she hear me?"

"Yes and no," I replied. I wanted to say, *Don't worry, she thinks you're here anyway.*

"That damn little pink pill is an issue," she said, switching into a serious tone. "She's always messing with her pills! Maybe we should start crushing it up and slipping it into her food?"

"Uh. Okay," I said, imagining me dusting the fine pink powder onto her food.

Gene Ann was on a roll. "Actually, that's another issue, I don't think she's eating."

Not taking pills, not eating, this isn't sounding like independent living. I was hit by a sudden feeling of unexpected resentment. I was already juggling my family, Mom's needs, driving between two cities, not to mention a recently empty nest. *Can't she just make it through the holidays!*

I stepped into the bedroom, out of Mom's ear shot. "I know, I know. Let me see what I can do about getting someone to come in every day," I said, defeated. "She's going to be pissed though."

"Yeah. She'll just have to deal with it," Gene Ann said, equally tired of hearing Mom complain about the helpers.

Running late, I sped down Texas Ave towards Mom's doctor's appointment. Mom's hands were firmly braced on the dash. "Watch out for that man!" she screeched.

"There's no man," I screeched back, not bothering to add, "You're hallucinating." I prayed the doctor's office wouldn't cancel the appointment. If they did, there was a good chance I'd break down crying in the lobby.

A woman sitting behind a protective plastic barrier looked up at me as I shoved the stack of appointment papers under the plastic trying to catch my breath. I felt a bead of sweat slide down my back from the sprint I'd just made through the parking lot. Mom, who I'd left in the dust, was just entering the lobby.

"Did they tell you to get here early?" the woman at reception asked, a bit irritated at our late arrival. Mom was off to my side digging through her giant purse looking for her ID. She pulled her wallet from the depths of the purse, then stared at the blank spot where her driver's license would have been. *Are you kidding me?* I'd completely forgotten to find where she'd hidden her ID and put it into my wallet.

"She doesn't have her ID. Honestly, I have no

idea where she's put it," I said. I could feel tears beginning to form in the corners of my eyes.

"It's okay. The doctor should be with you shortly," she replied. I could have leaned around the plastic barrier and given her a big, fat, germ-filled, kiss.

As the doctor entered the room, I was caught off guard. *How old are you? Did you graduate from med school last week?* My concern dissolved the minute he started asking questions that skillfully assessed Mom's disease without actually saying *disease*.

I heard Mom giggle before answering one of his questions. "Travis, her husband, knows more about my stuff than she does," she said, flippantly, gesturing towards me when she said *she does*. Hot anger filled my cheeks, I could have just ended her suffering right there. Travis had seen Mom one time in the last two months. *She*, her daughter, on the other hand had no life trying to accommodate her mom's needs. The doctor, who probably saw my irritation, jumped in continuing with another question.

When we stood up to leave, the doctor said, "I have another client with your same name, Kay Kovacs."

"That makes sense because one of the women

in the attic stole my identity," Mom said, giving me that "I told you so" look. The attic people were starting to annoy me.

Two days later, before 7 a.m., I picked up Mom's first voicemail of the day.

> Michelle, this is Mom and I've been robbed of everything! Everything! Everything! So, give me a call and let's start the process of canceling credit cards.

I wanted to call her back and say, "You should call Travis, he knows more about your stuff than "she" does." Instead, I called her back and reassured her she still had "Everything! Everything!"

Three days later, Gene Ann sent me a text to update me after a minor fall Mom had taken in front of the facility.

> Honey Kay has been with me ever since the fall. Joe helped her out the side door with her purse and into my car. She said she hadn't eaten in two days! She never drinks fluids. She ate a huge meal and went to bed very early even with all the activity in my house and there's a lot.

> She fell again tonight getting up out of one of my club chairs. Again, she hadn't eaten today, so I fed her potatoes, green beans and a chicken breast with green tea to drink. She is using my walker now and has gone to bed. I am trying to send you photos of pills.

My aunt's text message reminded me of my old elementary school's news channel that was broadcasted into the classrooms every morning with student anchors relaying everything from school happenings to the lunch menu. While I read her text, I heard in my head, *Today for lunch, the cafeteria is serving chicken breast, potatoes and green beans with milk. School pictures will be taken at noon. Back to you Kyle.*

The Fucking Little Pink Pill

August 23, 2021

"I read that if you're in the sun, the little pill I take at night can make you fall," I listened to Mom blame anything but her disease on her fall a couple of days ago. "It's the sun and the pill, it says so in the pamphlet they gave me." *Shit, I thought I threw that paperwork away.*

I didn't engage. I was sick of talking about that fucking little pink pill, it had become a four-letter-word in my vocabulary. Everyone had become fixated on the fucking little pink pill, like it would magically fix Mom. Between the conversation I'd just had with a client at work about the legitimacy of her opioid prescription where I'd wanted to point out she was sitting in detox and Mom's fucking little pink pill, I was ready to convince a doctor I needed a prescription for Xanax.

As I continued to cuss out the pink pill in my head, Mom continued, "The guy in the attic was down watching sports. He brought his daughter like I was supposed to babysit her. Can you believe that? I don't babysit!"

"Is she still there?" I said, choosing the attic people over talking about the pill.

"No, they went back upstairs. His daughter was wearing my clothes," she said, annoyed. "She blatantly just took them. Are you getting close?"

"I'm about an hour out." This was a lie. I was about ten minutes out and set to meet with Stacey, the director of Victoria Inn.

I gave the energetic, bubbly lady behind the

front desk an acknowledgement wave, then did a sweep of the lobby with my eyes, mostly looking for Betty. I figured Mom would be in her unit, but Betty was like the town crier. If she spotted me she'd march down the hall like a reporter who'd just been given a scoop to tell Mom I was there. I felt like an undercover agent, but with Mom's paranoia simmering constantly just beneath the surface, I could just imagine the fall out.

"Why are you meeting with Stacey?" she'd ask.

"To talk about you," I'd reply, sending her paranoia into full conspiracy mode.

My undercover rendezvous with Stacey was essentially to find out if Mom could stay or if I needed to move her into a higher level of care.

Slipping into Stacey's office, I took a seat. "She isn't eating, she doesn't remember her pills, it's not feeling like independent living," I said, like I was finally spilling the beans in an interrogation.

"It's a difficult decision," Stacey started, in an even tone. "I agree, your Mom isn't eating much, we don't see her down in the dining hall. We've tried bringing food to residents in the past, but with someone like your Mom, we run the risk of them forgetting about the food, then eating it later, possibly spoiled."

"Oh, I hadn't thought about that," I said,

remembering the fuzzy cheese in Mom's refrigerator from our Sunday dinners.

"We don't accept Lewy body in our next level of care," Stacey continued, pausing to give time for the information to sink in. "You have time, though. Just start looking for other options and we're here to support you in the meantime."

Stacey suggested bringing in helpers for a couple of hours each day, even offering, "You can make me the bad guy. Just tell her we're requiring consistent help from an outside agency."

I walked down the hall, the anticipation of the conversation with Mom forming beads of moisture on the palms of my hands. I noticed Mom's door was open into the hall. *She's seen me*, I thought, checking over my shoulder expecting to see Mom and Betty walking up behind me. The panic subsided when I saw Mom sitting on the sofa, her ceramic dog situated on a blanket next to her.

I dropped my purse on the breakfast bar. "Your pills continue to be a problem," I said. The nerves sent the words flying out before I could say hello or ease into the conversation.

"I take my pills!" she said, irritated.

Grabbing the pill container, I flipped open the daily lids and started counting. "You have to be able to take care of yourself," I said, dropping two pills into the correct day. "You don't eat regularly or take your medications." I trailed off when I saw Mom's eyes glaze over like I was speaking another language. I snapped shut Monday's lid and tried another tactic. "Stacy thought it would be good to bring someone in everyday to help."

"She doesn't know what I do," Mom spat. "I eat all the time. I'm fine!" She continued to mumble something under her breath that I couldn't quite make out but was sure was about me.

Another chicken fried steak at Cracker Barrel, made me want to suggest to them a chicken fried steak loyalty punch card where the tenth steak is free. After lunch, I headed back to Austin, updating Gene Ann while I drove. "I don't know how to have a conversation with someone who doesn't think they have a disease," I said, venting. "She's going to get mean about the helpers coming in every day. Be prepared."

First Catch of the Day

August 31, 2021

A week later, I was back in the car. I barely turned over the ignition before Mom called. "Well, I'm dressed and don't know where I'm supposed to be?" she said, as I picked up her call. *Well at least she's dressed on the right day.*

"I'll be there in about two hours. You have a doctor's appointment at 11 a.m.," I said, fiddling with the rearview mirror.

I'd packed the day with appointments trying to be efficient with my time in Bryan. Mom and I would start the day with labs and a urine sample at the doctor's office, then we'd be headed to a meeting with Mom's financial planner after lunch, at you guessed it, Cracker Barrel, and then finally a dental checkup. As I drove, I started second guessing my efficiency plan, thinking a crammed packed agenda for someone with dementia had "shit show" written all over it.

Mom greeted me at the door. "The first catch of the day is the best for bladder infections," she said, shoving a jar with sloshing yellow liquid into my face.

"Sounds good, are you ready to go?" I stepped to the side of the jar.

"I've been ready for hours," she replied, as she dropped the jar of urine into her purse. *Hopefully that doesn't spill,* I thought, as I heard it slosh.

"You should take your walker," I said, gesturing to the walker I'd bought her, that hadn't moved from the corner of the room.

"It's too wide, clunky," she said, heading for the door. "The other ladies' walkers are smaller." *Let the walker battle begin.* Mom had made it clear since I dropped the walker off that she didn't need a walker. At the end of the hall, I saw Betty and Violet perched in their chairs overseeing the lobby.

"Violet's is the same as yours," I said, showing Mom the walker.

"They're a standard width," Mom replied, in a condescending tone.

I know, that's my point.

At the first appointment of the day, Mom eyed the nurse holding a needle ready to take her blood. "What are you going to use the blood for?" she said, crossing her arms.

"Just standard blood work up," the nurse replied, smiling, not understanding the paranoia that lay behind the question.

"I don't know about that," Mom said, retracting her body into the reclining chair.

"Your doctor wants it Mom. I just did blood work up two weeks ago at my doctor's office," I said, giving the nurse a wink.

Mom then fished into the depths of her purse and pulled out the jar of urine. "Here," she said, jamming it into the woman's hand who had just drawn her blood. I watched the woman hold the jar like it contained uranium, then place it onto the tray next to the vile of blood.

The blood draw had gone so well, I figured Mom would think her financial advisor was running a money laundering scheme with all her money. To my surprise, other than the comment, "I have to remember we're talking thousands, not dollars" the meeting went off without a hitch. By the time we headed to appointment number three, the dentist, I was exhausted, thinking, *Forget the lady with dementia, maybe my efficiency plan was too much for me. I'm five minutes away from being the "shit show".*

Gene Ann called me on my drive home to express her concern that Mom had left her door open the previous night, after taking two of the fucking little pink pills and falling asleep. *At least she took the pill,* I thought, too exhausted to get upset.

Chapter 19
Resident Watching; Birds of a Feather Flock Together

September 6, 2021

I'd just confirmed the last memory care facility tour, when I saw a text message from Gene Ann.

> Your mom had a dizzy spell this evening and fell onto the kitchen floor. She laid there in place very alert until the EMS team arrived and moved her to the couch where they took her vitals and ran an ekg and a test for diabetes. Everything was in normal range. She responded to their questions coherently. She didn't want to go to the emergency room and I agreed.

> It's too scary with the Delta variant unless it's a life-or-death matter. We had not really eaten anything all day except sugar, key lime pie, cake. I fixed her a protein drink, the one I am supposed to drink twice a day, and warmed up all the leftovers from yesterday. We are now watching the Lifetime special series on Meghan and Harry which is pretty entertaining. There was no charge for the EMS call. The pill taking routine is back to being a trauma. She has taken them all out of the container and rearranged them again. She is dozing now, so I will try to get her into bed with Foxy (dog).

Gene Ann could do press briefings for the White House, her text messages were so thorough. Comments from friends ran through my mind.

"My mom's fall was really the end, she never recovered from that" one friend had lamented over lunch.

"My dad was never quite right after the fall, he died a month later," another had said one morning over coffee.

I'd felt unprepared back in April when I'd looked at facilities. I'd witnessed strung-out family members frantically dropping off loved ones, handing them off like relay batons. Back in April I couldn't have imagined being one of these frantic family members, but now I felt a strange kinship with them.

This time around, rather than just focusing on the facility, I was more concerned with the residents. Could I see Mom there? Became the question I'd ask myself as I toured. Resident watching, as I called it, felt a little like bird watching. Instead of peering into trees, I was peering into rooms. In those rooms I found:

Common name: Lucid
Scientific name: Cognitively intact
Common name: Bedridden
Scientific name: Non-ambulatory
Common name: Confused
Scientific Name: Delusional

Inside each of the three facilities I toured, I'd question, *Is this her flock?* as I popped my head in and out of rooms.

Also of concern was facility access once Mom became a resident. COVID was busy morphing into new variants, and I couldn't count on how facilities would respond. I thought back to the stories I'd heard where facilities had installed walls of plexiglass so families could view their loved ones safely. I envisioned Mom running into the plexiglass, like I'd done when I walked into my screen door, leaving the paper plate full of food I'd been carrying stuck to my t-shirt. The next image was of Mom and I pressing our palms against the plexiglass, like loved ones during prison visitation hours.

The morning I was set to tour the last memory care facility on my list, I received a text from Sherrie.

> Good morning, I just had a "conversation" with your mom.
> She seems to be very mixed up?

In my mind I could see Sherrie's hands making air quotations as she said *"conversation,"* her head tilted to the side, eyebrows arched. If Wikipedia were to define a conversation with Mom it would be a talk between two people, one of which makes a series of random, often unrelated comments strung together without context to another person, who tries to piece together the information to formulate an exchange.

I barely processed Sherrie's text before I noticed a voicemail from Victoria Inn. *When did that come in?* I pressed play to hear the voice of the bubbly, energetic woman behind the sign-in desk.

Michelle, it's Karen at the front desk here at Victoria Inn, can you please give me a call back?

I held my breath and hit the call back icon. My stomach tightened with anticipation.

"Is your mom going to lunch with friends today?" Karen said.

"I'm not sure. She mentioned something about lunch," I said, trying to remember what Mom had said. "I don't know when though."

"We're just checking because she scheduled a driver but didn't schedule a return ride." I heard residents in the background asking about Doughnut Friday, which always drew hordes of residents to the common living area. "We just want to make sure we're not just dropping her somewhere with no way back."

"Actually, this is her calling me, let me find out and I'll call you back" I said. I switched the call over and heard, "Well it's been a confusing morning!" Mom laughed. "Maybe lunch is tomorrow? Joanie said she'd call me before."

"Did Joanie call you?"

"That driver, he really has an attitude!" she

said, no longer laughing. "I'd be fine if I went to the restaurant, no one needs to check on me."

"He's just trying to make sure he's not dropping you somewhere, then leaving you with no ride home," I said, grateful he didn't just dump Mom at the restaurant. *Opportunity for Silver Alert,* I thought, then my mind played with the acronym (OFI) Opportunity for Improvement, *maybe I'd just start saying* (OFSA) *Opportunity for Silver Alert.*

Mom was consistently mixing up dates and days of the week. If I told her I'd be in town Thursday, she'd call me multiple times a day until Thursday asking, "Are you coming today?" Further confusing things, Mom would tell her sister I was coming into town on whatever day she could remember, which rarely was correct. Her sister, armed with the wrong information, would text me to coordinate plans.

(Gene Ann)

> Are you coming in today? Tommys' in town and I'm driving over to your mom now.

(Me)

> I'm coming in THURSDAY.

The "what day are you coming in" calls and text messages started to confuse the shit out of me and I started to lose track of days. *Is today Wednesday or Thursday? What day is it?*

Retail Shrinkage

September 30, 2021

I felt uneasy approaching Mom's unit, it had been a couple of weeks since I'd seen her. Unsure what I'd find, I slowly opened her door to poke my head in first. The TV blared the news, but I didn't see Mom. Her patio doors were cracked open, but no one was sitting outside.

"She loves going outside," Mom's voice came up behind me.

"God, you scared me," I said, placing my hand on my chest, as I turned around to see her creeping in from the bedroom. "Who loves going outside?"

"She does," Mom said, gesturing to the ceramic dog placed just to the side of the open door. A bowl of water and a small dog biscuit were placed at its paws. In no time there'd be water bowls in every room.

My eyes drifted from the dog up to a slight movement that had caught my attention. Hanging from the ceiling just above the patio door was a grasshopper that anxiously moved side-to-side gazing down at me. In the adjacent corner a light breeze caused a spider to bounce in the corner of its web, its long brown legs clutching the silky fibers.

"They're a bunch of bugs in here because you're leaving the door open," I said, as I batted a gnat away. Texans don't leave doors open in September, unless you're an Entomologist looking to classify the species that wander inside.

"The dog likes going out. Leave it!" she snapped back. I let it go.

"That guy still drops his daughter off here," she said. My mind scurried to figure out who the guy was. "She hangs out in my walker and just stares at me." I watched her eye the walker sitting in the corner. *Ah?, got it, attic guy and his daughter,* I concluded, then deduced that the daughter must be using the walker as a chair. Only fifteen minutes had passed since I arrived, it was going to be a long day.

Getting Mom into my SUV had become like a ROPEs course, with me standing directly behind her in a show of trust, as she scaled the footboard clutching the door, suspended between the seat and asphalt. Just before her door clicked shut, I heard, "Hi there" and saw Mom talking to the back seat. *Whatever,* I shrugged off Mom's new imaginary friend. Two minutes later Mom, her pretend friends, and I were off to lunch. A 900-calorie salad at Cracker Barrel had my name written all over it.

Target all but shared a parking lot with Cracker Barrel, streamlining my visits. However, once inside Target it was anything but streamlined, because Mom treated every department in the store like it was the first time she'd ever seen it. The hours I spent in Target led me to believe I needed something from almost every department. I threw a fuzzy throw blanket into the cart that I was convinced I'd be re-homing in the years to come, probably as a Christmas gift.

"Maybe I need stronger ones," Mom said, as she fiddled with a pair of glasses.

"Those are blue-light glasses, they won't help you," I said. An image of Travis wearing his ridiculous clear-framed blue-light glasses that made him look like he worked in a lab made me laugh. "They're for people who stare at computer screens all day."

"I don't see a blue light" she said, placing the glasses on the bridge of her nose.

"No, it's to help with the blue light of computer

screens" I said, knowing this would be five minutes of my life I'd never get back.

"I do see a lot of blue on my computer."

"You don't even use your computer. Never mind," I said and threw the glasses in the cart.

When we finally checked out and were in the parking lot, I noticed Mom had hooked the blue light glasses on the collar of her t-shirt, like a pair of sunglasses. How the glasses had made it out of the cart and onto her shirt was a mystery. Before I could even decide whether or not to be a decent human being and go pay for the glasses, Mom pulled a Giant Snickers bar from her purse. *What else did you steal?* I thought about all the news reports I'd seen on retail shrinkage and wondered if they had a risk reduction plan for shoppers with dementia.

Voicemail from Mom, October 6, 2021

> Hi Michelle, it's mom I was hoping someone could come pick us up? Michelle and I are up at Victoria Inn, um, we're there for this afternoon and realized we don't have a car to go back in. We just got that phone call, it's gone now. Anyway, I'll talk to you later.

I dialed Mom to tell her AGAIN when I'd be in town, although according to her I was already there.

"Mom, I'm coming tomorrow. Do you remember...," I started to say, but was cut off.

"I don't, because I'm in another reality," she said, speaking fast. "It's like I'm in one reality, then another, then I flip back. I'm in the house now, can you believe it?"

"What?" was all that escaped my mouth.

"That lady doesn't want me to go outside," she continued. "That's a little ridiculous, don't you think?" By *that lady*, Mom meant the helpers we'd hired to come in. Displeased with their presence, she refused to call them anything but *that lady, her*, or *that person*. Given she just described being in another reality, I understood why *that lady* didn't want her going outside.

"I'll be in tomorrow. We can go somewhere then," I said and quickly hung up. *Tomorrow's Thursday, right?* Mom's confusion was bleeding into my world causing me to slowly go mad.

Biting Off More Than You Can Chew

The next day I walked into Mom's living room to find the ceramic dog comfortably laying in the seat of the bright turquoise walker Mom never used. I'd recently taken her walker shopping, hoping if she selected the walker she would use it. The poor salesman pointed out all the different features, only to have Mom make her selection solely on color. "This will go with everything, and I've always liked turquoise!" she'd said. I pictured it bedazzled with colorful rhinestones in the future.

"You're letting every bug in," I muttered under my breath, closing the patio doors that were open for the dog sitting in the walker. I surveyed the corners of the ceiling, noticing the insect population had decreased. Only one measly mosquito hovered by the door. "Lunch time," I said, giving the spider I'd grown fond of a wink.

I felt Mom come up beside me. "Can you believe we're in our house?" she said smiling, gesturing with her hands around the living room like she was showing me a room I'd never seen. "The house, we're in it again!"

Intuitively I knew she was talking about our family home in San Diego. She really was flipping through realities. On a weekly, sometimes daily, basis Mom thought she was in Lakeway, or San Diego, or at other times she thought she was at my house in Austin. If there were frequent flier miles for mind travel Mom would be gold status.

Before I could respond she pivoted around and headed to the bedroom closet. "The girls upstairs are doing a skirt contest," she said leaning over to dig through a pile of pants and skirts laid on the floor. "They've been in here messing with everything playing dress up."

They sound cute. "Sounds like they're having fun," I said.

"One of them stole my skirt," she replied, her tone no longer playful. "The embroidered one that's expensive!" I could see the black skirt with colorful embroidery hanging towards the back of her closet, but I knew better than to engage.

An hour later, a plate of steak enchiladas sat in front of Mom. I thought I'd be happy we weren't at Cracker Barrel, but all I could do was watch her painstakingly stab a butter knife at the enchilada barely piercing the tortilla before the fork would fumble out of her other hand. *When did the hand shaking start?* I asked myself, as I watched her finally nab a piece of food onto the fork, only to see it fall just before making contact with her mouth. I desperately wanted to lean across the table and cut the enchiladas like I'd done hundreds of times for the boys when they were toddlers.

Contact! I rejoiced to myself, as a bite of enchilada entered her mouth. My celebration was short-lived when I watched her struggle to chew the large fajita style piece of beef. Quietly I went through the Heimlich Maneuver in my mind in preparation.

Back at Moms I eyed the bright turquoise walker lined up next to the first walker I'd bought, but she refused to use. "I'm going to donate that other walker to the facility, is that okay?" I asked Mom, gesturing to the walker that looked plain next to the bright turquoise.

"I don't need it," she replied.

I know, I know.

I pushed the plain gray walker up to the energetic, bubbly woman at the front desk. "Do you all have a use for this? It's brand new," I said, my body shifting slightly to accommodate the resident that had come up beside me.

"You could sell that," the resident at my side chimed in, his finger pointing at the walker. "Probably get a hundred bucks for it."

Another resident joined, flanking my other side. "There's a place just down the street that'll sell it for you," she said, touching the seat of the walker. Before I knew it, no less than four residents had gathered to debate how much money I could get for the walker.

I should have known from past experience

with Mom, never give something away for free that has value. "I'm just re-homing it," I said, pushing it behind the desk and out of sight. Once out of sight, the residents disbursed. *Out of sight, out of mind.*

Voicemail from Mom, October 10, 2021, 7:13 p.m.

> I just can't believe that I've gone all this time, it's like you just have no feelings for something, for us. I still hope for answers, some physically can't give um......

(voicemail ends)

Exhausted from driving four hours, I caved and called Mom.

"Well, where have you been?" she said, accusatorially. "People have been worried."

"I've been in Denton for Connor's birthday," I explained, wondering who the *people* were.

"You could have called when you got off the phone," Mom said.

Huh?

"Danielle and Ben were at Walgreens just walking around," she continued. "We were watching them." She sounded paranoid and I wondered who *we, us* and *people* were that she kept referencing.

In my mind I saw a group of worried imaginary people sitting all around her. I let out a long exhausted breath. "I'll call you tomorrow," I said and hung up.

Voicemail from Mom, October 11, 2021, 9:13 a.m.

> Hello, hello. I'm up and around and I have a lot of things going on with Ben and the people here. I think that he's just unfair, that he takes advantage of us. So, I'm having to fight the things, innuendos, that people are making while he's sitting out in the middle of the lounge just being you know himself. I see him going across the thing, but you know, it's not my place to clear him up. I don't know what's going on with it. Anyway, give me a call, I'll talk with you. I need to get in touch with Danielle, so give me a call.

Fuck the paranoia is back, I thought, figuring Danielle was about to get an earful about pretend Ben being disruptive to the Victoria Inn community.

Unstable foundation

Most of October I felt like my world was spinning out of control. The anxiety that had plagued me in my twenties returned with a vengeance. Nothing was off limits, I worried about EVERYTHING! Are the boys alright? Should I cut back at work? Did the dog have a horrible disease because he threw up? At night the worry seeped into my dreams disrupting my sleep with chaotic short dreams that woke me up several times a night. Some nights the dreams played out like horror flicks, abruptly waking me up scared, causing me to flip on lights.

Sleepless nights coupled with constant racing thoughts that played on a never-ending loop, sent me reminiscing about the nights I'd drank till I passed out. *Maybe if I just drink tonight I'll sleep,* my mind wrangled. *It wouldn't look like before. I'll just drink tonight,* the thoughts continued to make a case for a relapse. I pulled the covers up under my chin trying to rid my head of the thoughts. *Shit, Travis is in the living room. I'd have to pass him to get to the kitchen,* the thoughts continued. *Damn it, I don't think we have any alcohol in the house.*

The next morning, I considered that the simple lack of alcohol in the house probably saved me from relapsing. If I'd had access last night, I might have been hungover drinking my morning coffee.

"I'm so strung out," I blurted out to Travis the minute he stepped into the kitchen. "I feel like I'm in a constant state of worry." I left out my mental gymnastics about drinking from the night before. "Like I'm on the brink of a panic attack all the time!"

He placed his mug down and came around the island to the barstool I was slouched on. "Of course you feel that way. Your mom's your last living parent," he said, wrapping an arm around my waist. "Well, and she's really not your mom anymore," he paused. "It's like losing your foundation."

She's dying. Warm tears fell down my cheeks and before I knew it, I was sobbing.

Mind Travel Baggage

Voicemail from Mom October 12, 2021, 10:01 a.m.

> Michelle, it's your mom, give me a call. I've got some dilemmas going and uh, I'm getting on a plane. I packed everything I own in my closet before I left and now I've

> got to figure how to get it all back to something. Or to throw away, or to do something with it. But I thought that maybe you and Danielle could come in. I will pay for tickets. If you would come in and help me get out of here. Ben is the only person that I know and he is barely speaking to me. So, it would be nice if I had someone else to run things through and I'd love to see the two of you since nobody talks to me. I don't know how long but I'm, uh in my closet this morning and it's uh, its just to get everything out the door again. I'm afraid I'll be paying huge amounts for it and I'd just as soon pay for your tickets if you came out again. I know that's asking a lot and uh…that's the way it is right now. I will talk to you when you give me a call.

What? The utter confusion in Mom's voice made me feel sad for her.

"I think Ben is mowing the lawn," Mom said casually, as she picked up my call.

"Ben's in California with Danielle," I replied.

"I should be in California, you know, at the condo," Mom's voice was faint and cracked. *Damn it, I walked into that one.*

"San Diego is not a good option. Remember, there's stairs and no one is there to help you," I said slowly, feeling like I should be wearing a "Bad News Bears" t-shirt.

"I just wish I could sort things out. It's so confusing," she said, sounding distressed. "Like I'm here, but there."

I remembered Mom's purple paisley suitcase filled with a couple of items of clothing laying on the bed, then another image of the suitcase standing by the door filled my mind. *Is she packing for the mind travel?* I'd later learn from staff at Victoria Inn that Mom would pack and unpack her suitcase all the time. I felt helpless, unable to help her sort out her confusion.

Chapter 20
This is Your Flock

October 22, 2021

The conversation Cameron and I had driving back from Mom's the previous week replayed in my head. "Holy shit, watching grandma eat that fish taco was painful," he'd said. "She pretty much choked on the chips."

"I know," was all I'd responded, as my stomach did somersaults.

"Sorry, I know it's hard Mom, but she's worse," he'd added. "You need to move her."

Now I was frantic and out of options, because all the memory care facilities I had toured last month filled their vacancies leaving me back at square one. *I'm going to be one of those frantic, strung-out family members I'd seen back in April,* I thought. Even my inner voice sounded panicked.

In a frenzy, I'd broken down and called Leslie AGAIN. "I just put another client's dad in The Cottages," she'd said slowly, trying to calm the panic she heard in my voice. "I think you'd really like it."

The Cottages, a sign flanked by brick pillars welcomed me, as I pulled into the parking lot. I stared at the one-story red brick building through my windshield praying I'd find Mom's flock inside. Immediately upon reaching the front door, I saw the exterior door handle rattle. Out of reflex, I stepped back to allow whoever was leaving to come out, but the door didn't open. Again, the handle rattled. *Was someone inside trying to get out?* Ignoring the rattling handle, I stepped forward and rang the doorbell.

A loud alarm reverberated across the front porch, as the door opened to display a tiny, adorable, upbeat woman who stuck out her hand. "I'm Jannis, come on in," she said, as she led me past a man who paced, like a tiger in a cage, two feet from the door, focused intently on its opening and closing.

You were trying to get out, I said to myself, giving him a little smile as I passed. The door clicked shut, silencing the blaring alarm sound, which left classical music playing softly in the background.

I stood in a common living room similar to other facilities I'd toured. Pale yellow walls emanated warmth, giving the whole area a homey feel. To my right a mahogany grand piano sat in front of a window overlooking the parking lot. To my left, two well-dressed women in their eighties sat next to each other on a sofa talking, while a man snored in the adjacent lounge chair.

In front of me two large crystal chandeliers dangled like sparkling earrings, delineating the wide hall that housed business offices and terminated into what looked like an activities room. Dark oak tables were scattered throughout the activities room that overlooked a garden outside. At one table, residents sat with laminated cards in front of them while a woman called out numbers. *Bingo*, I heard several residents say.

I immediately was reminded of the two hours I'd spent at the state mental hospital as a class requirement helping residents play bingo. I'd only been given two pieces of advice that day. "Don't give anyone more than one cookie. ONLY one cookie! It'll be chaos if someone gets an extra cookie," the very serious staff member had said. "And everyone will ask you if you have the bathroom key. Just say no." I'd thought she was being dramatic until a man wearing noise-canceling headphones slid up next to me. "You got a cookie?" he'd said, like he was initiating a drug deal, the words whispered out of the corner of his mouth while his eyes surveyed the room. Now as I surveyed this group of cognitively impaired bingo players, I wondered if the same rules applied.

"We have all ages," Jannis's voice interrupted the memory. "There's two here in their fifties and one who will be 106-years-old soon." *Fifties? What?* All those times I joked about "becoming my mother" now sent a shiver down my spine.

"Did you lose your way?" Jannis gently touched the shoulder of a woman facing the janitorial closet door, wringing her hands. "Here, let me help. You were really close," Jannis said, then led the woman away from the door. "See your room is right here." The look of fear remained on the woman's face as she walked into her room and took a seat on the edge of her bed. Back in March, the distress of the woman would have sent me into tears. Seven months later, I saw Mom in that distressed woman and was grateful there would be staff to help her.

Buzzzzzzz. The blaring alarm sound sent a jolt

of cortisol through my veins when Jannis pushed open the door to the back patio. A group of painted rocks, some with pink hearts and others with painted flowers lay at the base of a rose bush. An image of the boys painting rocks in preschool was interrupted by the sensation of fur on the side of my leg. Leaning against my knee was a heavy brownish-silver lab panting like he'd just run a mile.

"He's not allowed inside anymore during meals, everyone feeds him," Jannis said, giving the lab a little scratch on the head. *My dogs would weigh 100 pounds.* At least the ceramic dog would have a real friend.

Buzzzzzz. The blaring alarm sound rang out overhead as we walked back inside. *I'm never going to get used to that.* My body went rigid until the door closed behind us. I looked back to see the heavy lab's nose pressed against the glass. On our way to view an available room, a man in his early fifties, with brown hair and a bushy mustache, stood outside a resident room. "Taking a tour?" he said, as we passed.

"He's one of our younger residents," Jannis quietly whispered, giving the man a wave. My mouth fell open in shock, I'd thought the man was staff. When I turned to look back, I noticed a key hanging around his neck, the same key I'd seen on numerous residents. "The halls that hold residents' rooms are different colors to help our residents find their way," Jannie said. Still struggling with the image of the young man, I took note of the green paint that covered the walls.

At the end of the green hall was a vacant corner room. Two corner windows came together spilling natural light onto the floor. I stepped forward to look out the windows to see a field of grass that abutted the wrought iron fence surrounding the facility's garden. "She'd love the light in here," I said. *This is Mom's flock.* Paperwork in hand, I made my way back to the parking lot.

Voicemail from Mom, October 30, 2021, 11:51 a.m.

> Hi Michelle, It's Mom, could you give me a call. It's just I'm not sure I have the right dates and things going, but I need to probably see my doctor today. Nothing urgent, just a matter of sequencing for what might be in the future needed. Talk to you then, love you lots.

Mom picked up so quickly I pictured her waiting with the phone in her lap. "I'm bleeding every time I wipe," she said, her words releasing images into my brain that I'd probably need therapy to get over. "It's not a UTI. I don't think so anyway," she continued. "You know I hate the shower. I haven't showered but once in a couple of weeks." *Ewww. No, I didn't know.*

"Is it a lot of blood or just irritation?" I said, then held my breath waiting for the reply.

"Maybe with all the wiping? It's not a lot," she said, sounding less concerned now.

"I'll be there on Monday, we can go to the doctor if you want?"

"Danielle's here, she keeps taking my stuff," she said, onto the next topic. "It's really starting to bother me."

"That's a hallucination, she's in California. Why don't you call Danielle."

Voicemail from Mom, October 30, 2021, 3:32 pm

> Michelle says that I'm hallucinating, and
> I'd like to have another opinion, so if you're
> around somewhere give me a call back, talk
> to you then.

Well, that backfired, I laughed at Mom calling me thinking it was Danielle.

The calls kept coming, one after another until I stopped answering them around 7 p.m. Maybe I should tell her someone is trying to steal her phone, maybe then she'd hide it like she hid everything else never to be found.

Tours Daily

November 1, 2021

A well of tears that had been building over the last couple of days, released with the thought of another hard "you're moving" conversation when I got into Bryan. Since I'd toured The Cottages, I'd been working feverishly behind the scenes with both The Cottages and Victoria Inn to get Mom moved two days from now. When I'd called Leslie two days ago, yet again for advice, she'd recommended saying Mom's lease was up, which was brilliant. Also, a "family script" was provided to everyone that had contact with Mom, which I found ironic, since we were moving Mom to memory care.

Agreeing to Facetime Danielle in for the

conversation, I sent her a text after finishing my greasy Cracker Barrel Cheeseburger.

> We're headed back to Victoria Inn now.

Her reply text appeared nano seconds after I'd hit send.

> Yikes!

Back in her unit, Mom dove into her closet, like an explorer. Flashlight in hand, she started searching for the missing underwear I'd heard about over lunch. "I bet those girls from the attic came down," I heard her talking to herself, while she flashed beams of light into the corners of the closet. I wondered why she needed the flashlight, since the closet light was on, but knew better than to ask.

I set up my laptop on the ottoman and dialed Danielle. "Mom. Can you come sit down?" I tried to coax her back into the living room. "I need to talk to you."

"What about?" she said, slowly walking out of the closet, with the flashlight now aimed at my face. *Highlight the positives,* I reminded myself.

"I've got Danielle here," I turned the computer

to show her, which drew her over to the sofa. "Your lease here is up and I've found you a great place closer to me."

Danielle quickly chimed in. "I'll also be coming to Austin to help with the move."

"It's like a dream come true," Mom clasped her hands together in excitement. "Is Ben's family okay with that?"Danielle looked confused, but I knew Mom had taken Danielle's comment to mean Danielle was moving to Austin. In the same way I'd shown Mom pictures of Victoria Inn, I was now showing her pictures of The Cottages.

Over the next two days Mom would confuse her surroundings. Giving new meaning to the sign that displayed TOURS DAILY outside, Mom would ask Karen, the energetic, bubbly woman behind the check in desk, "Can you show me around? I just got here." While she toured her current facility, I planned for the move.

Stealth Mission

November 3, 2021

According to Urban Dictionary, Stealth Mission is defined as an assignment that requires you to be stealth in order to have an advantage. We would need to be stealth in order to have an advantage over Mom's propensity to fixate and sort her belongings. The evening before the move, over pizza with Danielle and Ben, who had come into town, Travis mentioned we should split into two groups. One group would pack up Mom, while the other group distracted her at lunch. Our mission, should we accept it: Get Mom out, in the least amount of time, with the least amount of stuff.

"Team Packing! I want Danielle and Connor on my team," I said, like I was choosing a dodgeball team in elementary school. That left Travis, Ben and Gene Ann for Team Lunch.

"Do we have to do Cracker Barrel," Travis said. *Seriously?!*

"I've done it every week for months, I don't think it'll kill you," I said with little sympathy.

The next morning, moving day, I heard the rain before I saw it, starting as a pitter patter then turning into a torrential downpour. I pulled the blinds to see gusts of wind blow the tall oaks that swayed under the pressure. Sheets of rain formed small lakes on the golf course behind our house. The whole scene seemed ironic given Mom's fear of flooding.

The two-hour drive to Bryan turned into three hours, the rain forcing Team Packing to crawl at forty mph. Connor in the passenger seat and Danielle in the back seat, passed a bag of Sour Patch Kids back and forth nervously eating. My knuckles turned white from the brute force of gripping the steering wheel, while I used the car's tail lights ahead of me as a guidepost through the rain.

Somewhere outside Caldwell, Travis called. "Do you want us to wait till you get her before we leave for lunch?"

You're there, good lord how fast were you driving.

"Just wait for us," I said, screaming over the sound of the rain.

Wet and worn out from the rainy drive, Team Packing arrived to join Team Lunch at Mom's.

"I haven't eaten in two days," Mom quipped, as she headed for the door, purse slung on her shoulder, barely saying hello before she was halfway down the hall.

"I guess she's hungry," I shrugged my shoulders. Once Team Lunch was safely out of sight, our stealth mission commenced. Out came the large white trash bags and boxes, with everyone taking a room in a frenzy of activity.

"We're taking very little," I reminded Team Packing while I made a "to-go" pile in the living room.

I watched Danielle rummage through the laundry basket next to Mom's bed. "I wouldn't take that if it's in the laundry. She has a million blankets," I said, then watched her throw the blanket into the air in an attempt to straighten it.

"What are these brown flaky things on it," Danielle mumbled to herself, using her nail to pick at a spot on the blanket.

"It's probably shit," I said, casually. "The bathroom thing is the real deal. Just leave it." Recognition of the word *shit* spread across her face, then she released the blanket back into the laundry basket in horror. A couple minutes later, she carefully placed the blanket into a white, plastic trash bag, using a sharpie to label the front "trash".

The constant fear of Mom showing back up, left us acting like prairie dogs, our heads on a swivel, constantly on the lookout for Mom. In no time we had Connor's car pulled up to the side door full of "to go" items.

"Let's go, go, go!" I yelled, throwing the last box into the back and slamming the hatch shut. *Click, click, click.* Three car doors shut and we were off!

Welcome to the Zoo

We arrived at The Cottages just before dinner. I had been to the facility a couple of times before, but tonight the activity level was bustling. I watched as two ladies sat on the sofa engaged in a heated conversation that I couldn't quite follow. Just as we made it into the middle of the living room, one of the ladies got up and stormed off. Danielle shot me a look. I just shrugged my shoulders, like "who knows?" A few residents roamed the halls aimlessly, anxiously wringing their hands as if they were solving the world's problems. Men were slouched on sofas, passed out, mouths wide open and snoring. *Typical.* I turned to my left and saw a life-like baby doll dressed in a cute blue and white onesie, cradled in the arms of a woman who repeated, "I can't believe they just dumped this baby on me" over and over again. Her stress over this baby was palpable.

Danielle strolled slowly behind me as we made our way down the green hall, carrying a box. She was taking in the scene and facility for the first time. She looked like she might cry. Connor, brought up the rear, carrying a lamp and bags. A man tried each door in the green hall, jingling the handles, then looked perplexed when it wouldn't open. *He's probably lost*, I concluded, wondering if he knew his hall color.

Team Lunch was thirty minutes behind us. The goal was to have Mom's room substantially set up before she arrived. Mom's corner room now held a facility-issued bed next to a nightstand and lamp. Also supplied by The Cottages, was a dresser sitting opposite the bed. I had barely unpacked a box, when a tiny woman, whose head came to my chest, wandered in carrying a plaid stuffed bunny.

"Moving in?" Plaid Bunny, my mind couldn't help but give her a nickname, said. "I don't think dinner was right, just not right." Her hand softly petted the plaid bunny as she walked further into the room eyeing Mom's stuff. "Just not right, not right," she continued on, seemingly concerned about dinner. Before I'd even opened the next box another resident strolled into the room, his pants falling off his skinny waist. He picked up the lamp Connor had just placed on the nightstand, extending his arm to give it a good look like he was assessing its worth.

"Okay. Okay, let's go find your rooms," a staff member appeared in the doorway. I watched the staff member guide, Plaid Bunny and the man out into the hall. In less than ten minutes, no less than three people had come and gone from Mom's room. I thought about Mom's love of isolating. *She's going to freak out.*

I could hear a group of voices approaching from the hall. *Shit, it's Mom.* My body tensed. I had no idea how she would react to only having one room rather than a full apartment.

"Well, there y'all are," she said, as she came around the corner into the room. She eyed the room. "The windows are nice," she said, appearing to be in a good mood. She seemed to be reveling in the activity of having her whole family around. The change from Victoria Inn to The Cottages was dramatic and I knew at some point this would hit Mom.

"Let's get her out into the main area," I nudged Danielle. I wanted to integrate her into the community before we left for the evening. Danielle and I led Mom back out to the main living room area.

"Welcome to the zoo!" a resident said, who had come up on my side without me noticing. She had the most beautiful smile, the kind that lit up her entire face.

A zoo is a pretty good comparison. I wondered why this seemingly lucid woman was here. "Welcome to the zoo!" she said again, with the same enthusiasm as five minutes ago. She then repeated the same dialogue about her life verbatim three times in a row.

I couldn't help but stare at her perfectly applied lipstick that framed her megawatt smile. *Where is that whistling coming from?* The whistling was nonstop, no pauses or breaks, just whistling, whistling, whistling.

A man wearing classic grandpa suspenders mumbled as he passed us, "God damn it! Damn whistling. She never shuts up!"

Only then did I locate the whistler sitting alone at a table, lips pursed. My parrot would absolutely love The Whistler, as I'd call her from that point on.

Team Packing was starving and it was time to let Mom acclimate to her new surroundings. Travis was easy to locate as he was standing next to me ready to leave. Ben chatted with the young man I'd seen on the tour, the same key hung around his neck indicating he was a resident.

"Can you believe that guy lives here?" Ben said, walking over to us, baffled. I'd had the same reaction when I toured the facility. This man could hold a five-minute conversation pretty lucidly, was always well-dressed, and was young by comparison. However, past a couple of minutes he would start repeating the same conversation over and over and become frustrated.

"Mom, do you want to stay out here or go back to your room?" I asked. "We're going to head out, but we'll be back tomorrow, and we can take you out for lunch."

Leaving Connor, Ben, and Travis to fend for themselves in the living room, Danielle and I situated Mom, who was now exhausted, back in her room. As we came back around the corner, I noticed Connor was holding the extra lamp we'd bought for Mom's room but didn't need.

"The guys over there are eyeing me," Connor said, gesturing to the two men slouched on the sofa. "They probably think I stole the lamp, or they want it. It does kind of look like the lamps in here."

"Gma thinks everyone is stealing from her," I said, laughing. "They totally think you're stealing the lamp."

The next day, Danielle, Cameron, and I arrived back at The Cottages to take Mom to lunch.

"Oh good, the food here is awful," Mom said, as she opened the door to let us in.

Here we go.

"The ladies in the kitchen have a real attitude," she continued.

"Where do you want to go to lunch?" I said, trying to distract her.

"Uh, the people here, they're just zombies. Or crazy!" she snapped, not detoured by the offer of lunch.

Your flock.

Everyone stood staring at each other until Cameron broke the ice. "I'm starving, can we go?" Almost a year after he'd stepped off the plane looking like a skeleton, Cameron was not only eating, but often rushing the rest of us off to a meal. The last year hadn't been easy, but he put in the work and continues to maintain his recovery. I still cry every time I think about that time a year ago, because that kind of fear, the fear that your child could die, embeds in your cells becoming a part of you.

Mom devoured her chicken fried steak, this time at Cotton Patch, while she complained about absolutely everything. There wasn't a single positive aspect to The Cottages. I understood and had expected as much, but what I didn't expect was the resentment that bubbled up inside me as I stared at her across the booth listening to her rant on and on. I withdrew into myself and sat quietly. All I could think about was everything I had given to this disease AGAIN: Tours, paperwork, moving, packing, buying furniture, tremendous stress, and worrying, lots and lots of worrying. I knew the move had to be hard on her, but I wanted to run out of the restaurant, away from her, and let Danielle deal with Mom for the rest of the visit. After lunch, that's exactly what happened. The next day I stayed home and let Danielle and Ben go to the facility before they left town. I took a couple of days off from Mom, hoping I'd be in a better headspace.

You Still Can't Drink

Monday morning, I flipped Mom's cell phone in my hand, taking in the colorful daisies on the plastic case. On advice from The Cottages, I had confiscated her phone, but now a pang of guilt resided in my stomach. Guilt had me questioning if she'd feel lonely without it. I slipped the phone into my purse, and I figured I'd assess how things were going after I saw her.

Buzzzzzz. The blaring alarm sound startled me, as Grace welcomed me inside. "Your Mom is back in her room," she said, keeping one eye on the two residents that paced just behind her, keenly aware the door was open.

A lady wearing pearls with a red turtleneck sat

with perfect posture next to the window. I found myself curious about her back story. *Has she always worn pearls? Did her mother nag her about her posture?* I was still wondering about Perfect Posture Pearl when I turned down Mom's hall. I felt my stomach tighten at the unknown that lay on the other side of Mom's door. *Knock, knock.* "Who is it," I heard Mom say through the door.

"It's me, Mom," I replied.

Seconds later the door slowly opened. "It's horrible, just awful! There are people coming in all the time. It's just awful!" Mom said, breaking into tears.

I've never seen you cry like this, I thought, as the sound of whistling got louder down the hall. *The Whistler would drive me crazy.* Time seemed to slow down as I stood frozen in the doorway. Like a vortex, I felt my emotions swirl around quickly, then suck back into my body. *Hide in plain sight. Don't cry, don't cry,* I pleaded with myself. If I broke down, it would send the message to Mom that something was wrong.

"I know Mom. It's a hard change and everything is different." I mustered some words and walked inside. I felt faint making my way towards her bed to sit down. Weirdly, Mom was the most lucid I'd seen her in months. *Did I jump the gun moving her? Damn fluctuations.* Mom took a seat in the brown leather BarcaLounger, the only piece of furniture I'd bought for her new accommodations. The BarcaLounger swallowed her small frame, she looked like a child. A sad, crying child.

"This is where you need to be," I said, testing the waters. *Could I say disease?*

"I need to focus on the positives. Everyone is always so negative," she said, after a few minutes of silence.

"Do you remember Leslie coming down to Bryan to visit you," I said.

"I remember her asking me a thousand questions," she replied.

"Leslie did an assessment to see what level of support you needed," I said, carefully using the word support, not *help*. "You were assessed at this level of care." I steadied myself trying to keep my emotions in check. "You were falling, calling me all the time about your hallucinations, not eating, and not showering. It wasn't going well Mom."

"Maybe I could look for something like Victoria Inn?" she said, softly.

Deep breath, here we go. "I have looked. Most assisted livings don't take Lewy body. Plus, I'm trying to not move you a bunch," I said feeling absolutely helpless. The truth was I couldn't solve this, her options were limited by her diagnosis. "Give it some time. Do you remember how much you hated Victoria Inn at first too?"

"Okay. But maybe we could talk about it again?" she asked.

"We can do that," I said, grateful she wouldn't remember this conversation.

An hour later, Mom's Costco shopping cart looked like the board game CandyLand came to life. Peppermint bark, Madeline cookies, chocolate truffles, and oreos sat in one corner, while Mom held a tin of Almond Roca. *If this is what life looks like in my eighties, then sign me up.* At checkout Mom's face looked exhausted and I knew we were on borrowed time.

At past 3 p.m., the sundowners switch had been flipped, putting Mom into a zombie like state that sent her wandering from drawer to drawer in her room reorganizing items. "I'm going to take off," I said, watching her pull a TV remote from the drawer and point it towards the TV. Panic, shot through my body. Ever since Mom had unplugged all the cables on the back of her TV and tried to plug them into the lamp, I just couldn't have the "TV or remote" conversations anymore.

I pulled my seatbelt across my chest, clicking into place, feeling like I had been hit by an eighteen-wheeler. The tsunami of emotions I'd felt all day lurked beneath the surface, settling in as an uncomfortable numbness. I feared what lay beneath.

I threw the car into park in the HEB parking lot but found myself unable to move. *Nobody would know if I got wine,* my mind tumbled into risky waters. *It's been seven years, I'm fine. No one will care if I just have a couple of glasses,* I lied to myself. "I can't do this!" I said out loud, falling into sobs. *I can't do this sober.* Shaking my head in an attempt to get rid of the thoughts, my mind flashed back to an image of me sitting in an AA meeting. A woman talked about sitting in her car in the parking lot of the local bar after her son died, fighting off the urge to drink. I'd been in awe of this woman as I'd sat there thinking, *I couldn't get through something like that sober.* The movement of my car pulled me back to the present. I fumbled to steady myself at the wheel. I hadn't ever realized I'd put the car in reverse. Tears fell down my cheeks as I heard all the different voices at AA meetings say the same thing, "find strength from others."

Later that evening, I sat on the couch eating the peppermint bark that was left in my car, with tears pouring down my face. "I really wanted to drink," I confessed to Travis. "It scared me. I can see how people go back out after years of sobriety. I really can."

"I'm glad you didn't," was all Travis could get out, while he stared at me with scared eyes.

I'm grateful for every person who shared their personal struggles in AA meetings over the years. I heard your voices today. Your stories helped me navigate one of the hardest days I've had in sobriety. Thank you!

Chapter 21
Shit Show

November 16, 2021

Buzzzzzz. The blaring door alarm at The Cottages had barely stopped before I heard, "She's alive!" I turned to find the source of the angry voice. Standing two feet from me stood Mom, stone faced, eyeing me up and down. *Great, what did pretend me do?*

"What's wrong?" I asked.

She threw her head to the side looking back toward the kitchen. "You need to apologize to them."

"Why?" I said, still unsure who *them* was.

She inched toward me, leaned in, her face within an inch of mine. "They made a plate for you because you were supposed to be here hours ago for lunch!" I was distracted by her breath. *How long has it been since you used a toothbrush?*

"I never said I was coming for lunch," I said annoyed, reacting to the anger oozing out of her. I'd grown tired over the years of always apologizing for some offense I'd made to the social contract that lived in Mom's head. Whatever the social contract held it also required I keep up appearances. The resentment Mom's delusion triggered sent me spiraling into memories of my relationship with Mom after I'd become sober.

"Do you still go to those meetings?" she'd occasionally ask in a tone that let me know her disapproval. *Those meetings*, an unacceptable appearance. Although the comment always poked at the shame that lay just under the surface, it was the only time Mom ever acknowledged I was sober. Not only did she never talk about my sobriety or drinking, if I ever referred to myself as an alcoholic her body would visibly tense, and silence would follow.

I inhaled a breath to push the resentment aside and switched topics. "I want to take you to get your nails done, but first let's grab some stuff from your room." *And brush your teeth,* I thought, but didn't say.

Sun streaming through Mom's window, hit the sequins sprinkled throughout the colorful pattern of her skirt, casting little gold stars on the wall. Catching my eye, I studied the other patterns on the skirt that told the story of everything she'd eaten recently. A little dried gravy, something that looked like chocolate, and a light brown stain, probably tea, intermixed among the colorful floral print.

"Why don't you change into another skirt," I said, heading for the closet. "That looks like it could go in the laundry." A change of clothes and some basic personal hygiene behind us, we headed out for the nail salon.

Warm soapy water engulfed my feet, my cue to relax, so I slid back into the leather chair at the nail salon. Videos of baby animals played on the TV screens on the wall. *Why didn't The Cottages show baby animals instead of Fox News?* I questioned, thinking that would make more sense for a paranoid population.

"I want it to match the pink on my toes," I heard Mom sitting next to me, as I watched her hand grab the bottle of bright pink polish. My eyes narrowed, focusing on something brownish and flaky smeared across her thumb and palm. I couldn't take my eyes off it. *What a strange color brown.* My mind continued to analyze the substance. *Not mud, no, there was a twinge of rusk color, with a lighter yellowish brown in areas. Not gravy or chocolate.* The image of Danielle's fingernails flicking the same brownish substance of a blanket formed in my mind. *Oh my god, it's shit.* The recognition caused me to gasp audibly.

Just then, a lady pulled up her stool to start working on Mom's hands. My mind panicked. *Now what? Do I tell her? She'd be so embarrassed. What would I even say at this point?* The lady turned Mom's hand to the side, eyed the brownish smear covering her thumb, then continued filing. A burst of air escaped my mouth, I hadn't even realized I'd been holding.

Walking on my heels in pink, foam flip flops, I slid my credit card into the machine, *tip amount* shown on the screen. I looked at Mom's beautiful rose-pink nails on the hand smeared with shit, and thought, *How much do I tip someone who manicured around shit? A LOT!* And I did.

Voicemail from Mom, November 19, 2021, 5:13 a.m.

> There are twenty or thirty people, they appeared and they're cleaning house. I got

Did Mom Drop Acid?

my dog back by ladies that are here buying it back. But my house is sold, and I have to get out of it. I know you're going to think this is crazy, you need to come, come and get me. Come and get everything out of here that we can before they touch it or walk on it. Anything that is a trigger and this whole community is involved in it. If you come here leave everything you have. In fact, right now take off your diamond rings and put them where you can find them. Hide them because anything of value is out the door today. I have no idea how it's been handled or how it can be triggered. It has to be stopped, but I know that it's happening, and we need to really go through this day to find out about a lawyer. Don't treat me as though I don't know what I'm talking about, because I'm standing here looking at some of it going on. Uh, you can only get me on my cell phone. I would advise you, don't call in to any of the living areas because they've taken over the houses. Anyway, whatever you do, take those rings off, talk to you later.

People in her room taking things was probably true, memory impaired residents roamed the halls lost, like nomads with hoarding disorder, using their walkers for storage, collecting items from other rooms. On any given day, Mom's walker was a treasure trove of items that weren't hers. I looked at my phone to see ten missed calls from Mom and immediately started to plot ways to get her phone back.

Dating Prejudices

November 30, 2021

"Shoo, you've had enough to eat," a lady balancing lunch plates on one arm, ushered The Cottages resident Maine Coon cat out of the kitchen. Begrudgingly, the large cat slinked along the wall, then darted under the table where everyone was eating.

Smart cat.

At the end of the table a frail woman wearing two or three sweaters pulled over the top of each other, held a full conversation with herself while stabbing at diced carrots on her plate. Mom hadn't noticed me come up beside her chair. I leaned down and whispered into her ear. "I was going to take you to lunch, but it looks like you've already eaten."

She blinked, the *back-in-five* sign turned to *open*. "Let's get out of here and go somewhere," she said, scooting her chair back from the table.

As I drove to get coffee, I felt Mom staring at me. "Who are you dating now?" she asked.

"I'm married to Travis," I replied, puzzled. "I'm not dating."

She looked at me, then turned to look out the window.

An hour later, coffees in hand, we pulled back into The Cottages. Unloading the walker from the back of my car, I pulled the release handle to unfold the walker and watched a book, a beaded bracelet, hand lotion, and a shirt that had been stored in the seat fly out onto the parking lot. I was starting to understand why visitors didn't take their loved ones off site.

Upon entering her room, Mom immediately opened a dresser drawer and began to fold a pair of underwear. "Tell me about your life," she said, placing that pair of folded underwear back into the same drawer, then selecting another pair to fold and re-locate.

That's a broad question. "Travis is still working from home, Cameron's working," I said, relaying a summary of life happenings as I lay down on the bed. "Connors in college—" I continued but was cut off.

"Are you marrying that guy?" Mom looked at me through narrowed eyes, the question lobbed more like an accusation.

"What? What guy?"

"Travis is all over the news. Everyone is talking about it. I don't know what to tell them," she said, sounding genuinely exasperated.

"I'm not following." *Was "that guy" Travis?*

"That guy works here. Everyone is talking!" she said, after an uncomfortable silence. "What am I supposed to say?"

"Mom, I don't know what to tell you, I'm married to Travis and there's no guy," I said, irritated. The words, *everyone is talking,* triggered something in my gut. I thought about all the times Mom worried about what others thought, dismissing my feelings in the process. I wanted to scream, *"I don't care if everyone is talking"* but then remembered it was a hallucination.

"People need to stay within their income levels," Mom said, heaving herself out of the Barca-Lounger. "Stay in their place." Her words creating a caste system for the imaginary world she inhabited.

"That's very elitist." The words slipped out of my mouth. I felt the need to defend *that guy,* whoever he was.

My words now had her standing in front of me, her face hard and determined, two inches from mine. "I don't know where my money is," she said, through clenched teeth. "How much does it cost here?"

I took a deep breath. "Do you remember meeting with the lawyer?" I delicately trudged into the money conversation. "I handle all your money and you have plenty."

"Well as long as you remember it's my money, not yours!" she said, her finger pointing an inch from my face. The comment crawled under my skin, unearthing feelings of hurt buried long ago. The knife of distrust she wielded like a weapon, sent my blood boiling.

"I'm going to take off," I said, before I could say something I'd regret or fall apart crying.

A resident lurked by the door blocking my exit path. *We're all trying to escape buddy,* I thought, scrambling to locate a member of staff. I turned to find Mom with her purse placed on the seat of her turquoise walker standing behind me. Panic surged down my spine.

"Say goodbye to your daughter Ms. Kay," Jannis said, coming up on my side. *Buzzzzzz*. The sound of the blaring door alarm echoed outside until the door shut. Before I made it to the car, tears were streaming down my cheeks.

Chapter 22
Fight Night

December 7, 2021

*The weather outside is frightful, but the fire is so delightful...*I hummed along with Christmas Spirit, as I waved to the woman standing off to the right of the entry door, studying the door like it held the world's secrets. Just beyond the grand piano, Perfect Posture Pearl sat by the window wearing her trademark pearl necklace with a tasteful red Christmas Sweater. I wondered what she thought about while she gazed out onto the parking lot. Twinkling warm lights wrapped around a tree that almost reached the ceiling decorated in jewel tones. A plate of untouched food sat in front of Mom, whose *back-in-five* stare fixated on the tiny woman across from her that was a dead ringer for Nancy Reagan. Nancy's twin looked up and smiled. *She's new.* I was curious if she complained to her daughter about Mom being crazy. The newbies were easy to spot as they always looked a little shocked by their surroundings, just like Mom had a month ago.

"Hi Mom," I said, coming up on her side. I started to pull a chair up.

"Let's go sit in the big room," she said, before I could sit down. When she pushed herself away from the table, half of a torn dinner roll tumbled from her lap onto the floor, catching the attention of the resident Maine Coon cat, who waited under the table.

Distracted by the cat, I trailed behind Mom who was already sitting on the sofa, mesmerized by the twinkling lights of the tree. "Do you want to grab coffee?" I took a seat. "Or get your nails done?" No response. *Weird,* I thought to myself, *usually you're eager to go outside.*

A gaggle of women sat in a cluster of chairs off to our side. One woman looked half asleep, another carried on an animated conversation with herself, and the third looked upset, muttering angrily under her breath. Mom who I'd almost forgotten about, turned to focus on the woman having an animated conversation with herself. "I think that's

Did Mom Drop Acid?

my sweater," Mom blurted out, which was ironic because she made the accusation wearing an adorable snowman sweater that wasn't hers. "We need to get a lawyer."

Because she's wearing your sweater? "We don't need a lawyer," I said.

I watched her eyes move to the left of the gaggle of women, then land on a woman who had just emerged from the lunch area. Her eyes narrowed. "There she is," she said, like she was picking someone out of a lineup. "She's bad news. She came into my room, so I hit her." *Great, you're going to get kicked out of here.*

"Why did you hit her?" curious, I asked. Something in Mom's demeanor made me believe she'd actually hit this woman. Waiting for her answer, I also waited to be called into the principal's office or in this case Jannis's office. I was reminded of the time Mom had been called into the principal's office when I got caught drinking in the locker room in eighth grade. *Payback, I guess.*

"She tried to take my jacket," Mom answered. "She fights with everyone. She deserved it!" I started to think if the staff wasn't constantly redirecting this population, it would quickly become "Fight Night". The woman Mom hit looked more stable than other residents in thick-heeled white sneakers. *I bet you can hold your own,* I thought, eyeing her like I was going to wager money on a fight. Sun had left her face etched with deep creases, giving her a weathered, ornery appearance, like she'd seen a few fights in her life.

The common living area felt tense, like at any second the delicate balance at play could turn to chaos. I suddenly longed for the painstaking routine of getting Mom out of the building and into my car.

"I had a strangest thing happen this morning at breakfast," Mom said. *I can only imagine.* "The married couple here, you know the ones that are usually so loving to each other?" Mom said, leaning into my face, her voice changing to a whisper. "Well, I thought he ripped her nose off!"

"Jeez?" slipped out of my mouth, more as a reaction than a reply. In my mind, I immediately changed my wager to this man. He sounded like Mike Tyson in the third round of the Evander Holyfield fight.

"I made a bit of a commotion about it," she said, shrugging it off with a "what are you going to do" attitude.

In twenty-four hours, Mom had hit someone and made a commotion at meal time over a hallucination. I was definitely going to be pulled into

Jannis's office. My mind started filing through back up facilities, when my thoughts were interrupted by Mom's voice.

"Are you ready for the baby?" she asked.

Do I look fat? I thought about all the sweets I'd been eating.

"I'm not pregnant," I replied, placing my hand on my stomach, as I pictured myself telling Travis, "Guess what? We're not empty nesters."

Thirty minutes ago, I'd come into the facility sane, but was now ready to check myself into a psych ward. Out of the corner of my eye, I watched the woman Mom hit, who'd I'd already nicknamed Fight Night, approach the gaggle of women. Her thick-heeled sneakers came to a stop alongside the woman who had been angrily muttering under her breath moments earlier. *Shit, we need to get out of here.* I practically ripped Mom up from the sofa to exit.

Safely back in her room, Mom plunked herself down in the BarcaLounger. "Do you remember the snow that morning?" she said, her eyes taking in the picture of our family in Sedona, AZ, that hung on the wall next to her bed.

"I do. It was gorgeous." I turned to look at the picture. Morning sun had illuminated the copper and pink of the red rock, shining a beautiful coral hue onto the fresh white snow. Our lodge, consisting of small individual cabins, sat atop a mountain of red rock.

"That was a good day," she said, her words fading off.

Leaning on the steering wheel for support, I tried to gather myself, feeling like I'd been side swiped by nostalgia. Memories of Sedona unlocked a release lever that flooded my mind with memories I hadn't visited in decades. An image of Mom showing me how to do the tedious layers of baklava, my hands covered in sticky honey. Mom and Dad coming to pick me up when I was in my early twenties, because a panic attack had left me unable to drive. Decades of memories made the past feel present. *You'll be gone soon. What then?*

"You come into this life in diapers, and you leave this life in diapers." - Bill Kovacs (Dad)

December 11, 2021

Juggling a cup of coffee in one hand and my purse in the other, I climbed into the car. A voicemail from Mom played on the phone tucked between my ear and shoulder.

> Hi Michelle, It's Mom and I need you to call me. We have a problem with the German Shepherd and probably other ones. They're obvious, anyway I'm trying to get together to get something done on saving these animals. So, Michelle here comes...god that's crazy.

Mom's voice quieted to a whisper, then trailed off at the end of the message, as if someone was coming towards her and she was hiding with the animals. *I'll see you in a few minutes*, I thought and turned on the radio.
Buzzzzzz. The blaring alarm sound frayed my nerves until the door clicked shut and returned the common living area to the sound of faint classical

music. The two residents that stood two feet from the door approached me. "Uh, hi. We just need to get something out of my car," the man said, pointing to himself and the woman standing next to him wearing a plastered smile. "You can see the car right there," he continued pointing towards the window. "We'll be quick." Two sets of eyes locked on me waiting for an answer, while I glanced down to catch sight of a stuffed fox tucked snuggly under the man's arm. At first glance, they were a convincing pair, except for the stuffed animal looking up at me that gave them away as residents.

"I don't work here. Sorry," I said, thinking, *You two are pretty slick.*

I spotted Mom creeping along down the green hall. I waved to the man I'd nicknamed One-Step-At-A-Time man, because he always seemed to be standing in his doorway, taking one step out into the hall, then immediately stepping back into the doorway. He'd do this over and over again, wearing a pattern into the carpet. As I continued to close the gap between Mom and me, I came upon Megawatt Mary, the woman who'd welcomed us to the zoo on the first night with her beautiful smile. Stranded, she was stuck halfway into the hall bathroom with her wheelchair caught on the transition ledge between the hall carpet and bathroom tile.

"Looks like you're stuck," I said, then pushed her over the transition.

"Oh, thanks! I was just hanging there," she said, flashing a smile with perfectly applied pink lipstick.

Mom entered her room, just as I came up on Plaid Bunny, the short woman who'd entered Mom's room the first night with her plaid stuffed bunny. Her plaid bunny clutched to her chest, standing just outside her room, she muttered, "Hard day. It's a hard day" over and over. I smiled at all the characters that inhabited the green hall and wondered what characters inhabited the other colored halls.

"Hi, I've got to go to the bathroom." I passed Mom who was sorting pillows on her bed. My fingers were just about to unbutton my pants, when I heard Mom yell, "Get out! No!, No! You get out!"

Is she talking to me? I stepped out of the bathroom to find Mom and Fight Night face to face in a stare off. Mom raised both hands and started shoving Fight Night towards the door. Fight Night, steady on her feet, held her ground.

"Okay, okay," I said, peeling Mom away from Fight Night, as I placed my body between them. Fight Night remained firmly planted in place with her eyes now fixed on me. *Seriously lady, you're going to fight me?* I asked myself. *Could I take her?* I looped my arm into hers and started to move toward the door. Fight Night was tougher to move than I'd anticipated. I too found myself shoving her towards the door. When I finally got her out of the room and into the hall, I closed the door and flipped the lock. "You really should shut your door, " I started to say, then heard, "I wet myself" from behind me. *What?* My mind was still reeling from Fight Night. I turned to see a large, dark wet spot spread over the crotch area of Mom's navy-blue sweatpants.

"Well, let's see," I said, moving toward her underwear drawer. "Do you want me to help you change?" I handed her fresh underwear and pants.

"No, I can do it," she said, giggling like a little girl, as she headed for the bathroom. An absurd amount of time passed before Mom re-emerged from the bathroom. Bored, I'd almost started sorting drawers just like Mom.

I'd intended for this to be my first trial "under thirty minute" visit, but it felt like I'd been here for a lifetime. "I've got to get going," I said, leaning in to hug her. As I pulled out of the hug, I reached down and quickly zipped up her jeans. *At least she was dry.*

On my way out, I popped into Jannis's office to write her a check for rent. My intent was to fill out the check and go, but instead I found myself talking. "My mom wet her pants." I could hear my voice coming out flat, emotionless, like a robot. "Should I get her Pull-Ups?"

"Yes. Just bring them next time you come," she said, placing her hand gently on top of mine. "We have plenty she can use in the meantime."

In a daze, my body slipped into the driver's seat. Dad's voice reverberated in my head, *You come into this life in diapers, and you leave this life in diapers.* One of his favorite sayings, I could see him throwing his head back laughing. Mom's incontinence marked another milestone in the progression of the disease. Through broken sobs, I pleaded out loud with Dad. "Just take her, please take her!" I cried. "Dad, it's so awful. She'd be so horrified. Please come get her!" I felt out of options. Mom's disease was a puzzle I didn't have the pieces to solve. I didn't want to lose her, but I hated what Lewy had done to her life. In my car alone, the most compassionate thing I could do was beg Dad to take her before she had to endure worse.

The aftershocks of these visits rippled through me for days as waves of emotions that at times crashed violently onto shore. Those waves rippled through my relationships. The tension that had been building in my marriage crashed against the shore the evening after my most recent visit. Travis and I hurled hurtful comments at each other, skipping them like stones across turbulent water, until he slammed the bedroom door headed for the living room with his pillow tucked under one arm. Alone in bed, my anger morphed into an all-encompassing whole-body sadness that left me curled up in the fetal position, shaking and sobbing.

Chapter 23
It Takes a Village

December 25, 2021

Travis placed his phone upright on the kitchen counter, so we could both hear Mom's voicemail.

> We can't get in because we need so many cards to get in, otherwise, you're eliminated. So, if you want in somebody has to get the cards or you can try and talk your way in. Whatever. We're just wandering around here, talk to you later.

Otherwise, you're eliminated, her words replayed in my head as I sipped my coffee picturing a scene from Hunger Games.

"I'm off to go grab her," Travis said, stepping out into the garage. "I better make sure I have my card." I heard him laughing as he popped the locks to his car. Travis definitely drew the short straw on Christmas morning.

Gene Ann arrived from Bryan just prior to Mom and Travis returning. The wolf pack, which consisted of my two terriers and Cameron's dog Charli, rushed Gene Ann as she came through the door. In the background Nigel bossed the dogs. "Sadie NO!" and "Get down!" he said, followed by barking sounds.

I saw the bright turquoise walker come through the door before Mom. A large canvas bag hung off one of her wrists, slapping the side of the walker with each step.

"Are you doing okay with everything that's going on?" Mom asked, as she approached her sister.

Gene Ann's eyebrows arched, and she shot me a confused look. "Sister, I'm doing great," she turned to Mom. "Merry Christmas!"

Mom heaved her canvas bag onto the counter, then I felt her come up on my right side. She leaned in to whisper in my ear. "Her trial just started," she said, her breath tickling my ear. "I bet the family of the person she murdered isn't great."

What? She pulled away and gave me a look that conveyed she had just placed a secret in my care. I watched her walk back to the canvas bag, reach in and slide out a book. "Merry Christmas. I didn't know if you had one?" Mom said, handing her sister a tattered Webster's Dictionary.

Gene Ann held the book out in front of her eyeing the worn cover that was holding on by a thread. "Thank you," she said. "I can always use one of these." Mom's hand slipped back into the canvas bag like Santa Clause, then out came a stuffed elf wearing a red and white Christmas sweater. Bulging blue eyes stuck out of its plastic face, making the elf look more creepy than festive. Mom jutted the stuffed elf towards Connor's girlfriend, who quickly plastered a smile on her face. Connor's girlfriend turned the elf from side to side, taking in its strange features. The room fell silent. Chucky from Child's Play came to mind, and I was convinced this elf would come to life as we slept. Just as Mom had Christmas shopped in her house the year before, she'd Christmas shopped at the facility, grabbing whatever items she could throw in her bag before coming over.

Throughout the afternoon, Mom mostly faded to the background, happy to sit among the conversations. As dusk fell and sundowners took effect,

Mom started asking, "Who's going to drive me home?" Code for, "I'm ready to go." Travis, Gene Ann, Mom, and I left for The Cottages.

Gene Ann and I stood on the porch waiting for someone to open the door, while Travis helped Mom out of the car. *Buzzzzzz*. Save for the blaring alarm sound of the door, an eerie quiet blanketed the common living area. No residents lingered by the door looking for escape, no one slept on a couch, even the resident Maine Coon cat was absent.

Directly in front of us, a woman wearing yellow rubber gloves flipped a cushion off one of the chairs onto the floor. A pungent but familiar smell lofted under my nose. *Shit and sanitizer*. I identified the odor before locating the source. Next to me Gene Ann curled her nose up, but neither of us said anything.

"God, what's that smell?" Travis said, dramatically, as he and Mom walked up behind us. I turned and shot him a look nudging my head towards the cushion on the ground.

"What? Ohhhhh!" he said, drawing out the word slowly. The cushion flipped onto the floor had large brown marks running like stripes down the center. It looked like skid marks made by a tire, only these skid marks were made by someone's ass.

The smell faded as we came around the corner of the dining area, where a bright orange cone marked a pool of liquid on the floor. "It's been a bit of a crazy evening," another yellow gloved staff member said, as she threw a kitchen towel down on the liquid. I hoped the liquid was tea and not another bodily fluid. There had to be a special place in heaven for the staff that worked at these facilities.

The green hall was dim and quiet, no One-Step-At-A-Time man wearing a pattern on the carpet or Megawatt Mary. I even found myself listening for The Whistler. The door to Mom's room was open at the end of the hall. I pictured at least two residents roaming around in the room, but instead found a life-like baby doll perfectly tucked into Mom's bed wearing pink pajamas. Lying next to the life-like baby doll was the ceramic dog.

"What a cute baby!" Gene Ann said, heading toward the bed.

"Everyone is opting for these nowadays," Mom replied, nonchalantly gesturing to the life-like baby doll.

"Well, they're cheaper," Gene Ann said, sarcastically.

I thought about all the different places I'd seen

this life-like baby doll in the facility and the proverb, *To raise a child, it takes a village,* came to mind.

Mom and Gene Ann, who held her real dog, Foxy Lady, on her lap, sat on the bed with the life-like baby doll and ceramic dog in the background. "I think I need to give up my dog," Mom said, petting the ceramic dog. "I'm just not around that much and it's not fair to her."

No one had time to respond before a nurse walked in holding a small white cup. Inside the cup was one fucking little pink pill. Just the sight of the fucking little pink pill caused Gene Ann, Travis, and I to tense. Without hesitation Mom flipped the cup towards her mouth and swallowed the pill. *Are you kidding me?*

"What did we do last Christmas?" Mom asked, while she repositioned the ceramic dog onto a pillow.

"I think we were at your house," I replied and could feel the energy in the room turn somber.

Has it only been a year? It was as if we all acknowledged the enormity of change one year had brought. It seemed impossible that in one year, Mom had gone from celebrating Christmas at her house in Lakeway to living in a memory care facility.

Days after Christmas, a thank you card arrived from Gene Ann. In her beautiful cursive handwriting, I read, "We both need to shampoo our hair and I wish she would put on a touch of blush and lipstick."

I burst out laughing, as my mind countered, *I wish she'd wear Depends.*

Chapter 24
Let Them Eat Cake

January 10, 2022

I asked Nana, 93-years-old at the time, "What sticks out to you over the course of your long life?"

Her initial, off-the-cuff answer was, "People. There are so many damn people now." After more thought, she said, "What you care about changes over time. As I age, I spend my time with the people I want to spend it with. And I guess, the experiences with those people."

I thought about this as I planned Mom's eighty-first birthday. Would it be her last birthday? Which people would she want around her? What kind of experience with those people would she want to have?

I shot off text messages to Mom's close friends in the area, as well as her brother and sister. Within minutes, all responded, eager to join. I thought back to all the birthdays I'd had or attended and taken for granted. Life was teaching me that not all birthdays are guaranteed. That lesson was a double-edged sword. On the upside, I was being more present and grateful, but at the same time I was becoming more aware of just how fragile life is. *I should definitely eat more cake!*

The morning of Mom's birthday, Connor and I headed to Costco to pick up the birthday cake we'd pre-ordered. Connor muscled the huge sheet cake, big enough to feed fifty, through check out and out to the car. I knew better than to bring a small cake into a memory care facility. That would all but guarantee Fight Night, not the woman, but an actual Fight Night event. As we drove, I wondered if I should engage Mom in a battle over wearing her Depends or just bring a change of clothes. I decided to go with the flow, no pun intended.

As Connor and I entered the living area of The Cottages, the usual suspects lingered by the door. Connor, still lugging the cake, exuded his typical chill vibe as he sauntered through the facility with two huge crystals hanging off a string around his neck. Following him, I watched as residents started to take notice of the cake. This was subtle, but noticeable, as they snuck in glances and stopped talking just long enough to acknowledge its presence. It was as if they were making a mental note, *Cake on premises.* Mom, who was sitting at the lunch table, smiled immediately at the sight of Connor.

"Hi Grandma," he said, stopping next to her chair, which caused a stir from the residents at the table.

"Is that cake?" I heard from somewhere at the end of the table. One by one, I watched heads turn and eyes fixate on the white bakery box. Just then, a hand gently grabbed Connor's arm.

"Let me take that and put it in the fridge for you for later," Jannis said, swooping in to grab the cake. I'm sure she could sense the flurry of activity building. Out of sight, out of mind. Once the cake was out of the immediate area, the table settled back into eating.

I relaxed when I saw Mom wearing a cute knit sweater that perfectly matched her tan corduroy pants. *Those pants are cute. I wonder who she took them from?* Her face was pale, but she was wearing a simple pink lipstick. *Gene Ann would be happy.* A quick glance around the room and I spotted the turquoise walker with Mom's purse hanging off one of the handles. I couldn't remember a time when Mom was not only dressed, but in clothes suitable for a luncheon. AND, her walker and purse were in the lunch area. Today was a glorious day indeed.

On the way to the restaurant, Mom talked with Connor about her time at the University of North Texas. "You know we didn't have air conditioning back then..." she started a story. I heard, *And I had to walk up a hill, through snow, barefoot.* I marveled at her memories from the 1960s, but mostly I was grateful she and Connor could share this little mostly lucid moment.

The hostess greeted us as we walked into the restaurant. "You must be here for the birthday party?" Mom smiled and followed the hostess, rounding the corner with her walker leading the way. She came to a complete stand still when she saw a large table filled with twelve of her closest friends and family.

"There's the birthday girl," one friend said and jumped up to give Mom a hug. I watched as others stood, forming what looked like a procession line to greet Mom. Her eyes were beaming, and I saw a glimpse of the Mom I had been missing since Lewy joined our lives. Her siblings saw their sister, *Honey Kay.* Her friends saw a glimpse of Kay, the fun friend with whom they'd had countless lunches with. She had several groups of friends who met for lunch regularly. One group she'd coined the Lunch Bunch. It was befitting that everyone had gathered for what might be a last lunch with Mom. We joked that Mom's job was "professional luncher."

Mom took a seat at the head of the table surrounded by gift bags. Everyone talked and laughed as Mom enjoyed chicken fried steak. A birthday brownie holding a single flickering candle, with Happy Birthday scrolled in caramel on the plate, was placed in front of Mom. She took a heaping spoonful, then passed the brownie around for all to sample. COVID be damned. It was a gooey chocolate brownie covered in a decadent sauce; if exposed, we'd all die happy.

Once lunch started to wrap up, I took the opportunity to use the bathroom. When I exited the bathroom stall, Mom's friend was washing her hands.

"I have to ask this, I'm sorry if it's too private," Karen said. "But your Mom told me, and, uh, I guess I'm just trying to see if it's true? Are you and Travis getting a divorce?"

"No," I replied. "She thinks I'm having an affair with a guy that works at the facility. I'm not. I mean, not divorcing and not having an affair."

I said goodbye to those not joining us back at the facility for cake. As I leaned in to hug one good family friend, he whispered in my ear, "Seeing her was hard at first. I thought we were losing our Kay." His voice broke. "But then I could see little glimpses of her in there." I knew exactly what he meant. I'd seen little glimpses too.

Back at the facility, staff had tied three Happy Birthday balloons to one of the chairs at the dining table. The huge sheet cake now bearing a handful of lit candles, was brought out to the table. As we sang happy birthday, I noticed residents starting to slowly circle the table, eyeing the cake. It reminded me of a TV segment I'd just watched during Shark Week. The residents came in slowly for a first pass to check the cake out. Then they grew in numbers and became more aggressive, pulling out chairs and sitting down for the feeding frenzy.

Delusional World Feelings Get Hurt Too

Voicemail from Mom, January 14, 2022

Hi, Michelle, it's your mother and I'm

trying to figure out how we can get back together. I've been hurt, solidly hurt, by all the talking that was happening about me, you were obviously aware that I was there. Anyway, if you want to give me a call. If you don't give me a call, well, that seems to be part of the problem, that we can't seem to get a phone call through half the time. But anyway, I heard it all. I just can't believe that someone would do this to me period, much less my daughter. But enjoy whatever freedom you have at this time and I hope to see you someday in the future.

Three days after her birthday lunch, I listened to this voicemail. Knowing it was delusional didn't stop my hurt. *Freedom, what freedom?* I felt completely caged by my responsibilities to Mom.

Feeling like my eight-year-old self again, I said to Travis, "It's always about her and I'm always doing something to her."

"You know it's not real," he said, giving me a little smirk.

"I know! God, it just stirs up so much shit."

"Hey, don't call her back. This doesn't need a response from you."

"I'm not going to," I pouted, aware that now I sounded like an eight-year-old. "She can just deal."

I decided to jump on the Peloton and peddle out my feelings. *Call from Mom,* read over the speaker of my Bluetooth headphones. Trying to tap the button to ignore the call, I unintentionally picked it up.

"I'm at the hotel across from your house, it's scary. I can see outside," Mom said. My stomach sank. *I really hate these headphones.*

"Mom, I'm on the bike," I said, out of breath. "Can I call you after I get off?"

"I'm watching two men ducking down behind —" she started, but I cut her off.

"I'll call you back," I said, quickly pushing the icon to end the call. I enjoyed fifteen minutes of peace before Mom started rapid fire calling me, each time hanging up before reaching my voicemail. *Why did I give her that damn phone back?*

As I pedaled, I remembered sitting across from my therapist seven years ago, four months sober. "Are you familiar with boundaries?" my therapist had asked.

What the fuck are boundaries? I'd thought.

"It sounds like you need to set boundaries with your mom." She'd handed me a *How To Set Boundaries* worksheet on my way out.

Reading the worksheet, I'd thought about the time Mom had pulled up a folding chair six inches from the stationary bike I'd been riding to be alone. Rather than expressing my needs, like the worksheet said, I'd pulled the headphones out and talked to her for an hour. Months before getting sober, I'd purchased another home that lacked the guest wing Mom would set up residency in for a week at a time, which according to the worksheet was passive aggressive. "You need to convert the garage," Mom had said, walking through the kitchen of my new home for the first time. "That bathroom," she'd said, gesturing to the powder bath, "could easily be opened up and accessed through the garage." In that moment, I'd known if I wanted to stay sober I was going to have to set boundaries.

Now as I watched my phone continue to light up with calls from Mom, I wondered if there was a *Setting Healthy Boundaries With a Loved One With Dementia*, worksheet.

The eleventh time, *Incoming call, Mom* scrolled across my caller ID, I picked up.

"I'm still here at the hotel across from you, she said, jumping in where she'd left off. "There's a couple of guys here that are up to something."

I took a deep breath. "Mom, that's not true," I

said, falling into a familiar trap. "There isn't a hotel across from my house."

"Well, it's the same place I've been and they're looking at me."

Hello paranoia.

"Maybe you could call Danielle or talk to the people there about what you're seeing," I said, my voice catching on a lump in my throat. "These conversations are hard on both of us?" I struggled to fight back tears. *I should be a better person. Why am I doing this when she won't even remember?* My mind instantly shamed me.

"It's hard on me Michelle!" she said, angrily. "It's not hard on you!"

A wave of adrenaline washed through my body. *Here we go. Of course, you're going to bring it right back to you,* triggered thoughts flowed in on autopilot.

"Okay?" was all I could utter, before I heard, *click,* then the line went silent. I thought about all the times in my life when Mom had hung up on me during conversations. If she wasn't getting her way on something I'd hear, *click,* followed by a silent treatment that lasted days or longer. If I pushed back to express my feelings, I'd hear, *click,* followed by a call from Dad to broker peace, which always ended with me apologizing. Throughout my thirties the *click* was so frequent I would shrug it off.

The voicemail on January fourteenth was the tipping point that sent me into a funk. Over the next few days, the funk crawled in slowly, each emotional encounter with Mom taking its toll. My inner dialogue turned morose and zeroed in on all my insecurities. Not only was I fatter than I had been on Friday, but I was also old. If I had the energy to get in front of a mirror, all I saw was my skin hanging off my jaw in little flaps, not to mention the dark spots that riddled my hands and cheeks. As my inner dialogue grew darker, it took aim at highlighting my purposeless life. The simple act of getting out of bed was an achievement. Like a dark vortex, my energy permeated everything around me.

"You're kind of like a black hole right now," Travis said, as I sat slumped on the sofa. *BINGO!* I thought about the actions I'd need to take to start lifting myself from the funk, but instead settled on eating brownies, while my mind told me I was fat.

Working to shake the funk, I deliberately took a break from Mom. During this time, Danielle checked in on Mom. "She thinks you're mad at her," Danielle would say, giving me updates.

Don't get sucked in. Don't get sucked in. Ignore it, I'd tell myself.

Chapter 25
We're Still Living with COVID

January 24, 2022

The appointment for Mom's COVID booster marked the end of my break. The cold air of January sent a shiver through me as I waited on the front porch of The Cottages to be let in. Minutes passed, so I pressed my face to the window to peer in. *Where are the door stalkers?* Shifting from one leg to another trying to stay warm, I started to dial the main number. *Buzzzzzz.* The sound of the blaring alarm caused me to jump as the door slowly opened. A staff member I didn't recognize stood blocking my entrance with her body.

"I'm Kay's daughter," I said. I watched the woman frantically look around. "I just came to grab her for an appointment."

Just then, Jannis came up behind her. "We were just getting ready to call you," she said, also blocking the door. "Your mom and a few of the residents tested positive for COVID. She's fine though. We just can't have visitors."

I remembered the time shortly after Mom was diagnosed with LBD. It had been the thick of the Pandemic and everyone was wearing gloves and masks in stores. Not Mom, she touched everything at Target.

"I'm ready to go," she'd said, dramatically. "If I die, I die." I'd waited for her to lick her hands for effect.

Maybe she just got her wish?

Later that day I received an update voicemail from the facility.

> We've quarantined all the positive residents in the green hall. Your Mom is sharing a room with another female resident who tested positive. She's up and wandering around the isolation wing.

Listening to the message, I quietly hoped the other female resident wasn't Fight Night.

Say What You Need to Say

February 14, 2022

One positive COVID test after another, Mom remained in isolation, granting me more down time. I'd also taken a break from work, the combination of people in early recovery, Mom and my lack of patience was at best 'unpleasant' for those who encountered me. During a deep dive through my garage in search of a document, I found a blue metal lockbox the size of a shoe box, with combo lock on the front. One, four, one, my fingers rolled the little dials to display Mom's birthday month and year. It popped open.

Inside held documents so old the paper had turned to an aged brown hue. Wedged between the documents were what looked like mailed letters and photos in various sizes. A treasure trove of historical information, the box was like an unearthed time capsule that mapped the lives of both sides of my family. Nana's passage into America was stamped in blue ink on her passport. Her young, beautiful face stared back at me. *I never knew this woman*, I thought, as I pictured her as a young immigrant coming into the bustling city of New York all alone. *I wish you had told me more about this time in your life.*

An aged light blue envelope with my grandfather's Hart Furniture logo in the upper left corner held handwritten letters. Carefully, I unfolded the delicate paper of the letter. My grandfather's handwriting bore a resemblance to Gene Ann's beautiful cursive. They were written to *Honey Kay*, my mom, while she was away at the University of North Texas. Each letter signed, *Daddy*.

You were Connor's age, I marveled. The letters depicted a loving relationship between a young woman just starting out in life and her dad.

Mom idolized her father or Daddy, as she called him and intentionally told Danielle and I stories about him to give him life in our memories. I'd been a newborn when he'd suffered a major heart attack at fifty-six-years-old. Mom, who'd been living in Pennsylvania at the time, flew to Texas, leaving two babies under eighteen-months-old with Dad. When she recounted this story, her voice still broke. "I knew he wasn't going to make it and I just wanted him to see you girls (referring to Danielle and I). I showed him pictures of you two," she'd said. "He just would have loved you both." She constantly talked about the sparkle in his eye and how funny he was. "He'd have the whole room laughing with a story," she'd say with a huge smile, like she was transported back in time, sitting in the room with him.

An old, discolored photo with scalloped edges showed Mom, with a time period beehive hairdo. She stood with her friends on what looked like the front steps of a high school. I thought about myself at the same stage of life, just starting out in the world with all the new adventures and struggles to come. I wished she'd talked more about those struggles with me, maybe it would have helped me understand her better.

As I became an adult, I'd speculated that some of Mom's behaviors likely rooted out of some kind of trauma or dysfunction. The toddler-like fits and silent treatments displayed when she didn't get her way, or the quick flip to anger that acted like a pressure cooker releasing rage into the air had left me asking, *What happened to you?* I flipped the photo in my hand and wanted to understand the complexities of this woman. I would have hugged that young woman in the photo.

I moved another photo out of the way to see my own handwriting staring back at me. *Dad, I remember everything*, I began reading my own words, feeling suddenly transported back to 2006, the year Dad was dying. More than fifteen years had passed, but I could still see myself on the sofa, alone, with tears running down my face as I wrote this letter to Dad.

Given six months to a year to live, a friend encouraged me to write a letter saying everything I would want him to know. "Leave nothing unsaid," she'd suggested. I still cry every time I hear the song Say, by John Mayer. The lyrics, *Say what you need to say,* guide my relationships today. I'd known when I wrote the letter that our time together on earth would soon end. Now, as I read the letter, each word layered with cherished memories, I could feel the raw emotions like it was yesterday.

"Oh my god, what's wrong?" Travis said, his comment pulling from 2006 back to 2022. I hadn't even realized I was crying.

"I found the letter I wrote Dad when he was dying," I said, catching my breath. "I didn't realize he'd kept it." A heaviness settled over Travis's face; he remembered me writing this letter too. *I missed the window to say what I needed to say to you,* I thought, wishing I'd written Mom a letter while she could have still grasped the words.

Chapter 26
Outdoor Cat

February 17, 2022

Incoming call, Danielle, scrolled across the caller ID, as I frantically tried to make coffee.

"Are you ready?" Danielle said, knowing I'd be nervous about seeing Mom this morning.

"Not really. It's been a month," I said, then a nervous laugh slipped out. "A lot can change in a month."

In and out of my car two times to retrieve items I had forgotten from inside left me frazzled by the time I got on the road. A bite of the toast I brought on a napkin in my lap caused me to choke, which then caused me to spill the coffee I used to wash it down all over the cup holder. *I probably shouldn't be driving.*

Buzzzzzz. The blaring door alarm sound didn't seem to bother the two residents standing directly in front of the door, blocking my path through the common living area. "Excuse me," I said, navigating through them. Out of the corner of my eye, I caught a glimpse of Mom. Standing in front of Jannis's office, her stark white hair looked like someone had said, "Boo!" and scared all the color out of it. She wore a white, long-sleeve shirt that hung off one shoulder, exposing her bra strap, looking like an aged scene from Flashdance. *At least she's wearing a bra.* As I got closer to her, I thought, *You look like Doc Brown from Back to the Future.*

"I didn't recognize your face," she said, as she approached.

You don't recognize me as your daughter, or you don't recognize my face as anyone you know? I pondered.

"Hi Mom. How are you feeling?"

"Oh. Michelle. It's you. I have a lot to tell you," she replied, like a teenager with good gossip.

Waving my hand to grab the attention of staff to let us out of the building, we started walking towards the door. If there were a recipe for falling, Mom's new way of walking would be the key ingredient. I watched her raise her knee awkwardly high, like someone in a marching band, then bring her foot down, slapping the carpet as it made contact.

"Where's your walker?" I asked, amazed she was still upright.

"I don't have the foggiest idea," she said. "I'm working on training myself not to use it." *That sounds like a horrible plan.*

As if she'd been listening to our interaction, a member of staff shoved Mom's walker in front of her. Mom shot her an annoyed look.

Just in front of the door, a woman with long silver hair contorted her body over one side of her wheelchair, straining to pick up the hairbrush that lay on the floor just out of her reach. Wanting to give this poor woman a win, I gently used the side of my foot to nudge the brush within her reach. Within seconds, her gnarled hand wrapped around it. She lifted her head and began to brush her hair in a zombie like state.

Buzzzzzz. "How do I tell the two Michelle's apart?" Mom asked, over the blaring sound of the alarm.

"I don't know," my voice sounded like I was screaming, as the door shut behind us. "What does the other Michelle look like?"

"She has dark hair."

"Well, I'm blonde, so there's one way," I said, curious who the other Michelle was.

"How old is her mother?" Mom asked, as I hoisted her into the passenger seat.

"Who? The other Michelle?"

"Yes."

"Early eighties," I said, figuring she meant my mother, but really, I had no idea which Michelle we were talking about.

"She looks good for her age."

I'm pretty sure you just gave yourself a compliment, I chuckled to myself.

One look at the bustling Target parking lot and I knew I'd made a mistake. Impatient drivers trying to exit, waited for Mom to inch across the parking lot headed for the entrance.

Inside, Mom floated aimlessly from one aisle to the next, until we stumbled on the baby department, where Mom came to a stop in front of a row of diapers. "Some of the people at the hotel wear those," she said.

Like you, I hope.

Once we made it to the grocery department, I reached to grab the Oreos off the shelf. "Those give me diarrhea," Mom said from behind me. *God, I hope you're wearing Depends today.* I slowly pushed the package back into place on the shelf.

Roaming through nuts and snacks we came upon shelves full of every kind of chip. "Oh! I like the really hot ones," Mom said, with excitement.

"These?" I pulled the bag of Flamin' Hot Doritos her eyes were fixed on off the shelf.

"YES! Those really kick you in the ass," she said, laughing.

No pun intended; my mind automatically finished her sentence. *If the Oreos give you diarrhea, I can't even imagine what these will do.*

Zeroing in on checkout, Mom got distracted by the bright lights of the makeup section, where she detoured to find lipstick. The women in my family were obsessed with lipstick. Twisting tube after tube to inspect the various shades of red, she landed on the brightest red shade possible. With one hand she threw the tube in the basket, while simultaneously reaching between her legs with the other hand. "I think I just wet myself," she said, casually, like an observation. I felt panic surge through me as I frantically gauged the distance to the bathrooms. Removing her hand from her crotch she continued, "These things catch a lot. It's amazing what they absorb." My mind was still calculating the distance to the bathrooms when I realized she was wearing Depends.

"The restroom is right there," I said, gesturing

to the two doors marked 'M' and 'W' that were a stone's throw from the checkout lane we'd just entered. With one eye on Mom, who walked towards the bathroom, I unloaded the cart. *Why is she going into the 'M' restroom?* I questioned, then sprinted to catch her right before she entered.

"You want the 'W'," I said, using my finger to trace a W in the air for emphasis. "When you come out, just stand here and I'll come to you." Returning, to finish checking out, I inserted my credit card. As I waited for the beep sound to remove my card, I caught sight of Mom headed for the exit.

"MOM!" I yelled, frantically throwing the last bag into the cart.

"Do you want your receipt?" I heard the checker say as I ran with my cart to catch Mom. My cart came up alongside her walker just as the automatic doors were opening and a gust of wind almost knocked me over. A front had blown in while we were shopping that dropped the temperature almost twenty degrees.

"It's freezing," Mom said, then literally froze in the middle of the crosswalk.

"Let's go," I said, grabbing the walker still attached to Mom. Like a small train, I pushed my cart, while dragging Mom and her walker through a flurry of cars. All the skills I'd learned as a child playing Twister started to pay off, when I hoisted Mom into the car with one hand, while hooking my right foot around the wheel of the shopping cart to keep it from rolling in the wind. Another strong gust of wind sent my hip jutting to the side to block the walker from blowing off.

Fighting the wind, I shoved the shopping cart into the return bin. Cold wind hit my butt cheek, sending my skirt flying up in a less attractive interpretation of the famous Marilyn Monroe picture. When I finally jumped in the car, I found Mom facing me, talking in mid-conversation. She paused at my arrival, looking confused. "I've been talking to you this whole time," she said. "You weren't here though, were you?" We both burst out laughing.

Back at The Cottages, Mom stood looking out the window. "The kids are re-building the bridge," she said, her finger pointed at the grass area. "There's that cute little dog just playing and playing."

A seismic shift had occurred in Mom's level of engagement with the real world in the weeks since I'd seen her last. With sundowners now in effect and aware that my presence made no difference, I decided to leave.

Alone in my car, I let the past several hours

sink in before I headed home. Mom lived almost exclusively in her delusionary world and although hard for me, she seemed to be more at peace. The underlying frustration and discord caused by living in two worlds seemed resolved. I thought about the constant supervision that had been required today. It was exhausting! When I really thought about it, Mom seemed most content in the familiar setting of The Cottages.

I was reminded of the evening a friend of mine recounted a story of her friend placing her father into a facility. That friend had been concerned with her father not being able to go outside. She'd argued with the facility that her father was an outdoor cat and that outdoor cats needed time outside. I'd laughed at the analogy at the time, but now I understood. *Indoor cat*, my mind played with the phrase. *You're an indoor cat now*.

Providing comic relief to my drive home, Danielle remarked, "She's going to look like the Joker," to my description of Mom's stark white hair and bright red lipstick.

Depressed, But Wearing Lipstick

The separation from Mom that Lewy had caused, hadn't been jarring, but subtle, happening slowly over time. Like strangers with a lifetime of shared memories, I struggled with how to grieve someone who hadn't actually died. A friend once told me that his divorce was like a death, the only difference was that he still had to see his ex-wife. I wondered if Mom and I had gone through a divorce.

Later that afternoon, I received an email from The Cottage's psychiatrist looking for historical information for Mom's psych evaluation. Prior to her new content attitude, Danielle and I had requested an evaluation for anxiety and depression.

Sadness crept in when I started to fill out our family history of depression. Childhood memories rushed in, dredging up time periods I'd long forgotten about. All the times Mom had retreated to her bedroom, ceasing to interact with the world, sometimes for days at a time. As a child, I'd thought she was tired or maybe sick. As an adult, I could see the depression that came and went in cycles. *Suicidal ideation*, the words inked on paper caused a chill to run down my spine. Years ago my sister had struggled with depression, confessing to me that she'd been suicidal at that time. The fear that I could have lost my sister became real as I wrote out our family history. All the funks that had left me barely being able to get out of bed were easier to admit than the suicidal ideation also in my past.

Estrogen, the common denominator linking the depression that ran through my family. Three women, depressed, but wearing lipstick.

I wish you'd talked to Danielle and I about your depression? The thought left a bitter taste in my mouth, while I wondered how life might have been different if she had. I thought about all the help I'd received with therapy over the years since getting sober. Peeling through the layers of shame, I'd gained understanding and insight that positively changed the way I interacted with my boys. *If you'd gained insight into your behaviors, would it have drastically changed your relationship with your daughters?*

What if? was Mom's go to retort to almost anything. Filling out the anxiety section of the evaluation I could hear Mom's voice. "What if you get fired because you'll be new to the company?"

I haven't even started yet, I'd thought when I told her of a new job.

"What if you get in a wreck and die?"

Then I'll be dead, I'd always wanted to say every time she worried about me taking a road trip.

"Geeshh Kay," Travis had said one afternoon,

fed up with Mom's cautionary remarks. "You have a lot of fears."

"I do. There's lots to be worried about," she'd replied. She was serious!

Completed, I sent the form back to the doctor, emotionally exhausted.

A Dance With Time

March 2, 2022

Out to eat with a friend, I glanced at a text message from The Cottages.

> Hi Michelle, Mrs. Kovacs needs a set of pjs. She only has one and her incontinence is getting a little bad at night, having to change her briefs and clothes as well. Please reach out if you have any questions, Thank you.

I forwarded the text to Danielle and continued my lunch. Later that evening, I received a text back from Danielle.

> Jen said three to six months for her mom when she started peeing and shitting herself.

I leaned over to Travis, who sat next to me on the sofa, to show him the text from Danielle, explaining that Jen's mother had died from LBD. The directness of the text sent him into a full belly laugh and I couldn't help but laugh too. Everyone handles grief in their own way. Every time symptoms presented, my sister estimated how much longer Mom had to live. I understood, essentially doing the same thing by obsessively searching for what stage of LBD Mom's symptoms fell into. For me, the act of trying to gauge time to death, grabbed back some sense of control.

When Dad was dying, I obsessively searched online for the life expectancy of Merkel Cell cancer. It was a dance with time itself; Slow down time, and I'm not ready for you to go, speed up time and the pain will be unbearable when you're gone.

Three days later I received a voicemail from The Cottages.

> This is Carla from The Cottages, I'm just calling with an incident report on your mom. She okay, she just fell last night trying to sit down for dinner. We assessed her and she seems fine, but we just wanted to let you know. Please call me if you have any questions.

In what stage of the disease is falling? I asked myself, then hit enter key on the search "Stages of Lewy body dementia & Falling."

Pretend Me Gets Around

March 25, 2022

I dunked a breakfast churro into Nutella and dialed Mom.

"I didn't realize it's surrounded by a moat," I said to Cameron, gesturing towards the grandiose Plaza de Espana in the distance. He rolled his eyes, throwing back his espresso shot.

"Hello," Mom's voice in my ear interrupted the sound of the Flamenco dancers' shoes clacking in the distance.

"Hey Mom, I'm just checking in on you," I said. "Do you remember I'm in Spain with Cameron for a few weeks."

"I saw your partner, he's cute," she said, not registering that I was out of the country.

"I'm still married to Travis," I replied, picturing what the guy pretend me was dating looked like. Cameron shot me a questioning look.

"Okay," she said slowly. "I get it."

No, you don't.

"How is everything going?" I said, switching the topic off my dating life.

"I'm staring at a red walker in my bathroom," she said. "I think I like red better than my blue one."

Whatever.

"I've got to get off. I just wanted to check in on you."

"Is your partner there with you?"

"What? No. Travis is at home," I said, laughing inside because I knew at some point Mom would combine my pretend dating life with Spain to create an international love affair.

"Well, that call was pointless," I said to Cameron after I hung up. I shoved another bit of churro into my mouth thinking, *Pretend me is really getting around.*

Bras Optional

April 17, 2022

"MOVE!" I yelled at the terriers, who seemed to always be camped in front of the oven. The smell of Easter ham filled the kitchen, while I set up for our dinner with Mom and the Smiths, our good family friends. I ran through all the scenarios that could go wrong in my head. *I should probably have Depends at my house in case of an accident.* I remembered the conversation I'd had with Mom last week. "I can't believe Craig left her with only $152 a month," she'd said, her voice cracking. "Just, destitute. You can't make it on that. I don't know what to do."

"Who?" I'd asked, thinking $152 was weirdly specific.

"Sherrie!" she'd said, tears streaming down her cheeks. "Can you believe he did that?"

Whistle, Nigel focused my attention back on my preparations. "Whaaaat!" Nigel said, as if he heard my thoughts, drawing out the word like a dramatic teenage girl.

"I know Nigel. Whaaaat is right. Hopefully Gma won't yell at Craig," I talked back to my parrot who loved drama and probably hoped Gma would yell.

The lemon bars, I'd already been into for breakfast, sat next to an espresso chocolate bundt cake and a vanilla bean bundt cake. Beyond stress baking, my reliance on sweets was starting to look like an addiction.

Travis and Cameron appeared in the kitchen, ready to head out to pick up Mom. "You'll need more time than you think," I started in. "She might be dressed, or she might be in sweat pants and a t-shirt with no bra." Judging from my observations, women over seventy-years-old viewed bras as optional. I envisioned myself older sitting on the sofa eating Oreos and Flamin' Hot Doritos with no bra. That sounded like a little slice of heaven.

"Ooookay," Travis said, probably trying to figure out if getting Mom to put on a bra was a battle he'd pick. About an hour later I heard a text come in.

> Not dressed, no bra. We're headed back with clothes. She can change there.

I laughed, it was pretty good problem solving.

Travis came through the door looking like he'd been through a war. His baseball cap was turned facing backwards, his shirt hung half untucked, and his face looked frazzled. He dropped a bag full of clothes on the counter that looked like it weighed a ton, then started ranting. "We sent her into the bathroom with clothes. It seemed like she was in there forever, so I asked her through the door if she needed help," he said, taking off his hat. "Of course, Cameron and I both were hoping she didn't." He took a breath, trying to dump all the information out before Mom got within earshot.

"Anyway, she finally walked out wearing the same clothes. What does she do in there?!"

I've asked myself the same question many times. Once, I considered strapping a GoPro on her just to see what she did in the bathroom, but then reconsidered, *No, that would end with you needing therapy.*

I was engulfed in making homemade biscuits when I caught my first glance of Mom, who was now walking inside with Cameron. I did a quick double take. *I just saw you not that long ago.* Her face looked ancient and drawn, features jutting out sharply, giving her a skeletal appearance. A bend in her back hunched her forward. Wearing a short sleeved stained t-shirt over another long-sleeved t-shirt and jeans, her stark-white hair stood out on end everywhere, like it hadn't seen a brush in days.

"I need to brush my teeth," Mom blurted out, holding up a toothbrush. I guessed Travis must have crammed it into her hand at some point, literally arming her for personal hygiene. Loose strands of white hair clung to her shirt and jeans as she walked to the bathroom. I desperately wanted to take a lint roller to her.

As soon as she'd closed the bathroom door, Travis leaned over to whisper in my ear. "I solved the locked closet mystery," he arched an eyebrow.

"One of the nurses told me they lock it, because your mom kept packing all her stuff into a suitcase."

"Ah." All I could think was, *Thank god I married this man.*

Like a coach hyping his team for the big game, Travis quickly updated me on new delusions. Apparently, Kelly (Sherrie's daughter) was using hard drugs and going to die. Travis had won some election, perhaps for Mayor. Someone at Mom's place had stolen her phone. Danielle had cancer and was dying. "I think that's it," Travis joked.

The Smiths arrived minutes after Mom emerged from the bathroom, now wearing the change of clothes Travis had packed for her. I quickly surveyed her chest for a bra. *Score!* She was wearing one.

Mom saddled up next to me at the island as I cut out the biscuits. "Did you hear?" she whispered in my ear, as if she was imparting a secret. "Travis won the election."

"I did. We're all really excited," I replied, grateful for Travis's forewarning.

Dinner went off without a hitch. No one wet their pants or screamed at each other. It wasn't a high bar, but it qualified as an enjoyable evening. After Travis had helped Mom into the car to take her back to the facility, I shoved a tupperware container full of lemon bars onto her lap. Then I sat down in the living room with Cameron, who'd had enough Gma time for one day.

"She's kind of obsessed with death," Cameron said, as I shoved a tart lemon bar into my mouth. "Or at least with people who are sick or dying."

"I know," I said, wiping powdered sugar from my chin. "She told me the other day Danielle was dying of cancer, Tommy was too skinny, and Gene Ann, apart from her constant delusional legal battles, was also dying. It's awful, she started crying when she told me about Danielle." I'd seen Mom cry more times in the last two weeks, than I'd seen in my whole life. The tears would come on suddenly, then disappear almost as quickly as they'd begun.

"I think she's processing her own death," I offered. The prospect was making her, understandably, sad, and the sadness was leaking out everywhere.

Chapter 27
Could Recovering Meth Addicts Aid LBD Patients?

May 6, 2022

"You need to put more time between your visits," Travis had pleaded with me after my last visit with Mom. Ironically, Mother's Day was around the corner, but he was right because my limited bandwidth had transformed me into a bitchy, irritated and often angry woman. I'd felt like an outsider on the last visit. Mom's world felt like a snow globe that I stood on the outside of, peering in through the glass. An observer to this whole little world I could witness, but not truly enter.

Taking Travis's advice, I avoided visiting Mom for two weeks knowing she was in good hands with the staff at The Cottages. It took about that long for my body to relax. Enjoying some freedom, I found myself at my favorite restaurant, laughing over dinner with ten other recovering alcoholics and drug addicts. These people were my flock! We had all met trying to get sober and tonight, almost seven years later, we laughed at stories from our past.

At the end of the table sat Gerry, whom I called the storyteller. He could hold an entire room in suspense with his tales of the times when he was still using drugs, predominantly meth. I watched him laugh at a comment someone else made, then continue on with his story. "I'm watching her go through my living room pushing a shopping cart full of my clothes, some of my financial papers, and a chainsaw," he said, hands acting out pushing the shopping cart. "We're both high, so I didn't think anything of it. A chainsaw in a shopping cart! Can you imagine? And nothing, not even a question from me." Everyone broke out in laughter. Later he would recount spending time while high with imaginary people. "We'd have full conversations sitting on my couch. I mean I *knew* these people."

Hm. *That sounded like Mom.*

Two years ago, I would have laughed at Gerry's stories because they sounded outlandish. Tonight, I was laughing because they sounded familiar. Mom constantly gathered random items in the basket of her walker. Not a chainsaw, but only because she didn't have access to one. She too hung out with imaginary people and had full conversations with them. I felt like I knew the imaginary people because Mom talked about them with me all the time.

It got me thinking. I was now back working limited hours at an inpatient rehab facility where I worked with recovering addicts called "techs". The techs were popular and highly effective with the clients, because they could relate, having been through similar experiences. It occurred to me that memory care facilities were missing out on an opportunity. Recovering meth addicts could be highly effective with dementia patients for the same reasons. They could relate to the delusions and hallucinations while exhibiting the patience only someone who has lived it can embody.

No Amount of Key Lime Pie Would Fix This Mother's Day

Mother's Day, May 8, 2022

> Happy Mother's Day, I'll call you later.

As I read Connor's text, I felt resentment creeping its way back into my psyche. Why can't I just spend Mother's Day with my kids? *I'm a fucking mother too.* For fifteen years, Mother's Days had revolved around Mom. Now it was as if my being a mother didn't count.

Just as I started to get comfy in my resentment, memories of the previous year's Mother's Day at Martha's Bloomers filled my mind. *That was only a year ago.* I could see the delicious piece of Italian cream cake I'd had that day, as Mom, Gene Ann, and Gene Ann's two daughters sat around a table talking. The scene was an adult version of the tea parties Mom had organized for me as a kid. That afternoon, Lewy had made quick appearances in the form of random comments, then ducked back into the shadows—a stark difference to Mom's delusionary world of late. I couldn't even imagine what another Mother's Day would look like. My

Did Mom Drop Acid?

resentment faded as I asked myself, *Will she even be alive next May?*

Travis had agreed to go with me over to Mom's for Mother's Day, a sort of Mother's Day gift to me. Waiting for Travis, I stared at the Madeleine cookies and key lime pie I'd bought for Mom on the counter and felt anxious. I didn't even like Madeleines, but now I was thinking about breaking into the container to feed my anxiety.

"You ready?" Travis asked, startling me.

I reached for my car keys and the Madeleine cookies. I thought about leaving the Madeleines for myself for later but resisted. "Yeah. Why am I so anxious?" I asked, following Travis to the door.

Travis blocked my path to the door with his body in an effort to snap me out of my hyper energy and get my attention. "I think it's understandable," he said, making sure he had eye contact. "You're going to see your mom, who doesn't know she's your mom on Mother's Day."

I felt a lump form in my throat as I fought to blink back tears. *She doesn't know me anymore.* My whole life, those two words, Mother's Day, meant celebrating my Mother. *I didn't know Mom anymore.*

We pulled into The Cottages. Travis put the car in park and turned to face me in the passenger seat. "Are you okay? Do you want a minute before we go in?" he asked, waiting for me to break into tears again.

"Let's just do this and get it over with."

"That's the attitude," he said, giving me a sarcastic smile.

Buzzzzzz. Vivian, the weekend nurse, opened the door with a big smile. "Your Mom's been up here looking for you. I told her I knew you would be here." I assumed Mom had been looking for me because of Mother's Day. *Maybe she will remember me,* I thought, hopefully.

One look at Mom, who stood with her walker in the middle of the TV area and I knew I was wrong. Her face looked confused, as her eyes darted around the room. *Is she lost?* Travis and I approached her, but she just stared blankly at us. Travis broke the silence. "Hi Kay. It's Travis. Happy Mother's Day."

Her expression went from confused to fearful. "I've had a really bad time, it's really bad!" Mom said, wringing her hands. My stomach sank. I could feel Travis lightly place his hand on my back, as if he could sense my tension.

I thrust the key lime pie out in front of me. "We brought you key lime pie," I said nervously, knowing there was no amount of key lime pie that would fix this situation. Travis and I always seemed to be armed with pie. Mom remained silent, just staring at us with wide eyes.

Travis took the lead. "Why don't we all go outside with the pie?" he said, starting to move towards the door. "It's a beautiful day out."

I left Travis and Mom by the door to the patio to hunt down a staff member to let us outside. *Buzzzzzz.* The sound of the door alarm blared, sending my heart racing, but didn't faze the residents who acted as if nothing was happening. Mom slowly made her way outside. My butt had barely hit the seat of the wooden rocker, when I heard Mom say, "I was raped three times last night."

What?! Did I hear that right?

Travis sat down next to me and placed his hand on my leg. We both stayed silent. Our silence was a reaction to not knowing how to deal with this delusion. Mom's voice sounded scared. I wanted to acknowledge how scared she must have been, but also didn't want to feed her delusion. I kept waiting for Travis to speak, but he looked like he was in shock. I'm sure he was thinking the same thing.

Mom, now sitting in a patio chair next to Travis, continued, "I'm never going to that house again." Her eyes filled with tears. "He and his mother, um, it was bad." I felt tears form in my eyes. *Please don't cry, Mom, I don't know what to do.*

"Kay, I'm so sorry, I know that had to have felt real to you," Travis tried to form the right words. "But you were here last night. You don't need to be scared. It's just a hallucination."

Mom began to roll up her sleeve exposing her forearm. "I have bruises all over my arms from him beating me," she said, rubbing the skin on her forearm.

Travis and I fell silent again. *What a horrible hallucination.* I turned and looked at Travis, my expression conveying, *I'm so glad you're here.*

After several failed attempts to redirect Mom, only to have her elaborate with more horrible details I said, "Mom, I think that was a really scary hallucination. Um, I'm not seeing any bruises." I prayed this would work.

Rubbing her forearm Mom was undeterred. "They're fading some," she said, moving her fingers up and down her arm and then onto her hand. "I have scars right here. My finger is still broken and bruised." *Damit, she's pointing at a real scar.* Mom had focused in on the thumb of her left hand, which was half its original size. It was discolored and covered with scar tissue from an accident fifty years before, when she'd rolled her car and the steering wheel had torn her thumb off.

Travis sat silent, staring at the rose garden. I couldn't blame him. We were only twenty minutes into the visit, and I could feel myself shutting down, quietly going inward. I waited for the numb, full-body anesthesia that typically followed.

Mom leaned forward and locked eyes with me. "Did the police call you?" she said, her question filled with expectation. "I thought you'd be here earlier; I made a report."

This is a very elaborate hallucination. I realized she hadn't been looking for me earlier because it was Mother's Day, but because she thought the police notified me of the rape.

"The police didn't call me," I said, unable to figure out how to get her off this delusion. "Why don't we go put the Madelines I got you in your room." I was ready to start shoving the cookies into my mouth. I hoped a change in scenery and the walk to her room would distract her enough to get her off this topic.

We made our way through the dining room where two residents were engaged in heated debates, not with each other, but individually with themselves. As we entered the green hall, I spotted Megawatt Mary wheeling toward us. Megawatt

Mary always looked alert and put together with her hair perfectly coiffed and full makeup. I leaned down and wished her a Happy Mother's Day. I didn't know for sure where Mary's kids lived, but I knew she was a mother.

"Oh, you too dear," she said, her perfectly applied lipstick outlining her megawatt smile.

At least someone remembered.

I caught up to Mom who was already in her room rummaging through her nightstand drawer, in search of who knows what. Travis grabbed my arm and leaned into whisper, "I think we should go pretty soon." There was no argument from me. I couldn't wait to get the hell out of dodge.

"Mom, I'm going to put your Madeleines with the Doritos," I said, opening the cabinet to her TV stand. "I guess we'll just give the pie to the staff to put in the fridge." She looked up from her nightstand drawer and stared at Travis who hadn't moved much since entering the room.

"This thing I have, um, with my head," she said, pausing as if to search for the words. "X-rays, there are X-rays you can take, I think? I don't understand what's happening up here," her hand gestured towards her head. I stood frozen. She never talked about her disease, let alone asked questions about it.

Travis jumped in. "Kay, in one area of your head, your memory is not very good," he said, laughing a little.

Mom chuckled too.

"But your imagination area is super charged. Like off-the-charts active causing you to see things." Travis did his best to put it on a level she might be able to grasp.

I waited for the angry defensive response, but it never came. Mom just stared blankly. *Is she thinking about what he said?* This moment of recognition from Mom made me incredibly sad. It would be awful to know your mind wasn't right, but not understand why or be able to do anything about it.

Like a switch, her face went from stone to a smile. "Don't you have golf today?" she said to Travis. "You really need to get going." It felt like she was ushering us out.

Travis took the cue, "We're going to get going. We love you." I leaned in and gave her a hug, as she almost shoved us out of her room.

I heard Travis's seat belt click then, "Holy fuck," he said, releasing a deep breath. "Now I know why you're a wreck for days after seeing her. That was awful. I didn't know what to say. God, what a horrible hallucination."

"That has to be the worst one." I agreed. "I feel so bad for her. She thinks all of it is real." My body felt like jelly in the seat. "I was at a total loss. I basically just shut down, sorry."

"Hey, you really need to talk to your sister about coming out to see her," he said, hesitating. "I know it sucks, but that's not the mom she remembers. That mom is gone."

I know.

Chapter 28
The Attic Family is Real

May 24, 2022

The flicker of the fluorescent lights caused me to blink as Mom and I entered the local grocery store. Mom froze in the entry, the shopping cart in front of her acting as a walker. *Gosh it's loud in here.* I questioned my decision to come, as I watched the chaos of people darting from aisle-to-aisle shopping.

An hour earlier when Mom had wanted to go to Target, pleading, "Let's get out of here. I'm just going crazy!"

I'd thought, *Outdoor cat* and felt guilty. I'd entered Mom's room, to find her talking to herself.

"She's always in here," she'd said, waving her hands around the room. "She's going to take my stuff," she'd continued, her eyes fixed on the open bathroom door.

"Mom, the attic family isn't here. They're not real," I'd said, my patience with the attic family long gone. Mom had just rolled her eyes. "I'm going to use the bathroom. I've had a ton of coffee," I'd continued, as I headed to the bathroom. I'd shut the door, then mumbled under my breath, *I really can't deal with the attic family again.* My body started to lower to the toilet seat when I'd heard a wrestling sound behind the drawn shower curtain in front of me. *Forget it, it's nothing.* My butt hit the seat, then I'd seen a ripple of movement in the shower curtain. *What the fuck?* When I'd ripped the curtain back, a lady stared back at me, her face as startled to see me, as I'd been to see her. I'd recognized this frail woman who roamed the building aimlessly after a fall that had left her with a traumatic brain injury.

"Oh, God. You scared me," I'd said, clutching my chest. I'd looped my arm into hers to guide her out of the shower, then we'd passed Mom arm in arm.

"Told ya!" Mom had said, arching an eyebrow.

Fuck! I'll never be able to convince her the attic family isn't real.

Now an hour later, I was in a crowded grocery

store unable to get Mom to move out of the entry. Dragging the cart with Mom attached, we roamed the isles looking for Oreos. Mom stared up at the bright lights on the ceiling, like she was tripping on drugs everytime we stopped. I wished I were tripping on drugs. *We need to get out of here,* I thought as I grabbed a package of Oreos from the self, then headed toward check out.

My car, acting like a thought incubator, became a space for reflection after visits. *That trip was for me. Why did I feel the need to do that?* Initially I'd thought it was guilt, but realized I missed our lunches, trips to Target, and yes even Cracker Barrel.

Baby Obsession

May 26, 2022

In the middle of facilitating a group at rehab on coping skills for depression (I know ironic), I saw a text come in from Uncle Tommy.

> Michelle, we had a nice lunch. We are thrilled to know about yours and Travis's new baby. We think that's great. We ate at Red Lobster and she enjoyed it.

My aunt and uncle had come in to take their sister to lunch. The image of the three siblings eating cheese biscuits made me smile.

I shot a reply text.

> Travis and I are happy about the baby now that we're not divorcing

My mind drifted to the idea of a baby. *No, No. Definitely no!* Between Mom thinking everyone was pregnant and the life-like baby doll that floated around the facility, I seemed to be talking about babies more than when I was actually having them. The chime of another text, this time from Gene Ann, interrupted my family planning.

> Will she not let you make an appt to style her hair and dye her lashes and brows? I'll be glad to drive in and take her.

I wanted to reply, *I'm more concerned with her wearing Depends than dying her lashes*, but I ignored it. I wasn't about to take a hallucinating woman to get her eyelashes dyed. My aunt's heart was in the right place, Mom's appearance was startling in comparison to even six months ago and I knew that was hard for her sister to see.

Bearded Lady

July 16, 2022

June had been an uneventful month other than the visit Travis and I took to The Cottages where finding Mom had been a bit like the Where's Waldo book series. Only after thirty minutes of weeding through a sea of gray heads moving at the same slow pace, looking a bit lost, had we located her down the wrong hall and in the wrong room. Now, back from visiting Travis's family in Washington, I was feeling refreshed and ready for whatever I might encounter when I saw Mom.

    Perfect Posture Pearl sat in an armchair by the window, wearing a purple sweatshirt with her customary single strand of pearls. When I entered the dining room, a single resident sat in a wheelchair pulled up to a corner of the table, a piece of chocolate cake and a glass of iced tea sat in front of her, untouched. *That's a waste.* I considered sitting down next to her to sneak a forkful of cake. In front of me, halfway down the green hall, a tiny figure looked at one of the oil paintings hanging on the wall like it might come to life. *Maybe it had?* A sage colored shirt hung off Mom's bony shoulders, emphasizing her hunched posture that now leaned slightly to the left. Black velour pants that looked two sizes too big, displayed the outline of her Depends which helped fill out the pants.

I closed the gap, slowing down just before I reached her, scared to touch or startle her tiny frame. "Hi Mom," I said, gently placing two fingers on her shoulder. At the sound of my voice she stopped, then slowly turned her head like an owl, leaving her body in place. She studied me as if I were familiar, but she couldn't quite place me.

"I thought we could go somewhere, get you out for a bit," I said.

"That would be nice," she replied, her voice so soft I found myself leaning into her, almost knocking her over to hear.

Upon entering her room, Mom headed to the bathroom. A minute later I heard, "I don't know if I can get these off in time."

Cracking the door, I saw Mom pulling at the button on her pants. *Buttons are not your friend, velcro and elastic are friends,* I joked to myself and headed to the closet to look for friendly pants.

"It's like a community swap meet," I said to myself, sifting through shirts and pants that didn't belong to Mom. Mom emerged from the bathroom, causing me to turn around. She stood in the center of the room where the sun streaming in cast light on shimmery gray hairs on her chin and upper lip. Intermixed in the chin hairs were a couple of long, coarse, curly dark hairs. I made a mental note to grab a razor at Target. I'd figure out how to shave Mom later. Reluctant to take Mom off site, I knew I'd regret the decision, but guilt from being gone for several weeks won out.

The automatic door slid open and the bright lights of Target made Mom freeze in the entryway. We entered the pet section where Mom stood in front of the dog leashes studying them. "I need to get a leash," she said, grabbing a pink leash off the hook. "And some dog treats."

I thought about the couple of dogs that roamed The Cottages. "Is it a real dog?" I said, the words slipping from my mouth as I was thinking.

"Yes. She's small though," Mom said, putting her hand through the loop at the end of the leash. I had a mental image of Mom walking the halls of the facility with one of those trick invisible dog leashes.

I pulled a bag of dog treats off the shelf. "Let's get the dog treats and we'll get the leash another time." I felt like the moms I'd see at grocery stores who negotiated with their kids that pulled one thing after another off shelves. Mom found something she needed on every aisle and I tried to limit the number of items that would ultimately end up back at my house.

Just like the kids I'd seen at the grocery store, she'd say, "I need hamburger patties."

I'd try to reason, "You don't have a kitchen," just like the moms.

Then on the next aisle, she'd say, "Oh, I want fresh cookies," grabbing a tub of cookie dough from the shelf.

I'd negotiate, "You don't have an oven, but we can get Oreos."

This exchange would go on isle after isle. I detoured to grab a razor on our way to check out, leaving Mom staring at a display of reading glasses. "I need a pair of these," she said, putting a cute pair of bright red glasses on her face.

"Let's look in your drawers," I said, knowing I had bought her at least five pairs in as many weeks.

At checkout, I watched the cashier scan the lemon scones three times without the scanner registering the item. "Can you read those little numbers?" The cashier said, handing me the lemon scones. The tiny numbers blurred together. As I stuck my hand in my purse to fish out readers, I heard Mom say, "You need those red readers." Her memory made cameo appearances at times.

Back in Mom's room, I took the razor from the

bag and grabbed a cup of soapy water. "Mom, can you come over here?" I said, standing in the bathroom. She came around the corner but hadn't noticed the razor or cup in my hand. "You've got a few whiskers," I said, smiling. To my surprise she allowed me to shave her chin and lip. When I dropped the razor into a zip lock bag and put it in my purse, I realized my purse looked just like Mom's huge purse had before Lewy. Mom's purse had been a survival kit of snacks, first aid, and medications. My purse had become a survival kit for a caretaker; Two Depends, in case of an accident, wet wipes for a whole host of reasons, a copy of Mom's room key, individual packs of madeleines, and a zip lock bag with a razor.

That evening Travis and I sat on the sofa, with Finn's burrito shaped body across my lap.

"How did the visit go today," Travis asked

"Pretty uneventful other than Mom looking like the bearded lady," I said, chuckling.

"That's a visual I didn't need"

Chapter 29
Shit Show, a Sequel

August 22, 2022

I saw Uncle Tommy's car as I pulled into the parking lot of The Cottages. He and Gene Ann climbed out when I pulled up next to them. While we exchanged hugs, I tried to prepare them before they saw their sister. "When I saw her two weeks ago, she was pretty frail," I said, pressing the doorbell. "Sometimes she gets frozen in place..."

Buzzzzzz. The sound of the blaring door alarm broke my train of thought.

Inside, pre-lunch activity made the common living area bustle with energy. Like a dinner bell had been rung, residents started closing in on the lunch tables. Spotting Mom, we approached the table. "Look who..." I started to say, then was interrupted by Mom.

"I thought you were dead," she said abruptly to her sister.

"Nope, very much alive." Gene Ann didn't miss a beat. I watched a smile slowly spread across Mom's face, like a switch had been thrown in her mind, turning on recognition of her siblings.

Trying to fold Mom's walker around the treasures she'd collected in the seat left me throwing it half collapsed on top of Travis's golf clubs. When I rounded the car to help Mom get in, she stood stiff, frozen in the stance I'd started calling The Tin Man. Like oil for the tin man, if I assisted her physically, it would awaken her body. With my hand on her back and her hand clutched to the door, she raised her leg, but was unable to get into the seat. *Here we go.* I positioned myself directly behind her to lift her into the car. For as tiny as she was, her limbs turned into floppy extensions like a Raggedy Ann doll, making her remarkably hard to move. The whole effort of getting Mom into the car took more time than it would take us to drive to the restaurant.

Arguably the largest selection of hamburgers hung on a wall above two smiling cashiers. Mom took one look at the dozens of cleverly named burgers, then hung a left towards the bathroom without saying a word.

"She's been gone a while," her brother said, after we'd all ordered and were looking for a table.

"I know, I really don't know what she does in bathrooms," I shrugged my shoulders. "I'll go check." I found Mom, clutching her walker, standing by the automatic hand dryer. Her face told me she had no idea where she was. (*OFSA*) *Opportunity for Silver Alert,* floated through my mind.

Outside, Gene Ann and Tommy sat at a picnic table, trays of paper wrapped hamburgers and fries laid out like place settings waiting for our arrival. It took me a minute once I sat down to realize that Mom wasn't sitting with us. Standing behind me was The Tin Man. An image of her trying to get in my car an hour earlier sent me climbing off the bench to help her.

"I can't hear you," Gene Ann said, for the tenth time across from Mom, who now sat on the bench next to me. I was convinced she'd fall backwards and crack her head open. Conversations made up of, "What?", "I'm not sure I understand" and "I can't hear you," left everyone worn out.

Back at The Cottages and worn out from lunch, I watched residents surround the ice cream table in the activities room like bees returning to the hive. Always up for ice cream, we grabbed a table. Five minutes later, Mom abruptly stood up, grabbed her walker and started to head in the direction of the hall.

"Where are you going?" I said, jumping up from my seat.

"The bathroom." She waved her hand to dismiss me.

I polished off the end of my ice cream and looked at the time. *What was she doing in the bathroom?* "I'm going to go check on her. I'll be right back," I said to Gene Ann.

"Mom," I knocked quietly on the hall bathroom door. Nothing. When I pushed the door open, the smell of shit knocked me backwards. A gag reflex in my throat sent my hands covering my mouth. Hunched over, facing the toilet, was Mom with her pants and Depends down around her ankles. In one hand she clutched a paper towel covered in shit. Scattered, like fallen leaves were other paper towels covered in shit all around her feet. *What happened here?* I thought, as I noticed the toilet seat covered in shit smears. I felt the urge to block the door with yellow crime scene tape, because it looked like a crime scene where shit substituted blood.

"Ooookay, I'm going to just take a look at your bum." I said, lifting her shirt up. Remarkably she'd done a decent job of cleaning herself, which explained the dozens of shit smeared paper towels on the floor. Wishing she'd just used the Depends, I reached down around her ankles to pull up the unsullied Depends and pants. "You're going to need to throw that one away," I said, motioning to the paper towel still clutched in her hand.

"I can't," she said, her eyes confused. Careful not to touch the brown smears, I uncoiled her fingers from the paper towel and dropped it in the trash. Just then, a staff member poked her head in through the door I'd left cracked open unintentionally. "I can get that," she said, a bucket and a mop next to her.

"Thank you!" I almost cried with relief.

Back at the table, Gene Ann and Tommy looked at me with questioning eyes.

"Don't ask," I said.

"She's gone downhill," I said to Danielle, fighting back sobs as I drove home. "I think we're getting to the end." A surreal conversation with words like, *feeding tube* and *hospice,* followed.

August 25, 2022, Voicemail from Danielle

> I talked with Jannis. I'll forward the signed DNR. Also, she said she doesn't think a wheelchair yet but will let us know. As far as the feeding tube, they are all about quality of life, not quantity, so when it comes time we can choose the tube or not and just make her comfortable with hospice.

Voicemail from the Cottages, September 1, 2022

> Your mom had a fall, a caretaker found her on the ground. I had the doctor check her out but everything is fine. Feel free to call if you have questions.

    I tried to remember how often she was falling, *Once a week? Every couple of days?* Whatever it was, it seemed like a lot.

Dear Mom, I Love You. That is All

September 18, 2022

While I gawked at the thick white icing on a pumpkin scone, the barista busily steamed milk for the latte I'd just ordered. Caught off guard, I grasped my chest trying to calm my breathing which had suddenly quickened and felt strained. A tightening in my chest sent a tingling sensation to my fingers. *Oh my god, am I having a panic attack?* Ironically, my mind panicked. I grabbed a bag of coffee beans from the display and started squishing the beans with my fingers in an attempt to distract myself from the impending feeling of doom. *Deep, slow breaths,* I said to myself, then felt my heart rate slow. As fast as the attack had come on, it washed away with the same momentum. *Am I stressed?* I questioned, but then decided overthinking never helped anxiety.

Back in the car, I tried to think of the last time I'd had a full-blown panic attack. The memory of myself sitting in a folding chair, using my floral skirt to wipe the moisture off my tingling hands rushed to mind. I'd found myself in that chair after the substance abuse outpatient program I was enrolled in suggested it.

The counselor had said, "You wouldn't be here if your drinking was manageable," as she shoved a list of AA meetings into my hand.

I'd remembered the same words, *we admitted we were powerless over alcohol, that our lives had become unmanageable,* from the AA Big Book the night I'd tried to read it on my Kindle, one eye closed to focus because I was drunk.

The counselor had then said, "Listen to what's said, I think you'll find you relate."

I remembered thinking, *I'm not an alcoholic!* Sitting in that folding chair, I'd watched a handful of women, all who stated their names followed by "alcoholic" or "grateful alcoholic" which blew my mind, take seats around three long folding tables set up in a horseshoe. I'd continued to wipe my damp hands on the floral skirt the whole meeting, feeling trapped inside my head, as I fought off a panic attack.

In the middle of the mental gymnastics of trying to reconcile how my drinking had landed me in the room, I'd heard, "If you're like me, you've earned your seat here."

Earned. Had I earned my seat?

"I think I've earned a Starbucks," Jannis said, the word, *earned*, merging the memory to present. I looked down at the two cups of coffee, one in each hand, and gave her a smile. Mom sat on the corner of the lunch table, her meal untouched with the exception of being moved around the plate. A couple of green beans that had been thrown off were piled on the table next to the plate.

"Where have you been?" she said, annoyed.

I placed the Starbucks in front of her. "I've been visiting Cameron," I said, pulling out the chair next to hers. Three more green beans fell off the arm of her sweater when she reached for the coffee.

"Let's go anywhere, wander, get out," she said, waving her hands around in front of her. *Indoor cat*, I reminded myself and guided her towards the common living area. On the sofa, I leaned back and I pulled up pictures of Cameron on my phone.

As I started to lean over to show Mom, I heard, "Do you have a pen?"

A female resident wearing a green sweater and navy polyester pants that showed the outline of her Depends leaned over to meet my face. I didn't recognize this resident which sent my mind into overdrive thinking about all the scenarios for why I shouldn't give her a pen. *It's not a knife*, I thought. *How much damage could she do?* I watched her scribble something on a small post it note then politely hand the pen back to me. If sticky notes worked as reminders, this place would be wallpapered in them.

"Auntie, my auntie!" a visitor yelled, her legs doing a little happy dance, as a woman, presumably auntie, was wheeled out in front of her. I watched as staff handed the visitor auntie's overnight bag and reviewed medications. In awe, I couldn't imagine taking Mom to my house overnight. Forget the risk of falling or fear she'd leave the house in the middle of the night, I couldn't imagine engaging in her delusions for twenty-four hours. A sense of guilt took hold for a moment, then quickly abated as Mom nudged me, her eyes looking at something in the corner. "Over there," she said, gesturing to the corner. "That man doesn't like me." There was no man.

The resident who borrowed the pen slowly approached Mom's side, then quietly waited for us to glance her way. "Sorry to bother you," she said, leaning down to Mom's level. "Did either of you happen to witness the argument over there?" She gestured behind her.

"No," I said more forcefully than intended. I knew better than to sign up to referee Fight Night. At any given time, there were several disputes, fights, or arguments taking place between residents. It was a little like air traffic control, you had to always be on alert to keep planes from colliding. I hadn't factored engaging with other residents in my grand plan to sit casually with Mom drinking coffee in the common living area, next time we'd go to her room.

Sadness became my bed fellow in the days

after the visit. An acceptance that Mom would die covered me like a blanket. *I love you,* played over and over in my head, but wasn't followed by the usual denial, anger, and resentment. Just, *I love you and you're going to die.*

The "Why didn't you see me or hear me?" resentment turned into images of Mom with my boys, her eyes filled with unconditional love. Frustrations with what could have been turned into gratitude for the parent she was. Her limitations as a mom turned into understanding her as a woman, not just my mom. The petty feelings about our past seemed to evaporate, leaving death staring at me waiting for me to blink.

When I blinked, I saw forgiveness, like a friend sitting next to me saying, "Dah, I've been waiting for you."

Over the last couple of years, I've been through the gamut of anger, resentment, analyzing my childhood, critiquing my relationship with Mom, you name it, I've walked through those emotional valleys. It felt like a life coming full circle, the ending titled, *Dear Mom, I love you. That is all.*

Don't Drink, Don't Smoke, What Do You Do?

September 23, 2022

In a good mood, carrying brownies and vanilla ice cream in from the car, a belated fiftieth birthday treat, I heard the chime notifying me of a text message.

> Michelle, your mom fell backwards no visible injury but she is complaining of dizziness and hit her head hard. Sending her to Seton Williams for eval. EMS on the way here.

I felt my good mood fade as I read the text from Jannis. I called Jannis who reassured me the hospital visit was more precautionary than emergency and that they would call me with any significant news. My mind fumbled through thoughts, *Should I go to the hospital? Would my being there even with her not recognizing me be helpful? Do I pace myself? This would definitely not be the last hospital situation.*

As if reading my mind, Travis said, "Don't rush up there," he slid the containers of brownies toward me. "There'll be plenty of other things that come up. Don't wear yourself out when you don't need to."

An hour later I received a text from the hospital prompting me to do the online patient registration for Mom. A nauseous feeling took up residency in my stomach, as I completed the online forms. The thought that sweets would no longer soothe my emotions sent me into a pity party, where the lyrics to Goody Two Shoes, *Don't drink, don't smoke, what do you do...* played on a loop in my head. Sitting with my feelings sounded horrible. *Seriously, you're a counselor for fucks sake. Sitting with your feelings isn't breaking news*, my mind scolded me.

Just as I was playing out worst case scenarios, the hospital called with an update. "Her scans came back fine," the nurse said. "Just waiting for labs then we'll release her."

Chapter 30
The Decline

October 4, 2022

Skilled Nursing, in the subject line of an email caught my attention, as I waited in line at the grocery store. Seeing it was from Jannis, I opened it.

> MICHELLE,
> WE'VE BROUGHT IN SKILLED NURSING AND PHYSICAL THERAPY DUE TO YOUR MOM'S RECENT DECLINE. THEY ACTUALLY HAVE TESTED HER URINE AND LAB WORK, EVERYTHING IS COMING BACK NORMAL. SO, IT LOOKS LIKE HER DECLINE, WEAKER, MORE UNSTEADY, IS PART OF HER PHYSICAL DECLINE.

Jannis's words just confirmed what I already knew; Mom was declining. After the facility had called me last week to approve a hospital bed, I popped open my laptop to do an online search for, "hospital bed and LBD". Links to End Stage Lewy body dementia appeared, displaying several links I'd visited before. Scanning the list of symptoms, I mentally put a check mark next to, *hospital bed*, then wondered how long it would be before I could check mark, *feeding tube*.

BarcaLounger Regrets

October 16, 2022

A man, whose pants looked like they might fall to the floor at any moment, assessed the telltale blue Oreo package I was holding as I walked past him toward the dining area. When I rounded the corner, I heard a news anchor discussing Russia's invasion of Ukraine and longed for the Hallmark Channel. I figured Mom would think military tanks were surrounding the facility if she watched the news. Halfway down the green hall I spotted Mom. She struggled to lift her head which seemed to be permanently pointed towards the floor nowadays, like her neck muscles just threw in the towel. She flashed a little smile before her head gave way to gravity again. I started to smile back but couldn't focus on anything but her tiny frame that was so small she looked more like a ten-year-old girl. *How could you have lost more weight?* I pondered, baffled by how an already tiny frame could become tinier.

"Where have you been?" she said, managing to hold her head up.

"I've been in Denton seeing Connor," I replied.

"Oh," she said, pausing like she was going to say something else, but didn't, then started moving forward. I actually thought it would be impossible for Mom to move slower, because in my mind that would just be standing. I was wrong, there's a speed between painfully slow and standing, that was Mom's speed.

"I just get so tired," she said, stopping for a minute. "I can't breathe sometimes." My mind frantically tried to remember if *trouble breathing* was a symptom in End Stage LBD, then I felt like an idiot since end stage meant death, so of course there would be trouble breathing. We finally, and I mean FINALLY reached her room. When I stepped inside, I froze, like The Tin Man, in front of the hospital bed. The bed sat close to the floor, like a lowrider car. Handrails ran the length of the bed for safety, yet the fall from the bed to the floor was maybe a foot. Mom would more or less roll to the ground from that height.

Mom had positioned herself in front of her BarcaLounger with an expression that looked like she wanted to sit down but couldn't remember how. After some gentle attempts to bend her into the chair, I moved around her body trying to assess whether to take her out behind the knees like a wrestling move or to push down on her shoulders. I chose the latter which caused her body to mostly fall into the chair, where she then began to slide down the leather fabric like jello towards the floor.

Regretting the purchase of the BarcaLounger, I asked, "Can you push up?" Her lack of response sent my hands under her armpits to heave her off the floor. Her frail body was always heavier than I expected, causing us both to fall back into the chair stacking on top of each other. Peeling my body off hers, I grabbed a pillow from the bed and shoved it behind her back to stabilize her tiny frame in the oversized chair.

Thirty minutes later, I stopped the weekend nurse to let me out of the facility. I watched her punch in the code, feeling my body tense in anticipation of the blaring alarm.

"Your mom's lost weight," she said, as she pushed the door open.

"She's tiny, I just saw her a week or so ago," I said in disbelief.

The emotional dump truck pulled up after the visit, piling my messy emotions everywhere. When I wasn't crying, I felt numb. When I wasn't numb or crying, I felt irritated. I had no bandwidth to handle life's simplest tasks. Even the simple task of feeding the dogs turned into a catastrophe. A ripped dog food bag sent kibble all over the floor and left me crying, crawling on my hands and knees to pick up the little pieces, when the broom in the laundry room mere feet away would have done the trick.

Knocking on Death's Door

October 24, 2022

A week later, I found myself on a ZOOM call, with Kristy and Tamara, both senior care associates that worked with Leslie. When I saw myself on the camera, I looked like I'd aged in dog years. My stoic face on the screen listened to the women talk about specialized toilet seats, as my mind thought, *We're way past toilet seats, she wears Depends.* Then the words, *small cottage,* floated in and out of sentences.

"Michelle," hearing my name snapped me out of the trance. "Do you want me to talk to Jannis about moving her to the small cottage or do you want to?"

"I will," I heard myself say, but felt detached. I wondered what the small cottage looked like inside. Then my mind created images of Mom at the end of life. I saw her laying in a bed, lifeless, like the night I'd found her years before in the hotel room with her mouth dropped open in a permanent scream position. The word, *hospice*, drew my focus back to the women talking on the screen.

"With her recent weight loss, falls, and diagnosis," Tamara said. "They'll be able to qualify her."

Small cottage, hospice, weight loss... the words played on repeat in my head. *Is this the end?* I asked myself, but realized I had no idea what the end looked like. I spent the next hour online, my fingers frantically typing, *end of life, end stage LBD,* and *how do you know if someone is nearing the end.*

The next day I sent the following email to Jannis.

> HI,
> I MET WITH KRISTY AND TAMARA YESTERDAY TO TALK ABOUT MY MOM AND WANTED TO GET YOUR INPUT WHEN YOU HAVE A MINUTE. I SAW HER LAST SUNDAY, SHE HAD LOST A LOT OF WEIGHT IN BETWEEN THAT VISIT AND THE VISIT ABOUT TWO WEEKS BEFORE AND WAS REALLY WEAK. SHE SAYS SHE HAS A HARD TIME GETTING OUT OF BED AND LOSES HER BREATH WALKING.
>
> I STRUGGLED TO GET HER IN HER BARCALOUNGER, SO I ENDED UP BASICALLY PICKING HER UP. THE BARCALOUNGER, I GET, IS NOT THE RIGHT CHAIR NOW, BUT IT SHOWED ME SHE REALLY CAN'T GET IN AND OUT OF STUFF, TOO WEAK. I'M NOT SURE HOW SHE'S NAVIGATING THE BATHROOM, OR IF SHE IS. ALL PART OF HER DISEASE AND I KNOW YOU'RE AWARE OF THIS TOO. WE DISCUSSED THE OTHER COTTAGE AND HOSPICE YESTERDAY, IT WAS KRISTY'S ADVICE TO START LOOKING IN THAT DIRECTION. WHAT ARE YOUR THOUGHTS? I'M IN HOUSTON TODAY, BUT AROUND THIS WEEK OTHER THAN IF YOU WANT TO TALK, OR IF EMAIL IS EASIER THAT'S FINE TOO. THANKS!

Reply from Jannis:

> HI, MICHELLE. THANK YOU FOR REACHING OUT. I WANTED TO TALK TO YOU NEXT TIME YOU CAME TO VISIT. YES, SHE IS DEFINITELY STRUGGLING MORE PHYSICALLY THESE PAST TWO MONTHS. UNFORTUNATELY, SHE IS NOT WANTING TO USE A WHEELCHAIR. SHE STILL HAS GOOD DAYS, AND WALKS AROUND OKAY, BUT SHE IS HAVING MORE DAYS WHERE SHE IS STRUGGLING. WE ARE TAKING HER TO THE BATHROOM ON SCHEDULE NOW. SHE IS NOW INCONTINENT. WHEN WOULD YOU LIKE TO COME IN SO WE CAN DISCUSS HOSPICE AND LOOKING AT THE SMALLER BUILDING?

The email punctuated my feeling that Mom was knocking on death's door. When *death* would answer the door was anyone's guess.

"I think it'll be okay for a week while we're gone," I said to Danielle, as I ran her through an end-of-life practice run. Travis was scheduled to speak at a conference in Germany and I'd decided to join him. We discussed who would need to be notified if *death* said, "Just a minute" from behind the door.

Cottage Dollhouse

October 26, 2022

When I entered the small cottage, I was struck by how much it looked like a mini replica of the other cottage. If the other cottage had a dollhouse, it would be this cottage. The same floor plan, just scaled down in size. It quickly became apparent that most of the inhabitants were non ambulatory or barely ambulatory. When I ventured down a shorter version of the hall that held business offices, I found Jannis on the phone. Waiting, I watched a group of women in wheelchairs sit around a circular table in a small activities room.

"You ready?" Jannis asked, waving me to follow her as she started to walk towards a yellow-colored hall containing half the amount of resident rooms as the other cottage. As if reading my mind, Jannis said, "We have one resident that is moving over from the other cottage next week, then your Mom would be next on the list."

"What is a typical time for this stage," I started to say, but stumbled on the words. "I mean, end of life. I guess what I'm trying to say is, once they've moved over here, how long do people stay here?" The words felt insensitive, but I found myself desperately grasping to the illusion of control over time. Or control over when *death* would get up off the sofa, walk over, and open the door for Mom.

"Three years with us," she gestured with her hands indicating both cottages. "That's a really long time. Typical is one and a half to two years." Her warm eyes locked on mine for a response.

"I'm not in denial," I replied, and felt the protective armor take its place on my chest. "I know where we are in this."

She just gave me a smile that conveyed, you don't know, but that's okay. When we parted ways, Jannis informed me hospice would be assessing Mom tomorrow.

Germany

November 3-9, 2022

Motorized bikes with large plastic buckets over their front tires, carrying everything from small kids to pets, passed me on my left, as I made my way down a side street towards the Marienplatz. The smell of warm yeast and butter lofting from a bakery made me hungry. Once I'd tried a pretzel in Munich, I realized I hadn't really ever experienced a pretzel in the US. I stepped inside, then pointed at the turkey sandwich on pretzel bread. When I sat down to eat my sandwich, I saw a text from Danielle and one missed call from a number I didn't recognize. I shoved a bite of pretzel bread in my mouth and opened the text.

> Just talked to Mom. She sounded "good". Completely out of it, but in good spirits/delusional.
> Thought I was you and something was burning down. They were getting ready to eat their Thanksgiving and Mom was excited for the pies.

I'd forgotten the facility was celebrating Thanksgiving early and that I'd asked Danielle to call her to check in. Next, I hit play on the voicemail. I felt my stomach tighten as a hospice nurse introduced herself. The tension I felt eased as she continued to say she was just providing an update to let me know they'd received all the necessary paperwork to initiate care and she'd done an initial visit with Mom. I waited for the bad news, but none came. In fact, the nurse ended the call by saying, "I found her out in the living area talking with another resident. She's a little congested but was having a good day." And just like that, it was as if *death* had hung a "Do not disturb" sign on the door.

Be Careful Not to Catch Death

November 24, 2022

Thanksgiving was shrouded in what I could only describe as a "death haze." Images of my visit last week where Mom had been unable to stand, left me with the realization that I would never have a parent present at a holiday again. I felt like death was everywhere! Mom was dying, I'd received a call that a family relative had been diagnosed with stage four cancer, and Dad's death had seemed to lodge itself in my mind, stirring up old grief. Not to mention the countdown to my own death I'd started in my mind since turning fifty. Mostly though, my anxiety focused on the people I loved dying, as if death was contagious and once in the air, everyone would get it.

In one of my "be sure not to catch death" rants I said to Connor, "Be careful! I-35 is horrible with all those trucks," the morning he was set to drive home from Denton. "You have to be paying attention all the time!" *I'm turning into Mom*, I thought, realizing my fear sounded just like Mom's fear had when she'd worried about me getting in a wreck driving home from college. The impermanence of life left no family member safe from my rants.

"You need to get a colonoscopy," I told Travis, as he sliced the turkey. The sight of the knife cutting through the meat made me remember seeing Mom last week. Using a fork to hold a white paper napkin on the plate, Mom had used a butter knife in her other hand to slice away at the napkin.

"I'm going to give half of this to you," she'd said, trying to slice through the napkin until she finally gave up and placed the whole napkin in front of me. When I'd left the napkin untouched, she'd said, "Did you eat already?" to which I'd replied, "I'm good. I had something before I came." Then I'd placed the napkin that looked like it had been through a war, back on her plate.

Later, Travis and I sat on the sofa eating chocolate cream pie while Nigel, who'd spent the day saying "chicken" and "you're a good boy," sat on his tree perch next to us eating part of a turkey leg.

"You have to stop," Travis turned to me, his face serious except for the blob of chocolate pudding that clung to his chin. "Look, I get it, but obsessing about something happening to me or the boys, well, it's just a lot." He was right, but I just plunged my fork into the chocolate pudding filling and didn't respond.

Chapter 31
The Final Cottage

December 9, 2022

"It would be easier if she were gone," I said to Travis through sobs. "It's just so weird. It's like she's here, just up the road, but also already gone." Travis took his eyes off the road to quickly look at me in the passenger seat. I realized the tears I felt falling down my cheeks had taken my mascara with them.

"Are you sure you want to go to dinner?" he asked, as we pulled into the parking lot of the restaurant.

"Just give me a minute to pull it together," I replied, digging through my purse for a tissue to clean up my makeup. Coming up short, generally baffled that with all the items in my purse I didn't have a tissue, I considered using a Depends, but decided I'd make do with my fingers.

Over dinner, I tried to put words around what it feels like to wait for someone to die but found the words messy and vague. "It's like waiting for the body to die, because the person is already gone," I said, fighting back tears. Across the table, Travis's face told me he was scared to say the wrong thing.

The following day, while out for an afternoon walk, my bluetooth headphones read a text from Jannis.

> Michelle, your mom just fell. Complaining of dizziness, hospice will be here in twenty mins, she's alert no obvious injuries. She is talking. Do you want us to call 911 or okay to wait for hospice?

I texted back.

> I think hospice is fine. Thank you for letting me know.

Two days later Travis grabbed my shoulder which caused me to jump. He motioned for me to shut off the mixer. "Your sister is texting me to tell you to call her," he said. I grabbed a kitchen towel to wipe the cookie dough off my hands and grabbed my phone that was face down in the flour that had spilled out of the mixer. I blew on the screen to clear the flour and realized my ringer had been turned off. Seeing multiple missed calls and a text from Danielle, I tapped on the text message.

> Call me Mom is not good at ALL! Hospice is coming in. She fell and her lungs are filling up with fluid. I just talked to the nurse and she said it isn't good at all.

I stared at the text, baffled and dialed Danielle.

"The weekend nurse said her lungs are filling with fluid," Danielle said. "I was super straight with her, like she's dying, and we know she's dying."

"What? When did this happen? She was just a little congested," I replied. Images of Mom from four days ago at the facility's Christmas lunch filled my head. *That was a good day*, I thought, remembering Mom sitting between Travis and I in the activities room, smiling in her red Christmas sweater with the puffy snowmen.

"Hospice is coming to assess her, but the nurse said her chest had a little raspy sound and she has a fever," she paused to take a breath. "But she said she doesn't look good."

"Okay. Shit, well, I guess let's see what hospice

says and I can head up there if I need to," I replied, shoving the balls of cookie dough I'd put on a sheet pan while talking into the oven.

A couple of hours later, hospice called and gave Danielle an update that Mom had an upper respiratory infection that was caught early, and they'd do a chest X-ray in the morning.

December 12, 2022

The next morning, I awoke to a text from Jannis.

> We are moving your mom to North cottage today.

(Me)

> Thanks, how's she doing this morning?

(Jannis)

> Alert but pretty weak. Chest x-ray shows bronchitis. Hospice will start her on antibiotics.

As I sipped coffee the words, *upper respiratory* and *bronchitis*, floated around in my head, joined by the information I'd seen in one of my many online searches about pneumonia being a common cause of death in LBD. Before I'd finished the first cup of coffee, I was already online searching again for pneumonia and LBD.

Twilight darkened into dusk with me perched in a lawn chair on the back patio already in pajamas. "It's really happening," I said to Travis, more like a proclamation than a comment. "Like I really get that she's going to die." The words fell out of my mouth, but I realized the words were for me not Travis. Situated in the liminal space between life and death, the small cottage acted like a waiting room to the other side. After numerous moves, I couldn't ignore that there would be no more moves. The small cottage would be the final cottage.

At Least You Have Lipstick On

December 14, 2022

Like my own personal hype man, my thoughts repeated, *You can deal with whatever you see* and *You knew this was coming,* while I drove to visit Mom for the first time in the small cottage. Anxiety rode shotgun like an old friend, its presence percolating, sending each individual cell in my body into vibration. *I'm going to break out in a rash,* I thought, remembering the ocular migraine that had left me with kaleidoscope vision yesterday.

A fork split the entrance driveways to The Cottages. *You go left*, my inner voice prompted, fighting the inner autopilot that wanted me to turn right like I had since April. Once parked, I took a minute to calm myself before heading to the front door of the dollhouse version of the larger cottage.

Before I rang the bell, I glanced down at the door handle, but no one was trying to get out. I heard the familiar click of the door opening. "Hi, I'm Kay's daughter," I blurted out nervously to the poor woman who hadn't even opened the door fully. "She just moved over here."

"She's over here just around the corner," the lady said, gesturing for me to enter. The woman's bronze colored eyeshadow and dark blue eyeliner looked like she moonlighted as a cosmetics influencer, but also made me conscious of my own makeup or lack thereof.

"How you doin'?" a man's voice caused me to whip my head around. Slouched forward in a wheelchair, wearing striped knee-high athletic socks and shorts, a man looked up at me. "How you doin'?" he asked again, and seemed to flash me a coy smile. *You sound like Joey from Friends,* I thought and smiled back. I found myself wondering what the man had been like in his younger years. *I bet you were a player*, I reasoned, then remembered the article I recently read about STDs running rampant in assisted living facilities.

Moving on, I walked into the south wing of the cottage where a small kitchen opened onto a dining area with a rectangle table that could seat six. Just off the dining area was a small living area that had couches set up in the same configuration as the larger cottage, except for the cloth seat cushions were chocolate brown leather. I remembered the large shit stain on the chair cushion from last Christmas and thought chocolate brown leather was a smart choice. A TV played a Hallmark Christmas movie rather than news, which almost sent me into tears, but I held it together. At the end of a row of residents in geri chairs (padded, reclining chairs on casters designed for geriatric patients with limited mobility), intermixed with wheelchairs, sat Mom hunched over in a navy-blue wheelchair.

The sight of her took the air out of my lungs. *Breathe,* I reminded myself. Her collarbone looked like a plastic ring with skin draped over it. A sage colored sweatshirt that looked three sizes too big, showed her protruding shoulder bones. Every vertebra running down her spine was pronounced by the hunch in her back. Unaware of my presence, I took a minute to gather myself before approaching her. As I got closer, I saw someone had applied pink blush to her cheeks and just a hint of rose-colored lipstick. *Well at least you have lipstick on*, I heard Mom's voice in my head.

"She won't eat," a woman dressed in scrubs said, leaning over to strap a blood pressure band on Mom's arm. "I've tried several times." Before I could respond, a man in his young thirties, wearing a hospice badge approached.

"Hi, I'm Jim," he said, sticking out his hand. "I've been checking on your mom. We'd like to start her on a series of three antibiotic shots to hopefully knock the bronchitis out before it can get worse. Is that okay with you?"

"Yes. Of course, please give her the shots," I replied, stumbling over my words trying to take everything in.

Barely audible, I heard, "I have to go to the bathroom," then realized it came from Mom. I started to push her towards the bathroom but jammed her wheelchair into the guy's wheelchair next to Mom. "Sorry," I said, to the man who continued to snore.

Before I realized I had no idea where I was

going, I ended up in front of a locked door that I assumed was a bathroom.

"I got you," I heard from behind me. The lady with the bright eyeshadow grabbed a key and opened the door. "I put a little make-up on her this morning. She was so pale," she said, swiping Mom's bangs to one side. "I think it brightened her right up?"

"Thank you," I replied, as I pushed Mom into the bathroom. "That's really nice of you, I appreciate that."

"It's no problem, I love doing make-up," she said, then turned to deal with the resident who had rolled past in her wheelchair and turned into the janitorial closet.

It wasn't till I was alone in the bathroom struggling to get Mom out of the wheelchair, that I realized I had no chance of getting her to the toilet. I contemplated scooping Mom up like a baby, but was saved by the make-up artist, who had poked her head back into the room. "She probably has Depends or a diaper on," she said, then stepped into the room.

"I didn't even think about that."

"Let's check," she said, coming up behind Mom to pull the elastic waistband on Mom's pants to take a peek. It reminded me of all the times I'd done the same thing with the boys when they were babies to check if their diapers were dirty. "All good," she said, releasing the waistband. "She's wearing a Depends." I could hear dad laughing in my head *You come into this world in diapers....*

Already worn out, I situated Mom back into the line of residents in front of the TV. When I leaned in to give her a goodbye hug, she squirmed, then looked directly at me. "I think that was a turd?" she said, in a whisper. Now I hear two-year-old Connor's voice in my head, running out of the bathroom, *I did a poopy! I did a poopy!*

I had no time to react to the possible turd, before a different hospice nurse came over to administer the antibiotic shot. "I'll have to do it in your bum, so your arm won't be sore," she said, while preparing the needle. *You really don't want to do that.*

"I think she went to the bathroom," I said to the nurse.

"That's okay, we'll just do this down in her room," she replied, as she moved around behind Mom to begin to wheel her forward. "We'll get her all squared away."

Back at home, I searched online for, "how long someone with LBD can live without eating," then read through the results. Ten days seemed to be the general consensus, but some go without eating for several weeks.

Chapter 32
Celestial Send Off

December 23, 2022

I'm aware that I'm dreaming as I watch Mom float by me wearing a crimson-red sundress. We're outside with fields of yellow straw grass stretching as far as the eye can see. "Where's my heart?" I hear her say. "There it is." She points to a chandelier suspended in the sky, like celestial jewelry. Woven in the weathered iron arms of the chandelier was a red-jeweled heart dangling on a silver chain. I recognize the jeweled heart as an identical replica to the heart ring Mom wore for many years as an ode to her maiden name 'Hart'. Out of nowhere she walks up behind and grabs my shoulder, rather forcefully, to lead me away from the table, her finger pointing at the sky. "I see things in *the dark spots," she says, the words seem to float by my ear. I see a single puffy white cloud with a heart shaped hole in the center. "You're getting your sight back," I hear her say, as I focus on the light blue sky behind the heart in the cloud.*

"It's been back," I reply, both of us knowing the sight she is referring to is a psychic or otherworldly sight. Before I can say more, she's gone and another woman in a red dress is approaching me.

"Your mom's been such a help to me," she says, but all I hear is the past tense in her words and an overwhelming absence of Mom in the dream.

Suddenly I was awake, sucking in air with tears falling down my face. Morning light sneaked in through the blinds, but all I could do was lay there, motionless, trying to gather the pieces of me still scattered in the dream world. *Are you saying goodbye? Are you preparing me?*

Crying in My Car Meme

December 25, 2022

Tired of crying every time I got into a car, I tried to keep the conversation with Travis light as we headed to Mom's. The pecan tassies I'd made the day before, Mom's favorite just after key lime pie, sat in Tupperware on my lap filling the car with the aroma of pecan pie. A lump formed in my throat when we pulled to a stop at the red light before Mom's facility. *Not again,* I thought, trying to wipe tears before they started to fall. I could see myself as a car crying meme and it wasn't pretty!

"How are you feeling about seeing your Mom on Christmas?" Travis said, as the light turned green. *Are you kidding me?* The dam of tears broke.

"Dammit!" I blurted out when I pulled the razor in a zip lock bag from my purse. I continued to fish through a couple dozen lipsticks settled at the bottom of the purse, but no Kleenex.

"What!" Travis said, confused.

"Tired," I snapped. "Just really sad and tired. This has been the weirdest Christmas."

Travis is used to my ugly car crying. Heck he's used to me crying everywhere! "Weird in what way?" he said, sounding like a therapist.

"Weird, in the way I won't ever see my parents again on Christmas!" I said, sarcastically, then immediately knew the attitude was misdirected. "Sorry."

Upon entering, Travis stopped to take in the small cottage, reminding me I hadn't prepared him for the change. Standing in place, he surveyed the row of geri chairs and wheelchairs in front of the TV. "Wow. Okay," he mumbled, then moved toward Mom.

"She actually looks better," I whispered. "The antibiotics must be kicking in."

"That's better?" he replied, then switched his tone as we came up on Mom's side. "Hi, Kay. We brought you pecan tassies." Straining to lift her head, she gave us a little smile.

The sound of the kitchen staff preparing Christmas Dinner for the residents echoed in the background, while the three of us sat around the dining table watching Mom pinch off little pieces of the pecan tassies on the napkin in front of her. Each bit of pecan tassie that rolled from her lap to the floor made me miss the maine coon cat from the other cottage.

"What's with the makeup?" Travis said, as we walked out into the parking lot.

"There's a lady that works there that loves to do makeup," I shrugged my shoulders. "At least she's wearing lipstick!" We both laughed.

Avoiding me like the plague, my family deliberately stayed out of my path for the remainder of the holiday break. I couldn't blame them, they were staying clear of my temper that seemed to be always waiting to attack. Fortunately, in the same way they avoided me, I avoided them, wanting to be alone more often than not. Trapped alone with my thoughts, I continued to question my own mortality. What's the point?, seemed a logical question. Theorizing, if we're all going to die, even worse maybe from LBD, then why care about anything. Like any good alcoholic left alone in the darkest corners of her mind, I began to theorize that if I was going to die anyway, then why not die from drinking, rather than something like LBD. It's not sound reasoning, but I'm an alcoholic. Happy Holidays.

Chapter 33
I Can't Unsee That

December 31, 2022

A light flashed in the room, pulling me from sleep. In my sleepy stupor, it took me a minute to realize it was a text from Jannis. When I saw it was 3:15 a.m. on the screen, I knew it wasn't good.

> Hi Michelle, your mom was found on the floor in her room. Looks like she hit the wall and need stitches in her head so they called 911 and sent to Seton Williamson, hospice is aware.

A half coherent phone conversation followed, where I was told to check on her in the morning, because there was no reason to race to the hospital.

Before 8 a.m. the next morning, I was already having another half-coherent conversation with Arlene from The Cottages.

"I'm so sorry honey," Arlene started the conversation. "She's okay, but they had to put ten staples in the back of her head, so it looks worse than it is."

"Does she need anything?" I said, trying to visualize ten staples, but the only image that formed was of Frankenstien. "I'll come by later today to see her."

"There's no discharge orders from the hospital, so there's nothing you need to bring."

Celebrations were in order when I'd made it through an entire car ride without crying and didn't even fall apart when Travis and I pulled into the parking lot of the small cottage. The sound of staff cleaning up after lunch told me it was around 1 p.m. A blonde lady darted from Mom's room, as we turned the corner, stopping us before we could get any closer.

"They're changing her diaper," she said, quickly. Over her shoulder I saw two staff members lifting Mom's legs. An image of myself twenty something years prior, holding one of the boy's legs up, as I slipped a diaper under his bottom came to mind.

"We'll just go wait out in the TV area," Travis

said, shuffling backwards trying to put as much space between him and the room as possible.

"I can't unsee that," I whispered to Travis as we waited.

"There's not enough hours of therapy for that," he replied, laughing.

Five minutes later, the blonde lady reappeared in the TV area. "She's all changed if you want to go back now," she said, using her arm to gesture down the hall.

One cracker and a small plastic cup of applesauce sat on the nightstand next to Mom's bed. *Is she eating?* I asked myself.

"I just keep hitting walls," Mom said from the bed, turning her head to face us. Surprised to see no bruising, I approached to get a closer look.

"Yes you do Ms. Kay." A young woman wearing royal blue scrubs emerged from Mom's closet. "She's got some pretty good bruising on her hip, but other than that looks pretty good." My eye caught the blood stains on the corner of the wall to the left of the closet. On the carpet, a blood stain the size of a dinner plate rounded out what looked like a small crime scene.

"Michelle, can you grab me the napkin," Mom said, reaching towards the napkin holding the cracker and applesauce. Travis and I stared at each other in disbelief that Mom used my name. *Did she know who I was?* I pondered, as I handed her the napkin.

On our way out the blonde woman caught my attention. "Your mom has been eating a little," she said, giving me a warm smile. "Mostly sweets, but that's typical because the elderly lose their sense of taste." *All I do is eat sweets*, I thought and concluded I was going to end up like the young man in the other cottage wearing a resident key around my neck in my fifties.

I Need to Recycle

January 5, 2023

Leftover peanut butter cookies wrapped in foil in one hand, I rang the doorbell with my other. "Are you the hairdresser," Arlene said, opening the door then gesturing for me to come inside.

"I'm here to see my mom," I replied, a confused look plastered to my face. "I can promise you no one wants me doing their hair." I studied Arlene's face as she tried to place me. It occurred to me for the first time in all our interactions that she was the same age as some of the residents. My next thought was, *She's killing it for her age.*

Wheelchairs of all shapes and sizes were pulled up around a round oak table in the activities room adjacent to a TV playing an old western movie. I noticed Mom's hand shaped like a crab claw with her thumb and pointer finger holding a single Kleenex. Whereas I never seem to have a Kleenex, Mom always seemed to have one. A small amount of her gray hair poked out just over the top of her new high-back wheelchair. Just as I reached her, I heard, "Shut the door!" yelled sternly from the man sitting at another table to my left. When I looked for a door to shut, I saw a younger man kick the patio door shut with one leg while he continued to push a gray-haired woman outside. Over the last year, I've concluded that patience is spent over a lifetime and used up by the time someone enters memory care. In this loud man's defense, open doors at memory care are an (OFSA) Opportunity for Silver Alert.

Mom, who now noticed I'd come up on her side, caught a glimpse of me and let out a *harrumph*. My reflex was to pat my hair and check for lipstick, but then I remembered she could have been reacting to pretend me or a hundred other people that were or were not there, so I ignored it.

"Your sister asked that we call her today," I

said. "Let's go back to your room where it's quieter."

"Ouch," Mom said, as we headed down the hall.

"What's wrong?" I scurried around her wheelchair to face her. Three quarters of the way through a visual body scan, I noticed her foot, covered in a striped fuzzy sock, was partially under the wheel.

"Sorry," I said, dislodging her foot. I worried my wheelchair driving skills would dump her out onto the carpet causing bodily harm before we reached her room.

Just as the man had kicked the patio door shut, I flung my leg out behind me and kicked Mom's room door shut. I half expected to hear the loud man yell, "Shut the door!"

You've reached Gene Ann...

"It's her voicemail," I said to Mom, holding my phone out for Mom to see.

"Well, you have a boyfriend too," Mom said, giving me a scrutinizing look.

I wanted to scream, "For the hundredth time, I don't have a boyfriend!" but instead I said, "No. It's her voicemail, not her boyfriend." A smile twitched the corners of my mouth thinking I needed to remember to ask Gene Ann about her boyfriend.

"I'm going to make a lunge for the recycling," Mom said, leaning forward towards the bathroom like she was going to push off the seat of her wheelchair to stand.

Recycling? Then it hit me that she was talking about the bathroom. My mind immediately adopted the word exchange and I vowed to start saying, "I'll be right back, I'm going to the recycling" or "I need to recycle." Before my mind was done inserting recycling into bathroom sayings, Mom attempted to wheel herself in the other direction.

"Where do you want to go," I said, grabbing the back of her wheelchair.

"Back out there." I interpreted this to mean the activities room, as well as my cue to leave.

As I walked by one of the business offices on my way out, a woman got up from her desk and waved her hand to get my attention. "Are you the new physical therapist?" she said, walking towards me with a big smile.

"No. I was just visiting with my mom," I replied, thinking, *First I'm a hairdresser, now I'm a physical therapist, it's like career day here.*

End of Life Lifestyle

January 11, 2023

Golden crystal sprinkles decorated the frosting border of the specialty lemon cake I'd ordered last week for Mom's eighty-second birthday. *She'll love this,* I patted myself on the back. Remembering the shark feeding frenzy the cake had caused last year, I'd also bought a Costco cake for the small cottage.

Balancing the small lemon cake box on top of the large Costco cake box, I looked more like I was setting up for a banquet than one woman's birthday among people who barely ate.

"Where can I put this," I said, poking my head around the cake boxes as I entered the kitchen area of the south wing.

"How about we put the big one in the fridge," the woman slicing potatoes said. "We don't have a lot of room so we may have to take it over to the larger cottage." Arms free, I started to look for Mom and saw that most of the residents were fast asleep.

"That's nice of you to bring a cake for her," another woman said, stirring a large vat of stew. "We can cut the cake up for dessert tonight. They'll love that."

Instantly, a feeling of loss hit me. *You're an idiot,* my mind berated like my own internal bully. *What were you thinking?* In that moment I realized the cakes had been for me, not because I wanted to eat them, although that would happen, but because I was grasping at last year's birthday memories. I was trying to recreate the scene from last year with a community and Mom that were different from a year ago.

Determined to at least give Mom a slice of the lemon cake, I hunted her down in her room and rolled her out to the dining room table. Painfully unable to connect the fork to cake, I watched Mom push the lemon cake around her plate for fifteen minutes. The effort landed some cake in her lap, some on the floor, and none in her mouth. If the maine coon cat knew how much food hit the floor at the small cottage, it would feel cheated. Mom had little interest in me, and even less interest in the cake.

Arlene pulled up a chair and slid a piece of paper titled, Lifestyle Plan, in front of me. She proceeded to explain that it was a treatment plan for Mom moving forward. Really, it was an End of Life Plan, which left me wondering if there was an end of life "lifestyle."

I signed the Lifestyle Plan and looked at Mom,

whose face conveyed, "I'm over it." I took the cue and left with the rest of the lemon cake.

Back in my car I read through the messages on my work app to prepare myself for the afternoon group I'd be facilitating. The morning's update read like a reality TV show I'd recently watched where people were all trapped in a house together. The clients, also trapped in a house together, but with the added drama of being in early recovery were getting restless. One client had stormed out of group after getting into a verbal altercation with another client, only to then stand right outside the door she'd slammed shut, and scream. The previous evening two clients had crossed the common living area that acted as a border separating the male and female wings to "hook up" another message read. Part of me was grateful for the distraction of client drama versus Mom drama.

Chapter 34
My Three Girls

March 4, 2023

February was lost to the ice apocalypse, as I called the winter storm that blew through Texas. "Shit, it looks like the apocalypse," Travis had said as he looked down the golf course at a scene that looked more like a hurricane had ripped through the town rather than an ice storm. Outside of having to console Nigel (parrot) who said, "You're okay," to reassure himself everytime a large tree branch hit the pavement, we'd weathered the storm. The huge tree that fell and blocked my driveway restricted my visits to Mom, but the times I could visit I was relieved to find not much change.

Praying Mantis, that's what Travis had said

Mom's hands looked like since they were frozen in place. The unnatural bend at the wrist, with fingers that cupped together forming a c-shape, like someone had slid a piece of pipe out of her hand did fit his description. Yesterday, I'd seen those Praying Mantis hands resting on the arms of her new geri chair, her body reclined into a v-shape that left her head arched in an awkward backward bend. As I mulled over the contortions of Mom's body, I heard my phone ring.

"I'm coming into Austin," Danielle blurted out. "I was talking to Mom last night, just telling her to hold on for a couple of days." We continued to speak, but my mind wandered off. Yesterday, I'd taken one look at Mom and couldn't imagine what else was left for Lewy to take from her. I'd tried to FaceTime Danielle, because it occurred to me she might be waiting to see Danielle before she let go of this world. "I get in on Monday night," Danielle's voice caught my attention.

"That's great! She's going to be excited to see you," I said, feeling relieved.

March 6, 2023

If spending an hour on the tarmac at SFO waiting to take off hadn't been stressful enough,

Danielle finally landed in Austin without her bag, which apparently was coming in on the next flight the following morning. "When they're out of cars, they're out of cars," Travis mouthed to me, as he overheard my conversation with Danielle about a packed rental car facility where she had already been in line for over an hour. I decided that was information she didn't need and just said, "We can pick you up if there's any issue with the rental car." When she finally arrived at her hotel, bagless, but with a rental car, she sent me a text.

> My phone is about to die of course and my charger (metal part) is bent so it won't plug into anything so I can only text on my computer. I'll text you when I'm up and headed in your direction.With her visit off to a crazy start, I thought, today was the easy part, tomorrow you see Mom.

∽

How did I not know this existed? I considered, as I pulled up the next morning in front of a small white building that looked like a mix of bungalow and farmhouse. Off to one side of the "farmalo" was a white, two-story hotel with retro turquoise paint and dark brown wood accents. A small pool sat between the hotel and another stand-alone structure that looked like a modernized bungalow with a large deck overlooking the pool. Leave it to Danielle to find the cutest boutique Hotel in the town I'd lived in for over twenty years that I hadn't heard of.

"This is adorable," I said, as she climbed into my car.

"I know. I just looked for places close to Mom's facility."

"This would be a great place for Mom's Celebration of Life," I said, like it was normal to talk about a Celebration of Life when the person was still alive. We then climbed back out of the car to head into the reception area of the hotel.

Approaching the front desk clerk who looked like a teenager but was probably in his twenties, I said, "Can I get information on renting the little bungalow by the pool for an event?"

"Sure, what kind of event are you looking for?" the young man said, pulling out a brochure.

"A Celebration of Life," I replied, opening the brochure to see artfully displayed food trays.

"I'm sorry for your loss," the young man said, dropping the smile from his face.

I folded up from the brochure. "Oh, No. She's still alive," I said, clarifying. A large question mark took the place of the stoic expression. "Dying, but not dead," I clarified. Seeing that my attempt to explain didn't help, I grabbed the brochure and Danielle and I headed out.

"This really is just a smaller version of the other cottage," Danielle said, as we pulled up in front of the small cottage. Once inside, we made our way to the row of geri chairs and wheelchairs that were lined up watching the Hallmark channel. Singing the same line over and over again, the woman to Mom's right reminded me of a singing version of The Whistler. On Mom's left a man in a geri chair displayed the same arched neck as Mom, staring at the ceiling.

"There she is," I heard Danielle say, as she walked towards Mom. "Hi Mom, it's Danielle." Getting onto Mom's level, she crouched down and leaned forward to touch her.

Mom's *back-in-five* stare turned into a smile that spread across her face.

She knows you. I tried to fight back tears.

"Why don't we go over to the table," I said, grabbing the back of Mom's geri chair. It wasn't long before I was steering the chair into walls, then reversing in an attempt to straighten the vessel out, only to jam it into another resident's wheelchair. It reminded me of the shopping carts with the attached bulky plastic "car" front, where one of my kids would turn the pretend steering wheel, while I tried to keep the cart from knocking every canned good off the shelves. When I finally got the geri chair close to the table, Danielle and I took seats on either side of Mom.

Danielle pressed her body into Mom's arm, straining to hear her whispered words. Together, we caught every third word she spoke, then spent the rest of the time trying to figure out what she meant. I watched Danielle softly grab Mom's arm, giving it little squeezes meant to be affectionate.

"If you keep pinching me, I'm going to pinch you back," Mom said, looking at Danielle's hand on her arm.

Shit, I forgot to tell her Mom's skin is sensitive.

"She's in from San Francisco," Mom blurted out to a staff member carrying a white plastic bag with gloved hands. Danielle and I shot each other a look that conveyed, she does know who you are.

After an hour had passed, I considered abruptly standing up, slinging my purse on my shoulder, like Mom and Nana had done many times, code for "let's go", but instead shot Danielle a look to let her know it was time to wrap it up. "I'll stop by tomorrow too," Danielle said, giving Mom a little kiss on the cheek. "Do you want us to leave you here?"

"Let's move her back out to the main area," I quickly jumped in. Only hitting the wall once, I steered her back to the TV area then stopped to assess where to park her geri chair among the others.

"Can she see the TV from here?" Danielle said, crouching down to get Mom's view of the TV. An empty spot between a woman sleeping and the woman who was still singing the same line over and over again, looked tight. The same way one might eye a tight parking space, I tried to figure out if I could get the geri chair into the spot without hitting the other chairs.

"I can't navigate her back into that spot," I said, remembering I couldn't even parallel park. Danielle shrugged her shoulders, and I did my best to angle Mom towards the TV.

Sliding into the driver's seat, I heard, "It's just so hard" from Danielle before she broke into tears. *Welcome to the crying in your car club*, I thought, but didn't say. Her reaction was the same one I'd had almost every time I climbed into my car after a visit. I also knew that seeing Mom would rip open a whole new grief process for days to come.

Later that evening, I received a text from Danielle.

> Love you sis! I can't thank you and Trav enough for all you have done and do for Mom! Wouldn't be able to have seen her today without you by my side.

I shot off a reply text, while I looked at the picture Arlene had taken that afternoon of the three of us. Mom sat in her jeri chair, Danielle to her right and me on her left, all smiling into the camera.

> Love u too, I'm glad we all three were together before she passes.

That's the last time we'll all be together. I could hear Dad's voice say, *My three girls.*

Chapter 35
CARLAAAA!

March 25, 2023

Obsessed with how much more time Mom had left, I asked Travis to go with me to visit Mom so he could give me his assessment. I'd become desensitized to the decline, whereas Travis, who hadn't seen her in months, would be a truer gauge.

"I think she's napping," Travis said, as we stood side-by-side surveying the line of geri chairs and wheelchairs in front of the TV.

"That's what she looks like," I replied, unfazed by her pale, gaunt skin and the abnormal bends of her body.

"Oh," he said, his mouth gaped open just like Moms.

"CARLAAAAA!" the sound of a female voice screaming made me jump. "She's almost here," the same voice said. Sitting in a wheelchair facing the window that overlooked the parking lot, a small woman wearing two sweaters that looked like they had wrestled with each other, screamed "CARLAAAA" just like Sylvester Stalone had called for Adrian. Each "CARLAAAA" was followed by "She's almost here" roughly every two minutes.

"Geeshhh, I hope Carla gets here soon," I said to Travis.

"I'm sure everyone does!" he replied, also staring at the woman

Pushing a tray full of dirty plates and glasses, a staff member, who heard our exchange, winked, then said, "She's waiting for her daughter," as she passed us. I immediately felt a kinship with Carla but was also grateful Mom didn't spend hours screaming MICHELLE! while looking out the window for me.

As I considered asking for Carla's address so I could go pick her up, I realized Travis and I were the only ones that seemed to be affected by her screaming.

"Hi Kay," Travis said, as he and I walked up and placed ourselves in her line of sight. Travis's eyes tracked to the woman next to Mom, who sang a song I didn't recognize.

"That's The Singer," I leaned over and whispered in his ear. "I forgot to tell you about her."

"Let's go to Allen's," Mom said, so softly I watched Travis almost fall on top of her trying to hear. Shades of green in a paisley pattern on the pillow wedged between Mom's tiny body and the side of her geri chair caught my eye. It took me a minute to figure out that without the pillow, Mom's miniscule frame would have fallen into the crevices of the chair never to be found again.

"CARLAAAA!"

Fuck!

"Does she mean Jack Allen's?" Travis asks me. "Like the restaurant?"

Ignoring his question, I came around behind Mom's chair and started to push her forward. "Let's go somewhere quiet," I said to Travis as he stepped out of my way so I could pass. I heard, "She's almost here" loud, then fading out, as I rammed Mom's chair into the wall that led to her room.

"It smells like they're working on dinner," Travis said to Mom for the first time since he'd greeted her. Understandable, the geri chair alone would be an adjustment for him, add the tiny woman whose body was contorted in strange bends with Praying Mantis hands, and it was a lot to process.

"I could go for a meatball sandwich," Mom said, causing Travis to laugh. The image of a meatball sandwich being pureed in a blender filled my head. Before Travis or I could react to the meatball sandwich, she threw out another option, saying, "Let's go somewhere and get coffee." Travis and I froze. *You're an indoor cat. I can't get you in my car,* I reminded myself, feeling helpless. The sudden realization Mom will never go out to lunch again caused my eyes to fill with tears. After twenty minutes of strained conversation, where two of the three people couldn't hear or understand the third person, we said our goodbyes.

"CARLAAAA!" rang in my ears, as I parked Mom's geri chair back in front of the TV. "She's almost here," the lady by the window, who was now two feet from me, screamed. I wanted to scream, "CARLAAAA's not coming" but instead I remained quiet, understanding that she just wanted to see her daughter.

The minute the door shut behind us Travis stopped. "Holy fuck," he said, then released a long, deep, breath.

Silence blanketed the car ride home, until Travis started speaking his inner thoughts out loud. "I wonder if Washington is a right to die state?" he said, like he was asking himself. "I NEVER want to get to that stage," his tone took a serious turn, then he turned to look at me. "I mean it."

"Okay," slipped from my lips.

More silence, then his inner thoughts came out again. "Your mom looks like a corpse," he said, his face fixed on the road, again like he was talking to himself. "Sorry, but honestly, I've seen corpses that look better in open caskets. Probably because of the makeup they put on them, but still, you know what I mean." We drove again in silence for a few minutes, until Travis shifted in his seat and I waited for the out loud processing to restart. "I see why you want her to go," his voice said, now soft. "It's really mercy. No one should live like that."

We climbed out of the car and I felt Travis grab my arm. "Geessshh Michelle, I'm sorry," he said, fighting back tears.

Three days later, I listened to Nigel boss the dogs while he ate breakfast. "Sadie! COOOME!" Nigel said, sounding exasperated with the dog.

"Leave the dog alone," I told him, as my finger scrolled through emails.

Whistle. Door Squeaking Sound. Whistle.

I shot Nigel a, *that's still messing with the dogs,* look which sent him back to eating his hard-boiled egg. *Incoming call, Hospice,* scrolled across the screen.

"I was checking on your mom yesterday and she sounded really congested," Jim said. I heard The Singer in the background and knew he was in the living area. "I listened to her and it sounds like she has an infection in the lower lobe, probably aspiration pneumonia (food or liquid is breathed into the airways or lungs, instead of swallowed). I'd like to start her on antibiotics if you're okay with that?"

"Yes, please start antibiotics." Jim went on to explain that Mom's throat and esophagus muscles weren't functioning normally, which was common with late-stage LBD. He continued stating they would puree Mom's food. I'd been half joking in my mind when I'd thought about blending the meatball sandwich.

Change in Condition

April 2, 2023

Numb, would be the best way to describe my coping skills of late. Skipping dinner because, *who gives a fuck*, I scooped vanilla ice cream onto a brownie. A little flicker of light flashed on my phone displaying, *Incoming call, The Cottages*.

"Hi, dear, you moms had a change of condition," Arlene said, gently, but to the point. "She's just staring at the ceiling and hasn't really been eating in the last two days.

"Okay," was all I could get out. *Change in condition*, my mind started somersaulting through thoughts, *Is this the end? Are we talking days, hours? What should I be doing?*

"I don't think the antibiotics are working, but I've called hospice to assess," Arlene continued, filling the silence.

Just before 9 p.m., *Incoming call, Hospice* scrolled across the top of my phone. Part of me wanted to put my head in the sand and ignore it, but instead I took a deep breath and answered.

"She was in bed, responsive," Jim continued his update. "Vitals were all fine and I spoke with Mary, her caretaker, who said she drank a full Ensure." He said the last part, like drinking a full Ensure should be added to the Gutbuster's Guide to the Greatest American Food Challenges. I half expected to see Mom's picture on the wall in the kitchen next to an empty bottle of Ensure.

"Should I come up there," I said, feeling sick from all the brownies I'd eaten.

"Of course you're welcome to, but she's stable right now," he said. "We'll see about getting her up and out of bed tomorrow."

The whole conversation felt surreal, for as many times as I'd begged Dad to come get her, I also was in denial that at some point she'd actually be gone.

Walking the crazy terriers the next morning, I spotted a small white dog headed towards us. As we got closer, the terriers almost pulled the leashes out of my hand. With the small white dog, was the same neighbor who had referred me to in-home care over two years ago. Three crazy dogs circled our legs as she told me her mother had passed six months ago. "There was definitely sadness. I have moments of great sadness," she said, when I asked how she was doing. "But mostly I'm relieved."

Relieved, the word stuck with me as I continued walking the dogs. *Three years is a long time to watch someone decline*, I thought and like I was trying on a dress, I could relate to my neighbor's relief.

At 3:32 p.m. I noticed I'd missed a call from hospice. Thinking I might have missed "the call" I fumbled to recent calls and tapped the number.

"Just an update on your mom," Jim said, and I knew it wasn't "the call". "She's still congested and probably still aspirating. We could do breathing treatments, but at this stage they can aspirate their own saliva."

"Don't do the breathing treatment," I started to say and then fell silent.

"I think this is going to be her decline," Jim filled the silence, intuitively answering my next question. "I sat her up some and she coughed to clear her throat. She's responsive but I think we'll see a change in condition in the next twenty-four hours."

"I don't know how to ask this," the words slipped out so fast I couldn't concentrate. "Is she dying? I mean, I know she's dying. Do you know how long?"

"It's hard to say," he replied, slowly, as if choosing his words carefully. "We'll be keeping you in the loop and will let you know immediately if there's a change in condition."

Feeling like "change in condition" was code for dying I called Danielle to give her an update.

The following afternoon, barely back from seeing Mom, who'd slept in bed the entire time I was there, *Incoming call, Hospice* scrolled across the screen and vibrated the phone in my hand.

"The onsite nurse put in order for injectable antibiotics," Jim said, as part of his update. "I need your approval if you want to move forward with the antibiotics."

I thought about Mom rebounding for twelve hours, only to fall back into pneumonia, prolonging an already horrible quality of life. "I don't know what the right answer is here," I said, trying not to sound insensitive. "But I don't really want to be in a pneumonia cycle. That just sounds awful for her."

"That's why I wanted to check with you," he said. "Even if it did work, it would likely only buy her a short period of time and she would likely aspirate again."

"I feel guilty, like I should do everything to help her," I started to ramble. "But it just feels mean. I wouldn't want to live like that." The second my mouth stopped rambling, my mind went to morbid thoughts like, *Which one of my kids would give me the antibiotic shot? I need to make sure that kid isn't my medical power of attorney.*

"We'll continue with comfort meds of

morphine four times a day," he said, in a soft, reassuring voice. "We'll take it day by day and I'll keep you posted."

"Your path you must decide" - *Yoda*

April 5, 2023

My eyes ran up and down the line of geri chairs placed in a row in front of the TV. All but one of the people lying in them were asleep. From the corner of the room, a nurse waved her hand, motioning for me to follow her towards Mom's room. I fell into step behind her and as we rounded the corner, I could see dim light and hear soft music coming from Mom's room. *But it's the middle of the day,* I thought, my stomach tightening. The nurse slowed her pace, stepped to the side, and extended her arm to lead me through the doorway. As I passed, she gave me a sympathetic smile. "If you need anything, dear, just come find me," she said, then retreated, leaving the door cracked.

I stood frozen just beyond the doorway. A lamp not much bigger than a candle cast a soft light over the bed. Everything seemed to pause with me except for the soft music, which continued to play in the background. A tiny lump covered by layers of blankets lay in the bed. Just above the pastel-colored quilt, a small head peaked out from under the covers. I sucked in a gasp. Stark white hair frizzed out in wisps from the head, so thin I could make out the lines of the skull. Translucent skin stretched over the skeletal frame, rendering every facial bones unmistakable. I found myself fixated on the two protruding veins that ran down each side of the neck just under the surface. It was Mom, but also not Mom. She reminded me of the Egyptian mummies I'd seen at the British Museum in London.

Are you breathing? I wondered, leaning over to listen for sound. A *gasp*, followed by a crackling sound, escaped her wide-open mouth, so sudden it sent me jumping backwards. I placed my hand over my heart to calm my breathing. Composing myself, I cautiously touched her bony shoulder, so frail I worried it would break.

Feeling alone and vulnerable, I shot a text off to Danielle.

> With Mom.

I attached a picture of Mom with the text, not for shock value, but because I desperately needed someone else to be with me. I felt out of my body and wanted another soul to ground me.

Seconds later, three dots appeared suspended in a bubble, same as my body felt suspended in the room. The pending response helped pull some part of me back into my body.

> Um, you're up and at it early. She looks dead.

I wanted to text, *I thought she was dead*, but instead sent:

> I've been up since 5 a.m.

I noticed my shoulders shaking before I realized I was sobbing. I lunged for the nightstand and fumbled through the top drawer looking for a Kleenex. I looked at the latex glove I'd pulled out wondering if it would suffice for Kleenex. Tears streamed down my cheeks and out of my nose. When I leaned forward to open the bottom drawer, snot fell from my nose onto the floor. *Good lord, is there anything that's made of paper here,* I thought, giving up.

I felt my body fall into the BarcaLounger at the foot of Mom's bed, but my mind traveled elsewhere. I'd rehearsed this scenario in my head a hundred times. Each time, the picture-perfect scene had looked like Mom lying in bed, tired but aware, and me reading her a book or telling her stories as she passed into the next world. She wasn't supposed to be unconscious. She wasn't supposed to be struggling to breathe. *I'm not prepared*, my mind panicked. Just then, an elderly man wearing a red-striped jersey wandered into the room.

"How long have you been in the hole?" he asked, and I wondered if he meant prison.

"Too long," I replied, unable to muster anything else.

"Me too," he chuckled and headed back to the hall.

Paralyzed and unable to take my eyes off the figure that lay in the bed in front of me, I realized I was now the one with the *back-in-five,* stare. The sound of an incoming notification lit up my home screen displaying the time. *Forty-five minutes*, I marveled, unable to get my head around the amount of time that had passed since I'd arrived.

Without meaning to, I found myself standing next to the bed, like I'd floated over, looking down at Mom, but not Mom. "I'll be back, Mom," I said, unable to bring myself to touch her again. "I love you." My legs walked down the hall of their own accord. I knew this because I moved forward, but it wasn't a conscious action. At the same time, the walls seemed to be closing in and I couldn't get to an exit fast enough.

As I walked by the kitchen, I heard a voice break through the fog surrounding me. "I know it's hard to see them like that," a woman said, scooping carrots onto the tray in front of her. Her dark, brown eyes fixed on mine, and I choked back tears. "It's really a solo journey," she continued, using a huge spoon to spread the carrots out. "One they have to take on their own. Even with people around them, it's something they really do alone."

I heard the words, "Your path, you must decide" in Yoda's wise voice, and thought, *You're right, she's somewhere else.*

That evening, wrapped in a blanket up to my neck, just like Mom had been, I shoved M&Ms in my mouth. A text from Danielle came in just before I snarfed down three more chocolate morsels.

> I'm sure you're done for. Today must have been hard. Thinking of you.

I popped the morsels into my mouth then replied.

> Thanks, hopefully it won't drag out too long.

An hour later, another text from Danielle.

> I just got an overwhelming feeling that she may have passed.

Numb, I robotically replied.

> No one's called.

Chapter 36
The End

April 6, 2023

Periwinkle wisteria vines braid through a trellis, casting little rays of sunlight onto two towheaded young boys sitting at a table eating ice cream. Dad sits next to the older towheaded boy, whom I recognize as Cameron, while the other towheaded boy, Connor, climbs out of his chair. Mom stands off to the side with a camera. Click. The sound of her snapping the photo pulls me out of the dream, awake.

All morning I couldn't shake the strange feeling in my gut that had caused a corresponding and omnipresent lump to lodge in my throat. Images of Mom, some with the boys, others with Danielle and me as kids, flooded my mind, making it impossible to concentrate on anything. I tried to meditate, but the minute I sat down I got the overwhelming feeling that I needed to go see Mom. *I just saw her,* I thought, but the feeling persisted. Before I knew it I was behind the wheel headed for The Cottages.

Once again, I heard soft music coming from the dimly lit room at the end of the hall and got the unmistakable feeling of deja-vu. On my left I passed a room where a son was moving his mother in and thought, *As one comes in, another leaves.* Mom lay in the same place and position as yesterday, only now she wore a baby-blue beanie cap on her head, making her look like a gnome. I paused a couple of feet from her bed. The sound of her breathing sent my eyes to her chest. Gasping sounds formed as she sucked air in, reminding me of a goldfish at the surface of water. The image of the orange cartoon goldfish with bubble eyes flashed before me. Between gasps, long silent gaps left me wondering, *Is this the end?*

They say the heart's electromagnetic field is 100 times stronger than the brain's field. Standing there, I could feel Mom's and my heart fields exchanging information. Suddenly I grew lightheaded and saw the walls shift slightly, then fix back into place, like a glitch in the matrix. I tripped

Did Mom Drop Acid? 519

making my way to the BarcaLounger, crying uncontrollably, then fell into it and pulled my legs into the criss-cross applesauce position. Before I knew it, I was talking to Dad whom I also felt in the room. "Pleeeeassseee come get her, pleee-asssseee..." I pleaded, between sobs like a child. The sound of a text interrupted my pleading.

> Hey Michelle. It's Jim with Hospice, I checked on your mom today and she was doing okay. She was comfortable. I'm checking to see if y'all have funeral home info in the event she passes tonight.

We didn't yet have that information. I knew I needed to look it up. I decided to put some different music on while I studied and searched for The Carpenters in iTunes. Mom always played Karen Carpenter as she drove in our cream Buick. "Goodbye to Love" started.

I can't, I thought, skipping to the next song.

*Why do birds suddenly appear...*Karen's voice sang quietly from my phone where it rested on the arm of the chair.

Better. As I scrolled through funeral homes and cremation company sites on my phone, a field of bluebonnets on the homepage of one of the cremation company sites reminded me of my drives to Bryan, so I sent the link to Jim.

Gasp, gurgle, gasp. Mom's erratic breathing and The Carpenters were the only sounds in the room, until someone whispered, "*Say goodbye.*" I jerked my head up as I scanned the room for the intruder, but there was no one. *It's Dad,* I thought, *He's telling me it's time.* Again, I found myself standing over Mom, but not Mom. I saw her chest still moving even as I knew that she - the essential part of herself - was gone. "I love you Mom," I said, the lump in my throat almost choking me. I gently laid my hand over her heart, letting my heart field speak. "Thank you for everything. I'll see you on the other side."

I barely made it to the car. Suddenly, I was the one gasping for air. Through sobs, I dialed Danielle. "She's gone," was all I could get out.

"Oh my god! Do I need to pull over? I'm driving."

"No, no, not gone - but *gone*," I tried to clarify. "It's the end. I don't think she'll make it through the night."

That evening, I received a text from Danielle.

Did Mom Drop Acid? 521

> I can't deal!!! Just the thought
> that both mom and dad aren't
> physically here is so hard! They
> always say its harder for the ones
> left behind. Here comes all of the
> cliches. I've got dads four fingers
> up in my head right now as he
> was rolling into radiation.

The image of Dad holding up four fingers to indicate the four members of our family, as he disappeared down the hall into radiation, filled my mind. *You're going to be back with Dad*, I thought and saw the image of the two of them on their wedding day.

Asleep in a dream-like state I heard, *bing*. *You're gone*, I said to myself as I looked at the phone, I'd placed on my nightstand knowing I'd get 'the call' in the night.

11:48 p.m., voicemail, unknown number, displayed on the screen.

> Hi Michelle, this is Kaye with hospice, um,
> could you give me a call back when you
> can or you can text me, thank you.

Just below the voicemail was, *11:54 a.m., text message unknown number*.

> Hello, it's Kaye with hospice can you call?

I sat up in bed and took a minute to collect myself knowing she would tell me Mom had passed. I could hear the voice on the other end of the line, but it felt muffled and far away. I marveled that a woman with the same name as Mom would be the one to deliver the news that she'd died. The voice came back into focus. "Is there somewhere you would like us to take the body?" she asked gently. The words, *the body*, floated in my head as I gave her the name of the cremation company. After we hung up, we exchanged a few more text messages and wondered what people did without this guidance at the end.

(Hospice)

> Spoke with (cremation company)...said they would contact you tomorrow

(Me)

> Thank you, I appreciate everything you all have done with my mom!

> (Hospice)
>
> > Of Course…My prayers are with you…please text me, on call till 8 a.m., or Jim tomorrow if you need anything we are available anytime (three heart emojis)

I looked at the clock, 12:01 a.m., then left Danielle a voicemail and sent her a text.

> I just left you a voicemail, hospice called, she passed. It's a good thing, I was hoping she wouldn't hold on like I saw her today. I'll call you in the morning, love you

I spent the next couple of hours fading in and out of sleep. My phone lit up on the nightstand with a text from Danielle at 3:48 a.m.

> I'm up listening to my owl in the backyard. Love you very much!

As a side note, I dated this section April 6, the date we used for Mom's death certificate because she passed so close to midnight.

The next day beautiful arrangements of flowers started pouring in from friends and family as they were notified of Mom's passing. Still in a fog, I walked around in this new reality that Mom doesn't occupy, working through the logistics of death. Somewhere in the background, the body, Mom, was being transferred from the facility to the cremation company. Danielle waited for the form from the cremation company that would need to be notarized giving them permission to transform Mom to ash. As the weekend approached, Danielle called, concerned she hadn't been sent the form. "I know the body came over," she said. "The guy did say they aren't open on the weekend, but I feel like I should have the form."

"I'm sure it's kind of like island time," I replied. "I mean it's not like she's going anywhere and we're not going to move the body somewhere else." We both laughed.

Do You Want Mom's Head?

April 13, 2023

A week later I found myself back in the blue metal box of historical family information. Verifying the information on the death certificate was like visiting ancestry.com. I was wrist deep in documents on a mission to unearth something with Baba's maiden name when I heard my phone ring.

"Do we want to keep Mom's head?" Danielle asked when I picked up. Her tone was casual, as if everyone talks about keeping a dead person's head. I immediately saw an image of an altar with religious candles casting soft light on Mom's head.

"What? No! Do you want to keep Mom's head," I finally spit out, trying to shake the image.

"No. I just remembered us talking a while back about donating her brain."

"Oh, yeah. No," I said, remembering we'd talked about LBD only being able to be seen in the brain postmortem. "I forgot. We would have had to start that process before now." I started laughing. "You have to start with more than, do you want Mom's head, in a conversation." At this, Danielle started laughing too.

Epilogue

Then There Were Two

May 23, 2023

The morning of Mom's Celebration of Life, I woke up with a cloudy head and blurry vision from the sleep stuck in the corner of my eyes. Danielle and I had spent the previous evening fighting over nothing significant and I knew we would have to make up if we wanted to greet Mom's guests together convincingly. Before facing that task, I decided to go for a run to clear my head.

Outside, the morning was already hot and sticky. The humidity made my running shorts stick to my skin. My body felt heavy, more like a plodding forward than a run. Maybe the emotion from last night or grief was weighing on me, either way, the run felt like it took longer than normal.

When it was time, I slipped on a lightweight flowered chiffon tank top with black dress pants that were snug around the waist from all my dessert-eating, then piled into the car with Travis to head to the venue Danielle and I had picked out back in March. Some family members and friends were already in town. Others, driving in for just the day, were en route.

The venue looked as perfect that May day as it had the first time Danielle and I had lain eyes on it. Stumbling up the steps of the dark gray bungalow in my slippery heels and carrying a box full of tiny key lime pies and chocolate tarts, I again thought, *Wow this is really beautiful.* Towering old oak trees stood sentry around the building while the insistent songs of Barn Swallows filled the air. In the background, a deck overlooked Brushy Creek.

Once inside, I placed the boxes down on the rustic black stone bar to the left of the entry and took in the room. *I could live here.* Warm wood floors anchored the deep blue-gray walls that surrounded floor-to-ceiling sliding doors. Beautiful natural sunlight streaked the caramel leather sofas and mid-century-style chairs. Frosted glass and brushed bronze pendants hung like dangling earrings over the bar, illuminating the forest accent green tile along the wall. *Mom, you would have loved this,* I said to myself and felt a lump form in my throat. *Get it together Michelle, you can't start crying yet!*

I saw Danielle scurrying around, placing pictures we had pre-selected of Mom, family, and friends, throughout the venue. *Fuck, I don't want to deal with this today,* I thought, then approached her anyway. Danielle looked like she had passed a rough night. Her hair was piled on the top of her head in a messy bun, her eyes were swollen with day-old mascara smeared under them, and she wasn't dressed for the ceremony. Still, she agreed to step out onto the back deck with me and exchange words that put the previous evening to rest. Thus, patched up, we returned inside to finish setting up.

Friends from all over Texas started filing into the room, eager to share their unique memories from different time periods in Mom's life. Uncle Tommy and Susan joined Gene Ann and her daughter, who had arrived the evening before. Neighbors from Mom's cute little patio home joined the group. Little groups started to form, everyone talking and eating the little pies. So many little pies, I had to grab one and hide it for myself later. Mom would have loved looking around the room at the celebration, everyone she held dear to her heart in Texas stood in that room. I too, was grateful to stand among these people, each of them having supported either Mom or me at some point during the last three years.

With everyone assembled, it was time for me to make a speech. I find public speaking as desirable as hanging out in a pit of snakes, so I'd been feeling the anxious energy for the last hour and was almost lightheaded. Looking out onto faces I'd known for years, a memory of my dad's Celebration of Life caused my stomach to drop. Back then my alcoholism had prevented me from making a speech. While others had gotten up and talked about how awesome my dad was, I'd drunk my feelings down, scared I'd crumble if so much as a tear fell on my check. It was guilt I carried still.

I felt Danielle come up and stand beside me in front of the group, her presence recentered me in the room and then I could speak. "First, I just want to thank all of you for coming," I said. "Our mom would have loved this." I talked directly to Cameron and Connor, who stood in front of me. "Grandma loved you guys," I said, tears forming. "She thought you both hung the moon." When I was done talking about Mom, I felt relieved that it was over, but also grateful that I had been fully present and sober this time. In the rooms of AA, we call this a "living amends". Through my actions I was making amends for not being fully present at Dad's ceremony. I *love you guys*, I thought, feeling Mom and Dad's presence in the room.

∽

On an episode of Super Soul Sunday, Oprah interviewed Dr. Maya Angelou, who at the time was eighty-five years old, asking her, "What can you say about [your] eighties?" the talk show host asked the poet. Angelou's reply, "Do it if you can. If you have a choice, choose the eighties." Hidden in the simplicity of Angelou's answer lies life's essential lessons: time is a gift, perspective is everything, and tomorrow is not guaranteed.

This echoes through my mind now. If you're lucky, time slowly carves your family away, leaving you with just the memories.

My family of origin started with four members. First, time whittled away my dad, then my mom, leaving just two, Danielle and me. Like the urns that now hold our parents' ashes, my sister and I are also containers: of stories. Someday she and I will be gone, too, and I worry about what will happen to the stories we contain, stories I'm already forgetting. "Was that Mom's uncle that died cleaning his shotgun?" I asked Danielle recently; she didn't know. "Did Nana have a sister?" she asked me in return. "I think so," I said, "but I never met her." These memories, they slip through my fingers, fading like an old t-shirt, making the passing down of those stories I do remember-stories about my mom and dad-feel all the more urgent and essential. How much of them my boys retain, I can't say, but this, in the end, is the work. The reason we read, and write, and share.

Like all new chapters, this one has its challenges. Not only are Danielle and I still grieving our parents, but as the remaining two, we must also define our future as sisters without parents. For me, the grief process has been like a parable of opposites. One day I'm numb, apathetic, playing sad songs, trying desperately to feel the sadness I know lurks just below the surface. The next day, that sadness emerges from the depths, sneaking up on me, catching me in the produce aisle of the grocery store, leaving me sobbing and prompting a passerby to ask, "Are you okay ma'am?"

I have to remind myself that grief and love are two sides of the same coin. If I hadn't opened my heart to love, then I wouldn't feel grief. Everyone says time heals, and it does, but it doesn't forget. When I look back on grieving the loss of Dad, I see how the passing of time has allowed memories to inhabit space more freely. Early on after his passing, memories would gut-punch me with sadness. After more time had passed, the same memories were more likely to make me laugh or smile.

Today I thank Lewy for teaching me empathy, compassion, and forgiveness. Being witness to Mom's tremendous suffering, as she lost everything that makes someone human, deepened my compassion, allowed me to hurdle decades of hurt, find forgiveness, and be left with just love. When I find myself trying to hold back tears, I remember my tears honor Mom's life. Each little wet droplet says, *Thank you, I love you, and I carry you with me always.*

Acknowledgments

To my family, thank you for the continued support and love you showed during the three years we all traversed the delusional world of Lewy body dementia and for the years following as I wrote this book. Travis, I couldn't have made it through this without you. You are my soul and life partner.

To the Bass Ass Women in my life:

My Bad Ass sister, thank you Danielle for letting me cry, break down or laugh, sometimes all three at any hour. I look forward to being crazy old women together.

My Bad Ass aunt, thank you Gene Ann for taking your sister and my mom under your wing in Bryan, TX giving her precious more time as an independent person. Thank you for laughing with me at all the crazy experiences we had along the way.

My Bad Ass village, thank you Stephanie, Victoria, Karey, Tiffany, Jan, and Amber. I couldn't have gotten through this without the hours and hours of stories and support. You all are my flock!

My Bad Ass writing coach, thank you Jessica Bross, Cider Spoon Stories for all the hours of encouragement and guidance that helped turn memories into a story that could be shared with others.

My Bad Ass publisher and marketing duo, thank you Michelle Savage Sulit Press and Christy Jaynes. Michelle, thank you for seamlessly guiding me through the process from manuscript to published book. Your love of stories and writing shines through all your authors. Christy, thank you for your patience helping me get back onto social media and creating a wonderful brand that incorporates not only my writing, but my feathered baby, Nigel.

And finally my Bad Ass mom, thank you for showing me the strength of women. I feel you all around me through the women who have enriched my life.

There are many others who helped along the way. Tom, Mom adored you and talked about her 'baby brother' all the time. Thank you for walking alongside us during the last years of your sister's life. Thank you Stan for sharing your optimistic attitude with me and all the people you encounter. My co-workers who had to endure my stories and my ever changing moods. Lina, MIR Care, Mary-jane, Julie, Hospice, all of you who help care for us as we age and leave this world, you are the best of us!

Resources

Lewy Body Dementia Association
https://www.lbda.org

Lewy Body Dementia Resource Center
https://lewybodyresourcecenter.org

Dementia Society of America
https://www.dementiasociety.org

Care Giver Action Network
https://www.caregiveraction.org

National Council on Aging
https://www.ncoa.org/

Aging Life Care Association
https://www.aginglifecare.org

Service Referenced in Book:
Mir, Senior Care Management Inc.
https://mircareconsultants.com

About the Author
Michelle Cain

Michelle Cain is a writer who brings to life the extraordinary within the ordinary through her candid and often humorous style. Her debut book, Did Mom Drop Acid?, emerged from the unscripted, raw events of life. With a Journalism degree from Chico State, Michelle's path has spanned high-tech PR, real estate, and counseling, where her passion for people's stories deepened. Now based in Austin, TX, Michelle enjoys life as an empty nester with her husband, two "crazy" terriers, and the "terrier boss" Nigel, an outspoken African Gray parrot.

Bird House Publications LLC

Bird House Publications LLC. was born to gather and share. Founded to act as a nest for books that tell ordinary people's extraordinary stories.

Birds of a feather flock together. It's our belief, at Bird House Publications, that humanity is our flock and that when people are stripped down to their real authentic selves, true connection happens.

Just like stories passed down from one generation to another, we hope that the extraordinary lives of ordinary people are passed from one person to another, to another…giving others the strength to be real.

Be REAL. Share your STORY
www.birdhousepublications.com

Sulit Press

Sulit Press is a boutique publishing house committed to empowering women's voices and guiding authors through their transformative journey to publication. Founded by Michelle Savage, Sulit Press specializes in a Multi-Authored Book Program that consistently achieves best-seller status. Beyond publishing, we create a thriving community that amplifies visibility and strengthens the influence of our authors, helping them expand their impact and reach.

Then our Multi-Author Book might be the right path for you! Learn more at sulitpress.com/multi-author-books